What's the Story?
BORING GLORY

What's the Story?
BORING GLORY

Spurs fans experience mixed emotions

MARK JACOB

with Myles Palmer

Queen Anne Press

First published in Great Britain in 1999 by
Queen Anne Press
a division of Lennard Associates Limited
Mackerye End, Harpenden
Hertfordshire AL5 5DR

A CIP catalogue record for this book
is available from the British Library

ISBN 1 85291 613 3

Editor: Michael Leitch
Cover photograph: Mirror Syndication International
Printed and bound in Great Britain by
Biddles Ltd, Guildford

CONTENTS

This book is dedicated to
Ossie Ardiles, Danny Blanchflower, Paul Gascoigne,
Jimmy Greaves, Glenn Hoddle, Pat Jennings,
Jürgen Klinsmann, Gary Mabbutt, Dave Mackay,
Alan Mullery, Bill Nicholson and Steve Perryman.

I trust that current club captain Sol Campbell will
eventually rank alongside these Spurs legends.

INTRODUCTION

I grew up in Stamford Hill and Tottenham Hotspur were my local team. We always had star players, always had style, always had glamour. We were one of the Big Five clubs in England and had a worldwide following.

We believed that Tottenham were the classiest team in London. We were the Lillywhites. We had our own traditions, our own identity and our own unique history.

We were the first team to win the FA Cup as an amateur club in 1901, and after that we became known for our exciting cup exploits.

Arthur Rowe's innovative push-and-run side won promotion from the Second Division in 1950, and then became First Division champions the following year with the same team.

Then, guided by the great Bill Nicholson in 1961, we became the first team to win the League and FA Cup double this century.

That legendary Spurs team, starring Danny Blanchflower, Dave Mackay, John White, Cliff Jones and Bobby Smith, rewrote the record books, scoring 115 goals in 42 games. We were champions with the most wins in First Division history, and the most away wins in First Division history.

Jimmy Greaves, one of the finest goalscorers of post-war football, wanted to play in that magnificent team. He joined us from Milan in December 1961. Bill showed his class by having the cheque made out for £99,999 because he did want not to burden the young genius with a six-figure transfer fee. Greaves, perhaps appreciative of this small mercy, scored a hat-trick against Blackpool on his début.

In 1967, when I was two months old, we won the FA Cup, beating Chelsea 2-1.

We broke the transfer record again when we signed Martin Peters from West Ham for £210,000 in March 1970, with Greaves joining the Hammers in part-exchange.

We won back-to-back victories in the FA Cup in 1961 and 1962. We became the first British club to win a European trophy when we won the Cup Winners' Cup in 1963, beating Atletico Madrid 5-1 in Rotterdam.

We reached the semi-final of the European Cup in 1962, losing to a magnificent Benfica side after two tremendously exciting matches. Benfica then beat Real Madrid 5-3 in the final in Amsterdam.

We won the League Cup against Aston Villa in 1971, and again in 1973 when we beat Norwich. We defeated Wolves to win the UEFA Cup in 1972, and lost to Feyenoord in the UEFA Cup Final of 1974.

We scooped the world by signing Argentinian World Cup winners Ossie Ardiles and Ricky Villa in 1978. We won the FA Cup in 1981 after a 1-1 draw with Manchester City when Ricky Villa was substituted by manager Keith Burkinshaw. The replay was a 3-2 thriller, one of the most entertaining of all FA Cup Finals, and is best remembered for a spectacular goal by the aforementioned Ricky.

In the 1982 FA Cup Final we drew 1-1 with QPR. Glenn Hoddle scored with a shot from the edge of the box. In the replay Graham Roberts dribbled into the penalty area, was pulled down by Tony Currie, and Glenn scored the only goal of the game from the spot. The Falklands War with Argentina was on at the time. Ricky played up to the semi-final, after Ossie had earlier gone on loan to Paris St Germain.

In 1983 we were the first club to be publicly quoted on the Stock Exchange, and the following year we beat

Anderlecht on penalties to win the UEFA Cup.

We signed the brilliant, boisterous young Paul Gascoigne from Newcastle for £2.2 million in 1989. This was another English record transfer fee. Once again Britain's most expensive player was playing in a white shirt with a cockerel on it.

All of which brings us to the Nineties, which started on a high. We had Gascoigne and Gary Lineker, two of England's heroes at Italia 90, who starred in yet another FA Cup run in 1991, culminating in a 2-1 victory over Nottingham Forest at Wembley. This was Tottenham's eighth FA Cup, more than any other club at that time.

But what have we seen in the eight years since 1991? Mostly, a declining team and a shrinking status within the game. Also, and even more worrying, a systematic erosion of our precious and unique identity, our DNA.

Football remains Britain's No1 sport. It is the only sport that sells newspapers, and the only sport which sells satellite dishes and cable subscriptions. I have been profoundly depressed to find that, during a football boom, we have slumped. As the game in England has become bigger, we have become smaller. Tottenham are not news any more.

Most reporters fall in love with the game at school and become fans of a club. Some start their careers on local papers and local radio before progressing to national press, radio and TV, and over the years many reporters get to know fans of the various teams that they cover. This is of benefit to the game because these dialogues between fans and journalists help to give the media a wider picture, and balance the propaganda peddled by the clubs.

I knew a few journalists even before the Tottenham Action Group (TAG) was formed in 1996. For instance, I first got to know Harry Harris of *The Mirror* in 1993 when Alan Sugar sacked Terry Venables. I was one of the few supporters to back Sugar. I was very disillusioned with what Venables did with the team. I wanted him sacked because of what he did on the field. Venables signed far too many mediocre players.

To most fans a season is about players and going to matches and cheering goals and hoping to win trophies and reading the speculation in the papers and talking about what we have seen on TV. A season contains a lot of talk, a lot of anticipation, a lot of opinions, a lot of predictions and a lot of newspaper stories.

The 1998-99 season has been different because I wrote it all down, partly for therapeutic reasons. At first, in July and August, it was for my own personal reference. Then, as events gathered momentum, and dramatic things started to happen in September, I realised my diary might be interesting to other fans, and not only Tottenham fans.

Because I have a message for all football fans. It is: be pro-active. Don't be passive. Don't accept being treated as turnstile fodder. Don't accept poor facilities, useless managers and players who go through the motions. Don't just grumble, organise!

Football clubs are very important to each community, providing a focal point for social interaction as well as entertainment. Clubs brings people together in cities of seven million people and towns of 70,000. Unfortunately, local loyalties, rivalries and traditions are being destroyed by the mass media and the marketing men.

Why have I published this diary? Because I believe the traditional identity of Tottenham Hotspur is threatened. Our DNA is being eroded by a chairman who knew virtually nothing about football, or Tottenham Hotspur FC, before he bought the club.

INTRODUCTION

The diary does not need much more explanation, except to say that where I talk about going to games in the plural I am usually talking about going with my uncle Zak and my cousin Adam. Where I occasionally mention playing, it is for my Sunday team, MAL, the Maccabi Association London.

Chapter One

CHRISTIAN GROSS STRUGGLES

Wednesday 15 July

We visit Peterborough for our second friendly of the season. Peterborough are in the Nationwide Division Three, so a comfortable victory is expected. We lost our first friendly 3-1 in Zürich against Grasshoppers, Christian Gross's former club. Our World Cup stars are still on holiday: Campbell, Anderton, Calderwood, Grodas, Baardsen. Did someone say Ferdinand?

New left back Paulo Tramezzani scores the first goal and we lead 1-0 at half-time. Peterborough manager Barry Fry, the most happy-go-lucky manager in the country, replaces his whole team at half-time. We win 6-0. Did he bring on eleven traffic cones? Thanks, Barry. We owe you one. Can we play here every week?

Thursday 16 July

Quiet day all round, no world exclusives. Harry Harris must be on holiday. The recent diet of rumours regarding Kluivert, Dugarry, Mahdavikia, Ruddock, Sheringham and Klinsmann seems to have ceased. Share price down a penny. How many pennies does that knock off Mr Sugar's wealth?

Friday 17 July

Even Liverpool have a French manager now, Gerard Houllier. 1998 continues to be the year of the French. Arsène Wenger won the Premiership and FA Cup double, France won the World Cup, and our own David Ginola adopts the mantle of Princess Diana, campaigning against landmines. But Marcel Desailly at £4 million was obviously too old and too expensive for us, so he joined Chelsea.

———————

Saturday 18 July

Many rumours about Sol Campbell. Pressure on Sugar enormous. Should he take the money and run? If Spurs keep Sol, and have a bad start to the season, Sol will be unhappy and his value will go down. The decision is yours, Mr Sugar.

Still the Kluivert speculation continues. Our Director of Football David Pleat finally goes on record: Sol not for sale. 'We are not interested in selling any of our assets.' So Mr Pleat, how many assets do we have? And who are our liabilities? 'The media speculation is disconcerting for our fans.' We are told that we should only take notice of quotes specifically attributed to Christian Gross or a club spokesman. Yes, presumably like the purported offer of £120 million for the club at the turn of the year.

———————

Sunday 19 July

Our third-choice 'keeper Frode Grodas moves to FK Schalke in Germany. We are in the hunt for Lee Clark, a

Geordie lad who went to Sunderland because he couldn't get into the Newcastle team. Now we are said to be willing to pay double what Sunderland paid. We are also linked to Norberto Solano, a Peruvian right back playing in Argentina. Arsenal are also linked with Solano. I wonder which club he will choose?

On the 12th of this month David Pleat said that Ronald de Boer was 'ungettable' for our club. Pleat had dismissed an Italian news agency report linking us with Patrick Kluivert, and I did an interview with PA Sport saying, 'No-one should be ungettable for Tottenham Hotspur Football Club. Every player has their price and the club should be able to compete for the best in the world. The fact that Mr Pleat admits defeat shows the lack of ambition of the club and gives us reason to fear another season of mediocrity. It was Spurs who led the way 20 years ago by signing World Cup stars Ossie Ardiles and Ricky Villa, but it seems that kind of swoop is now out of the question.'

———————————

Monday 20 July

News filters through that we lost 3-0 to Brondby in the latest friendly. The bookmakers' odds on us winning the championship, 66-1, are a bit mean. More like 66,000-1. I wonder who is captaining the team in the absence of Sol Campbell? Surely not our Swiss roly-poly, Ramon Vega?

———————————

Tuesday 21 July

No major news. Ginola still aggrieved at being left out of the French squad for the World Cup. Well, David, you had better prove this season how wrong Mr Jacquet was.

15

France won the World Cup without you. Gary Mabbutt has still not found a club after being shown the door. Mabbutt was treated disgracefully on the last day of last season. He was brought on for nine minutes after 16 years' service, having joined Spurs from Bristol Rovers in 1982 as a 22-year-old midfield player.

There were calls for Mabbutt from the start of the game, throughout half-time and after. That shows the esteem in which he is held. Gary, you should always be welcome at White Hart Lane. I just wish Gary had realised that his playing days at top level had finished after his collision with John Fashanu. His comeback against Blackburn was another sign. He should hang up his boots and become a manager. Maybe if he had stopped playing he would now be a coach at Spurs.

News that Arsenal will use Wembley for European Champions League fixtures. Wembley was once a second home for us, we were there about ten times in a year. FA Cups, Charity Shields, League Cups – at least I have the memories. A pity for fans born after 1983, who have seen only a flirtation with greatness in 1987, allegiance to the Paul Gascoigne roadshow in 1991, and constant transition since. No wonder the local parks are full of Man United, Arsenal, Liverpool and West Ham shirts. As our former manager Keith Burkinshaw remarked when he resigned in 1984, 'I remember when there used to be a football club over there.'

Wednesday 22 July

We are linked with Ipswich wing back Mauricio Taricco. Who? Once upon a time we signed two Argentinians who had just won the 1978 World Cup. But now we are interested in an uncapped, unknown Argentinian playing for Ipswich. Once we used to send our reserves up the A12 to Ipswich and Norwich. How times change. And we now employ Charlie Woods, a Chief Scout from Ipswich, who has recommended Taricco.

———————————

Thursday 23 July

Fourth friendly, third defeat, 4-2 away at Birmingham. Our big names are still absent, Calderwood was out with a broken finger and we had a trialist Italian 'keeper Stefano Visi, as Ian Walker's wife is expecting their first baby this week. Mixed reports about the game: various people said that Vega was terrible, awful or atrocious. Nothing new there then. And we had a new captain, Ruel Fox. I thought the captaincy bottomed out when Steve Sedgeley was given the armband. Spurs captains of yesteryear have included tremendous heroes like Blanchflower, Mackay, Perryman and Mabbutt.

Paul Furlong scored after ten minutes, then hit the bar with a header and Jon McCarthy followed up for 2-0. Dele Adebola immediately made it 3-0. Rory Allen got one back, Adebola got his second, and Vega headed in a late goal from Edinburgh's cross.

The papers still suggest that Dunga, Taricco and Clark are on the horizon, but I'm not excited. (Then a phone call about Sol sends a shiver down my spine. Watch this space!) The share price is down to 66p. Bet of the season: do we have a goalscorer who can reach double figures? How many more weeks will it be before the Gross-Pleat double act is terminated? Garry Brady, our 21-year-old Scottish right winger, has walked out and joined Kenny Dalglish at Newcastle. He was at the end of his contract and we cannot demand a fee, although we may get compensation from a tribunal. We reportedly offered him £30,000 a year, which is what some players earn in a week.

Friday 24 July

Not much news. Clarke, Taricco, Dunga all still on the hit-list. Do we really want these players? It smacks of desperation. Season approaching. No major signings. Confidence? I have no confidence about this season. I'll be happy to be four points off relegation with a game to go.

Saturday 25 July

We play Celtic at Parkhead in a friendly, still with a depleted team. Wonders never cease, a goal after 11 minutes, Ginola to Armstrong, 1-0. We're on our way. But, with Scales and Vega at the back, we lose 2-1. Our big names are still on holiday. What did Ferdinand do in France that warrants three weeks off? England played four games, but he never made an appearance.

Sunday 26 July

Now we are linked with the de Boer twins, the World Cup stars who want to leave Ajax. Do we need scouts and Directors of Football to find players like the de Boers? There is only three weeks until the start of the season, but no good players have been signed. There is plenty of time to regroup, make some major signings and take the Premiership by storm. Last week the chairmen of

Europe's top clubs had a meeting to discuss a European Super League. Fifteen years ago Spurs would have been represented at that meeting.

Monday 27 July

Return of the heroes, fresh from their World Cup exploits. Once we had Gazza and Gary coming back from an England semi-final in 1990, and Ossie and Ricky arrived as winners in 1978. Sol and Dazza, a whole lot rests on you guys. Little to report. No chance that the de Boer twins will choose Spurs ahead of Barcelona or Real Madrid.

Tuesday 28 July

Share price down again, 64½p. I believe that it would improve dramatically if we had a new chairman, someone who could give a boost to the team, staff, supporters and the City, someone who would send a clear message once and for all that "We've got our Tottenham back".

Preparations for a game against Norwich on Wednesday, but our stars will not appear until Saturday's friendly at QPR.

Wednesday 29 July

Hans Segers is our new goalkeeping coach on a one-year contract. Baardsen to go? Apparently Segers read on Teletext that Spurs have offloaded Grodas so he phoned up Pleat to ask for a job. Maybe the club's phone number should be posted up in the Haringey Job Centre.

Sol flies off to Milan. Strange. Didn't he have his break? England's last game was 30 June against Argentina. I thought all the Tottenham squad were training this week. Has Sol been given extra time off to ponder his future? Or was he just buying a new wardrobe from Armani? Sol caught a British Airways flight, but he is definitely not signing for Inter or Juventus for £15 million. So we are told. Tottenham is Sol's club, and he is our captain. He is 23, has just played in his first World Cup, and might play for a foreign club later in his career. Anything is possible in football though, and we do get paranoid about the possible departure of our heroes. The club deny any official approaches for Sol and insist he is not for sale.

Thursday 30 July

We beat Norwich 3-1 at Carrow Road. Ruel Fox was our captain against his old club and a crowd of 16,000 turned up. Craig Bellamy scored the first goal after intercepting an Edinburgh backpass, but then Ginola created two goals. He teed up Moussa Saib for the equaliser, and crossed to give Armstrong a header which made it 2-1 at half-time. Vega got our third with another header from a cross by new left back Paulo Tramezzani. Walker made two late saves from Bellamy. Christian Gross said, 'It was good. It proved we are going the right way, even without the internationals who start back next week.' It was our first victory since Peterborough.

CHRISTIAN GROSS STRUGGLES

Gross has promised that Sol Campbell will be a Spurs player at the start of the season. A major transfer panic is over. Gross said, 'I can guarantee that, injury permitting, he will be a Tottenham player at the beginning of the season,' said Gross. 'He is under contract. He had an excellent World Cup, he is young and strong and he is the type of player that every club is looking for, but he is committed to Tottenham. He will be coming back on Sunday. I gave him these days off because he played a whole season and then had games for England. The trip to Italy is only for holiday reasons. He is not linked to any Italian team and is not there with his agent.'

I did a piece with PA Sport comparing our summer transfer activity with that of West Ham, who signed five new players including Ian Wright. Despite promises from the chairman, the manager and the director of football, we have only signed Tramezzani and Segers. 'It quite clearly demonstrates that we are not able to compete at the top level, both in terms of the Premiership and Europe. What is the problem? Is it the transfer fees? Is it the wages? Or is it because the players believe that Tottenham are now a second-rate Premiership team with aspirations only of League survival and a good Cup run? The buck must stop somewhere and the chairman, Alan Sugar, should either put up the money for new players to get us back to the top or he should put the club up for sale.'

A three-man arbitration commission has ordered the de Boer twins to honour their contracts at Ajax. The twins are 28 and each signed seven-year deals in March 1997, but then took the club to court. Their contracts run until 2004 and include a clause stating that they cannot ask for a transfer until 2001. Barcelona and Real Madrid wanted to sign them. Dutch players are notoriously opinionated, but if every player who signs a contract goes to court two years later it will be anarchy.

Saturday 1 August

QPR v Spurs at Loftus Road is 0-0 and a dreadful game. We were seriously bad. Titi Camara, a centre forward from Guinea who has been on a month's loan from Marseilles, made his début. He was poor and didn't sign. What a surprise!

Sunday 2 August

The *Sunday Mirror* backpage is 'SPURS FACE SOL PAY ULTIMATUM'. The article includes a league table of estimated weekly wages of Tottenham players. Ginola and Anderton were said to be on £15,000, Ferdinand £12,000, Armstrong £10,000, Scales, Vega and Fox £8,000. Calderwood and Walker were on £7,000. Campbell was on £6,500.

The match report by Graham Nickless said that Ginola was the main man in the first half, and Spurs struggled after he went off at half-time. Nickless reckoned Gross must be unhappy with the form of his team, which has only won two of seven pre-season friendlies.

Monday 3 August

Team flies to Holland to prepare for Feyenoord friendly at the end of the week. Why a week in Holland? Others play Inter Milan, Atletico Madrid, Lazio, we play Birmingham, Norwich , QPR.

Tuesday 4 August

Now we are linked with Darren Eadie and Craig Bellamy at Norwich, £10 million for both. Yeah, right! Phone fund manager at Equitable Life, who hold 4% of Tottenham shares. Asked him if they were pleased at the way things were developing for the coming season, to see whether they'd had any contact with the Board of Directors.

Equitable had had limited contact with the Board and I was given the bog-standard line: only one team can win the Premiership, only one team can win the Cup, so it's a balance between how much investment goes on the playing side and how much you take care of business in terms of the bank vaults and the balance sheets.

I explained to him that if you don't take care of business on the pitch, it doesn't matter what happens off it. Tottenham Hotspur PLC may be trading profitably and doing well, but Tottenham Hotspur FC certainly isn't. And I think he took that on board.

Wednesday 5 August.

Share price drops half a penny. Little news, team away. I have decided to write a sarcastic letter to Alan Sugar. In the meantime I did a piece with PA Sport saying that it is a farce that we are linked with so many world-class players but come nowhere near signing any of them.

I said: 'I am afraid that Spurs have become the club who cried wolf and we just don't believe it any more when

23

we are linked with a big signing. It does the club no harm when the headlines put them in for these players and maybe they hope it will help them sell more season tickets and attract sponsors. But we will not believe in the signings until we see the player unveiled in a Tottenham shirt. We have had our hopes built up a number of times and have become a laughing stock for not making any significant signings.'

Furthermore, I said that I do not accept the excuse that no international players will sign for a club that is not in Europe. John Collins has signed for Everton, Wim Jonk has gone to Sheffield Wednesday and Ian Wright has joined West Ham, while we have only signed an unknown left back and an ageing 'keeper on a free transfer from Wolves.

Thursday 6 August

Deloitte Touche Report. We made loads of dosh, but we want to see that money on the pitch! Team sheets are what matter, a quality team, a winning team. Not balance sheets.

Friday 7 August

The Pony deal is up at the end of '98-'99, so we have a new Pony away kit. That may only be for one year, so the fans will be ripped off yet again when a new kit deal is signed. A new company will obviously want to market two new kits immediately.

The David Mellor column in the *Standard* has a go at Sugar under the headline 'SPURS GUILTY OF GROSS MISTAKE'. Mellor says that we have had a bad week because Camara did not impress at QPR and Monaco playmaker Ali Benarbia decided to join Bordeaux because they have more ambition than Spurs, so we are seen as losers, a club no good player wants to join.

Mellor is surprised Gross is still our manager. 'I'm amazed he wasn't put on his bike at the end of last season. After another four months of mid-summer muddle, does anyone at Spurs still believe he's the business? But it's not too late to do something about it. I dimly remember another north London club a few years ago beginning a season with a sergeant major who wasn't taking their team anywhere. Anyway, they dumped him and brought in a Frenchman instead.'

Alan Mullery is quoted in a *Financial Times* piece by Roger Kelly. Mullery is a former Spurs half back who played 312 league games for the club and is now a Sky pundit. He said, 'It's now 37 years since they last won the championship and the last five or six years have been mediocre. The supporters still think Spurs is a big club, but you have to question it. Buying world-class players is the modern trend, but you have to pay big money. Look at what Blackburn, Manchester United and Arsenal have achieved by spending.

'You only have to compare Spurs to Chelsea. They have world-class players. That attracts a big crowd. They won a European trophy last season and had a respectable year in the Premiership. That makes it easier for them to attract other top players. The influx of players at White Hart Lane has not happened, we are told, because Spurs are not in Europe, but that is an excuse.' It is a shame that the club has to take this kind of criticism before a ball has been kicked in earnest, but it is hard to disagree with Mellor or Mullery.

Saturday 8 August

We draw 1-1 with Feyenoord in Rotterdam. Our goal is scored by Armstrong. Sol Campbell plays, but Anderton does not. I am still working on the letter to Sugar.

Sunday 9 August

The News of the World reports that Spurs have a new £40 million kit deal with adidas. £40 million? You could buy the club for that! If this was true, would it be in *The News of the World*? I wonder how much the share price will jump tomorrow on that news?

Monday 10 August

My letter to our wonderful chairman is now finished. It reads as follows:

Alan Sugar
Tottenham Hotspur Football Club
748 High Road
Tottenham
London N17 0AP

10th August 1998

Dear Mr Sugar

Given the recent rumblings of my fellow Tottenham Hotspur supporters I feel it is time to put the record straight, and offer you a vote of thanks. So I thank you for:

1. *Reducing my expectations so that I do not believe Tottenham will ever win a trophy under your leadership, or even compete at the top level.*
2. *Not buying Carlos Kickaballs like Bergkamp, Gullit and Zola who have not made the same impact on their respective clubs as the players you have signed.*
3. *Having a clear strategy in the way the Club is developing and in particular its investment in youth, the acquisition of Hans Segers and the sale of Garry Brady being classic examples.*
4. *Employing even more directors, consultants, coaches, scouts and other people behind the scenes, to establish a clear chain of command and always maintain another tier of administration between yourself and the 'decision'.*
5. *Ensuring that the Club does not qualify for Europe and so sparing me the inconvenience of passport renewals, days off work, travel arrangements, changing currencies, etc.*
6. *Turning our ancestral home into a corporate hospitality wonderland.*
7. *Not participating in the European Super League talks and saving me the cost of buying a digital receiver and paying to watch my club on TV.*
8. *Handing over Wembley to our arch rivals, Arsenal. I never liked the traffic jams anyway.*
9. *Reminding me that professional football is not about winning, but taking part, and, in particular, taking care of the elderly, lame and injured in the community, and giving them contracts.*
10. *Not winning any silverware for the last seven years, so I have not had to trek along to Tottenham Town Hall on a Sunday morning and therefore miss my local car boot sale.*
11. *My shares being worth half as much as they were worth last year.*

12. *Sending me those shareholders dividend cheques every year, which cost more to pay into my account than the dividend itself.*

13. *Ripping the heart and soul of our Club out by appointing custodians of our great dynasty who have no knowledge of the Club, its heritage and its values.*

14. *For what we are about to receive this season: another relegation dogfight. As we saw last season, that is always more exciting than mid-table mediocrity.*

15. *And finally, for being you. Someone I can look up to, respect and admire as a chairman who has the interests of the club at heart. Indeed, I endorse your comments on Klinsmann's shirt, Bergkamp being signed by Arsenal for cosmetic effect, and the stupidity of all of us loud-mouthed moron supporters.*

Nice one, Al. Keep up the good work.
Thanking you once again.

Yours sincerely,

Mark Jacob

PS See you at the shareholders meeting. Can't wait for your introduction of yet another new manager!

Tuesday 11 August

Directors Tony Berry and Douglas Alexiou resign. Or were they pushed? Alexiou was a director for 18 years, Berry for 12 years. So Sugar is now the longest-serving director. Important links with the past, with football as it was before the Sky-financed Premiership boom, have been severed. The Board now has no lifelong Spurs fans. They are all people with no THFC blood, no history, tradition or soul. What lies around the corner? The directors should be the custodians of an institution, not money men making profits. They are there to represent the community, not to satisfy the whims of corporations.

Sam Chisholm, former Sky chief executive, is appointed as a non-executive director. In 1992 Chisholm was reportedly phoned by Sugar and told to increase BSkyB's bid for the live football contract. Chisholm was Rupert Murdoch's right-hand man. What will Chisholm do for Spurs? Organise a wild card invitation to the European Super League? If you can't get in the front door, try the back one.

Once again we follow the lead of Manchester United. We used to set the agenda, to be pro-active. Now we are merely reactive, responding to what other clubs do, always trying to catch up. Will we ever be in the front rank of English clubs again?

I drive up to St Albans for the final friendly of the season. We win 6-2 with ease, just a walk in the park. There are 5,000 fans there. Our reserve matches will be played at St Albans this season, not at the Chigwell training ground, which is unsuitable. How much did we pay for Chigwell? Yet another own-goal. News that Barry Hearn is issuing proceedings following the proposed use of Brisbane Road for reserve matches. Decided not to send the letter to Mr Sugar yet.

Wednesday 12 August

Rumours of a takeover. Was the appointment of Sam Chisholm a sign that Murdoch is about to buy the club?

One of Chisholm's former Sky colleagues says, 'Chisholm was a rottweiler in the world of television. He gets things done and never takes no for an answer.' Sugar says, 'Sam's knowledge of international broadcasting trends in the industry will be a major asset to this club.' It all fits into place. Get rid of Berry and Alexiou and create a new board. The club knows nothing about these rumours, and Sugar is away.

I tried to contact Herbert Smith, Sugar's lawyers to find out who they were acting for, but they did not return my call. Share price down half a penny. So the City were expecting changes, but it made no difference to their perceptions of the club or its prospects.

Supporters must always act as a check and balance against the board. What directors regard as negative publicity is often, in fact, justifiable criticism. Fans will be treated as turnstile fodder for as long as they remain passive, acting like turnstile fodder. Fans have more power and influence than they realise.

Bill Pierce writes a piece for PA Sport saying that the club are amazed by 'negative' publicity on the Chisholm appointment. Sugar's spokesman Nick Hewer said, 'In Sam Chisholm we believe we have now got the top man to steer us through negotiations over television deals such as pay-per-view which are going to become very big business for football clubs shortly.' Hewer said the reshuffle was nothing sinister and that Alexiou and Berry have become life vice-presidents and will retain many privileges. Harry Harris reports that Sugar has started legal proceedings against David Mellor for the piece in the *Standard*.

CHRISTIAN GROSS STRUGGLES

Thursday 13 August

Pleat opens his mouth again about the influx of foreigners. Sorry, have we not just signed Tramezzani and Segers? And who reportedly tried to buy Ortega, Kluivert and the de Boer twins? I called White Hart Lane and was told that Pleat was abroad. Maybe he was signing an Englishman in New York!

And how many Englishmen now play in top European leagues?

Do we have anybody in Italy since Ince left Inter for Liverpool a year ago? Yes, one left back, Tony Dorigo, and even he he was born in Australia. Ince returned, Gazza struggled, Rush failed, Platt moved around for astronomical fees and Lineker suffered after Johann Cruyff realised he wasn't skilful enough to play down the middle and stuck him on the wing. So we have nobody in Spain or France. And only Brian Deane and Mark Pembridge at Benfica, taken there by Graeme Souness, a British manager.

David Mellor's piece in the *Standard*, saying that Spurs had a good opportunity to offload Gross in the summer and hire someone else, has upset Sugar. He should have laughed off a comment from an MP who wore a Chelsea kit while sucking an actress's toes.

For once Mellor was speaking on behalf of a lot of people, and at least he has the forum. Richard Littlejohn, a big Tottenham supporter, also has the forum but he has been quiet.

I remember Sugar's outburst in May 1997 on *Do I Not Like That*, Littlejohn's ITV programme, saying, 'You be careful what you say to me because I've been speaking to people behind the scenes here, and I may be the only friend you've got!' An astonishing TV moment.

Went to the pub at lunchtime and saw highlights of the 1997-98 Premiership. Francis hands over to Gross. Humiliating defeats: Chelsea, 6-1, Coventry, 4-0, Liverpool, 4-0. Coming soon at a shop near you, the video of Spurs season. Sixty minutes of non-stop action. Title? *The Great Escape.* Two days to go before Armageddon, Wimbledon away.

Friday 14 August

24 hours and counting. The team will probably be Walker, Carr, Campbell, Vega, Tramezzani, Fox, Nielsen, Anderton, Ginola, Ferdinand and Armstrong. This is it. Make or break, championship or some other brain surgeon can take over. I keep hearing the same old line: only a couple of teams can win something every year, you can't buy success, balance required.

No last-minute signings. Surprise, surprise. Every season you live in hope. What do I hope for? The Double and Sugar to resign. Realistically, Sugar to resign. If the core of our club is wrong, the rest of it will never be right.

Saturday 15 August
Wimbledon (a)

The season of reckoning is finally upon us, the moment of truth. Was Gross right not to delve into the transfer market? There have been no signings, which were promised by Pleat. Car journey to Selhurst Park is hell as usual. Will the 90 minutes of football be worth the 90 minutes' travel time to get there?

Spurs come out onto the pitch without a ball. Ferdinand remonstrates with the bench. Where is the ball? Kick off. Wimbledon launch the ball into orbit, we play on the deck, neat one-touch pass and move football. Ginola, stuck on the left wing, does not touch the ball for the first five minutes. And just when we think Tramezzani is going to throw the ball to Ginola it goes way over his hair.

They say it takes time to settle, it's the first game. Really? Everyone knew that the kick-off was on 15 August, 3pm. We establish some banter with photographers down below us, who seem more intent on capturing Gross in his black mourning suit and black shirt than they were in the action. Then one photographer read out the sign which Gross had been standing next to: 'EMERGENCY EXIT ONLY'. I wonder how long it will be till he uses it. We are outplayed, outfought, outwitted and out of our depth. We are beaten 3-1. Ginola is a disgrace. Dived all over, got booked, deservedly. Please come back, Jürgen.

At 2-1 down Gross switches Vega to centre forward, even though he had Rory Allen, a striker, on the bench. I don't blame you, Gross, not totally. You are just the wrong man at the wrong club at the wrong time. Astute appointment, Mr Sugar. You searched across Europe and settled for third best. You confirmed that at the shareholders' meeting in 1997. That you had been searching around Europe, went to Hitzfeld, who recommended Gross, went to Beenhaaker, who recommended Gross, and then you settled for Gross.

Outside the ground, traffic is at a standstill so we decide to have a quick drink in the bar. Not long after the final whistle our guardians leave en masse, the Sugar clan. AMS 1, A5PUR and YAW 1. The Sugars even act like royalty, Chief Al in one car, the heir apparent in another.

Seeing our custodians have left, perhaps without the courtesy of thanking our hosts and congratulating them on their victory, I decide to get a closer look at the cavalcade as it is stuck in traffic. I walk up to AMS 1, which has Sugar in the front passenger seat. Face to face with the man himself. Sorry, Mrs Sugar, and your guests, sitting in the back. You looked so radiant, elegant, charming and intelligent. This action was no disrespect to you.

I calmly say to Mr Sugar, 'I believed in you. I thought you would be good for the club. I was wrong. I love this club.' I kissed the cockerel on my shirt. 'You have ruined this club, this institution.'

'Fuck off!' says Sugar, in front of his wife and guests.

'How much would it take Alan, name your price,' I say as I mockingly take out an imaginary chequebook from my pocket.

He continues his conversation in the car, turning to me occasionally with another, 'Fuck off!' At this point a Spurs fan comes past and spits on the ground in front of the car. That fan's action showed the disdain felt for the man. For five minutes I stared at Sugar, and he could not face me. Eventually the convoy heads off into the sunset. I'm not proud of what I did, but love Spurs and I did it for the club. I have to stand up and be counted. I cannot allow this to go on.

———————

Sunday 16 August

Gross admits we were outplayed. 'More hard work required.' We have heard that one before. What were you doing over the summer? Spurs legend Alan Mullery, is being threatened over quotes which appeared in the *Financial Times*. Freedom of speech? Not in my backyard. Herbert Smith will presumably act on instructions from THFC and THPLC. I suppose my writ is in the post.

I wonder how Harry Harris will report this? Alan Mullery, former Tottenham legend, FA Cup winner, UEFA Cup Final goalscorer and winner, club captain. We are now linked with Kanu, the Nigerian striker at Inter Milan, who has been out of the game after an operation for a heart problem.

Monday 17 August

More of the same, *déja vu*. Gross out? Sugar out? Something has to happen. Share price down a penny. At this rate Sugar will have to pay someone to take the club off his hands. Still trying to get my head round Sugar's behaviour outside Selhurst Park. On the Internet, calls for demonstrations. One fan urges others to stand up for their rights and demand a decent team. He suggests, 'Why don't we march up the High Road and gather in thousands and demand that we get something back for our support?'

On the TAG site a guy called Jonny posts the following message: 'I truly believe that if results go badly or even averagely in the next few months, the discontent amongst supporters will be at its highest since as long as I can remember. But I don't think Gross will carry the can at all. All the media are saying that he's under great pressure, but I don't think he is.

'I think the fans anger will turn towards Sugar. Will anyone really demonstrate at a game and call for Gross to be sacked, believing that someone else can come in and do a better job with the players and money available? No, Sugar will take the heat this time. He has appointed three managers in a row who have flopped and Sugar will carry the weight of responsibility for that. I think when the heat is turned up Sugar will want out. Remember three years ago when we started terribly and Sugar was under fire for not spending enough (ie the Carlos Kickaball outburst).

'He threatened to sell up for £40m, although he was never serious. The criticism he got three years ago is nothing compared to what he is about to receive. He will go by Christmas, and whoever comes in, whether it's Murdoch or whoever, CANNOT do worse for the club than Sugar has.'

With every day that goes by, more people feel this way. In five days' time we play Sheffield Wednesday at White Hart Lane.

Tuesday 18 August

I speak to someone who posts Internet messages on the Spurs message board. We talk about a demo, a march, which got a response from a few people. I then suggested that, instead of a march, we organise a white handkerchief protest, waving handkerchiefs at the board. I suggested that this idea should not come from the Tottenham Action Group, and that the TAG could then be used to comment on it at a later stage.

The *Daily Mail* picked up the story about the planned protest, and what people were calling for. We hoped that 10,000 fans at the Sheffield Wednesday game would wave white handkerchiefs at the board. Of course, this was all dependent on the result. If Tottenham score two goals in the first ten minutes, nobody will be interested in demonstrating. Everyone will love the club, everyone will love the manager, everyone will love the chairman.

Our England players are at the get-together before the European Championship qualifier against Sweden in

Stockholm. Gross can use that as an excuse this week. Wait for developments on Teletext and in the papers, but there is an eerie silence.

Even a victory against Sheffield Wednesday will not paper over the cracks. It has gone beyond that. Once again I find myself in the position of wanting the team to fail in the short term, so that the future can be brighter, just like under Gerry Francis. He was the wrong manager yet we still had to endure Newcastle, Bolton, Liverpool and many other humiliations. But the voice of the people finally came through and Francis resigned. Of course Sugar wanted him to stay, which shows how much he knows about football. He said he was deeply disappointed to lose him. Today I was given Alan Mullery's phone number. I wanted to find out the latest news on whether a writ had been issued, but Mullery is away for two weeks. Still waiting for my writ.

Wednesday 19 August

Even money on Gross being out of a job at the end of the season. Odds look increasingly generous. Gross will not be there at the end of the season. But will Sugar still be chairman?

Thursday 20 August

We are linked with Ole Gunnar Solskjaer from Manchester United, if they sign Dwight Yorke from Aston Villa. Pleat opens his big mouth yet again: 'We are only interested in signing the best.' Really? You've changed your tune, after saying some players are 'ungettable'.

Pleat says £40 million has been spent by Spurs in the last four years. 'Make no mistake, we have enough money, as much as any other club in the Premiership. Over the past four seasons the club has spent in excess of £40 million. The chairman has made money available to bring in players requested by previous management. In the past players have been signed as cover, to appease supporters and the football disease of keeping up with the Joneses.

'This summer we have been prepared to match the highest price for the de Boer brothers and Kluivert. The last thing we need is a knee-jerk reaction and I make it clear that we will not pay crazy transfer fees again for secondary players. For Spurs now it is either the best from around the world or the most promising young British players.'

Do not kid us, Mr Pleat. We are not stupid. In a way I do not want anyone to sign, as they will be Gross/Pleat choices and may not be the players a new manager would want. That would be a waste of money which should be made available to our next manager.

Gross now blames the length of the grass at Selhurst Park. Apparently Gross walked into Kinnear's office and told him he would be making an official protest about the pitch, and Kinnear reminded him that Wimbledon are only tenants at Selhurst Park and Gross should direct his anger at the landlords, Crystal Palace. Was the long grass a Venables conspiracy?

Friday 21 August

Just 24 hours before the next game. I hope Gross has mowed the pitch. Other clubs must be laughing at us. We are a shambles, so unprofessional. Every time someone from the club opens their mouth they are ridiculed. We bid for Solskjaer, a player we could have signed for peanuts before he went to United. Well done, Gerry. Gross says, 'We are not selling Sol, not at the moment.' Very convincing. White-handkerchief demo idea picked up everywhere, hope it succeeds. We have to do something. Enough is enough. It's now or never.

Danny Kelly, who has a late night TV show and is the editor of *Football.365*, the online football paper, criticises David Pleat's defence of the club's half-baked transfer policy and his admission that money has been spent unwisely. 'He refused to name names but he must have been thinking about such big-money non-successes as Gica Popescu (£2.8 million), Ilie Dumitrescu (£2.5m), Ramon Vega (£3.7m), Ruel Fox, (£4.2m), Jose Dominguez (£1.5m), and maybe even the injury-ravaged John Scales (£2.6m) and Stefan Iversen (£2.7m).' Kelly said that everyone knows that Pleat and Gross get on worse than Mr and Mrs Alf Garnett, but nobody knows who is in charge of the team.

Meanwhile, Pleat has been talking to Michael Hart in the *Standard* about how the demanding Spurs fans want to see a team winning with a bit of style. Amazingly, he seemed to damn Gross with faint praise and faint sympathy when he said, 'He's a very hard working man, but it can't be easy for someone to come from abroad and work at the highest level with new players against unfamiliar opposition.'

On transfers, Pleat said that the three foreign players we made bids for (the de Boers and Kluivert) are still with their original clubs. He said they sat round a table with Steve Staunton, but he wanted to go back to Liverpool. Pleat said they made a big bid for a young Premiership player, and a big bid for a young Nationwide player. The Iranian, Mahdavikia, had to do military service and play in the Asian Games, so they were not sure he would be able to play in 75% of our games.

The *Daily Mail* reported that the fans on the Internet were demanding the resignation of the board, and planning a white-handkerchief protest similar to those seen at bullfights and at Spanish football grounds.

Saturday 22 August
Sheffield Wednesday (h)

I'm actually confident that we will beat Sheffield Wednesday and everyone will say: 'What was all the fuss about? The grass has been cut, the players have had another week of training, and Solskjaer looks like signing.' The *Daily Mail* headline is 'LID COMES OFF £5.5m SOLSKJAER DEAL'.

Team news: Nielsen in for Berti. We start brightly, Sol's header hits the post, then our defence goes AWOL as Atherton heads in Jonk's free-kick. We are 1-0 down and some white handkerchiefs are seen. Again, our central defence parts like the Red Sea, Di Canio puts us 2-0 down.

More handkerchiefs are unfurled. Big rush for the exits when the second goal goes in. Players booed off at half-time. Quite rightly. This was Sheffield Wednesday, not Manchester United, Liverpool or Arsenal. People keep saying: give it time, five or six games before protesting. No! By that stage we will be down. No shape, no pattern, no passion, no heart, no commitment, no hunger. Where will it end?

Vega had been jeered in first half and doesn't come out for the second half. A foot injury, says Gross later. More of the same. One by one fans get up and leave, many venting their frustration at the board. Andy Hinchcliffe curls a free-kick round the wall to make it 3-0. At one point we had four wingers on the pitch: Fox, Ginola, Dominguez and Anderton. Then Fox went off injured. When Gross took Vega off at half- time he brought Saib on in midfield and played three at the back. So he was not only admitting defeat in terms of his team selection, but also in his formation, going from 4-4-2 to 3-5-2.

We lose 3-0 and I am left in a state of disbelief. I had expected to win this game. Fellow fans looked stunned. Nobody knew what to say. You sensed unrest in the street. Fans were angry. Who would they blame? What would they do? About 1,000 fans gathered outside the gates. I tied a white handkerchief to the gates as a gesture of solidarity for the cause.

A week after telling me to 'Fuck off!', Sugar now says the same to reporters. Reaction afterwards is inevitable. Calls to Capital Radio, calls to Mellor on BBC Five Live. An hour after the game the demo is still going on. Police, stewards, horses, dogs. How did we ever arrive at this situation? Danny Blanchflower must be turning in his grave.

A PA Sport report by Bill Pierce later described the demo and the chants of 'Sack the board' and 'We've only got two men', and revealed that Sugar had been in the dressing room at half-time last week when we were 2-0 down. Pierce said that Sugar had criticised the *Daily Mail* report suggesting that Tottenham and Manchester United had lied about the Solskjaer deal and that it had already been completed. He quoted Sugar saying, 'This is a very spiteful report. We have only agreed terms with Manchester United for the player and we will not be speaking to him until next week. Tonight we are planning to speak to his agent.' Solskskjaer's agent is Rune Hauge.

Sunday 23 August

Headlines about the demo. 'FANS TURN ON SPURS' is the back-page headline of *The Mail on Sunday*. Peter Higgs described Sugar coming out two hours after the match finished, and long after the demonstraters had gone: 'Flanked by five security guards, he remained grim-faced and refused to discuss the developing crisis. Asked if he had a reaction, Sugar replied: "Oh, certainly." Then pressed as to what the response was, he delivered a curt four-letter word before departing.'

Solskjaer wants to stay at Manchester United. So all that self-righteous prose in yesterday's *Daily Mail* turns out to be the own-goal of the month. Where do we go from here? What will Sugar do? Try to be objective about yesterday. Was the demo right? What alternative was there?

Monday 24 August

Harry Harris reports that Sugar is ready to sell up. The shares are worth £80 million, and Sugar has 40%. If the story is false, will Sugar sue *The Mirror*? Unlikely. Sugar would be happy if the story boosted the share price, an effect which it could well have. Share price down half a penny however. Shows what the City thinks. I get many phone calls from journalists, television, it's going mad. Will Sugar sell? If so, to whom?

The *Daily Mail* said Sugar snarled and swore at the reporters after the game: 'Alan Sugar's response was as graceless as Tottenham's performance had been artless, a foul-mouthed, four-letter retort from behind a screen of orange-bibbed security guards.' After Sugar's Jumbotron response to the *Mail* on Saturday the paper was obviously going to retaliate, especially after a demonstration where fans chanted 'We want our Tottenham back!' outside the gates.

Encouraging to read a *Guardian* piece by Martin Thorpe, who also suggests Sugar may be ready to sell, up under the headline 'A CRISIS TOO FAR FOR WOULD-BE SAVIOUR OF WHITE HART LANE':

'Alan Sugar saw the writing on the Tottenham wall a long time ago. In May 1993, having just sacked Terry Venables as chief executive and with the first hostile crowd besieging White Hart Lane, the Spurs chairman exited via a side entrance saying: "I have done the right thing for the club but will I ever be able to show my face here again?"

'He did, of course, show his face again but it was never viewed in the same light. From that moment his image as the white knight who had rescued Tottenham from the jaws of bankruptcy two years earlier was irreparably tarnished. It was not just because he sacked Venables. That was the starting point and from then on Sugar's now seven-year stewardship of Tottenham Hotspur was a fight to gain credibility with the fans in the face of constant failures on the pitch.'

Thorpe recalled that Sugar had reminded us in August 1995 that if he had not come along White Hart Lane would now be a Tesco supermarket. After Saturday's protests Sugar said that he has invested more than £50 million in players and spent £30 million redeveloping the stadium.

'Now this proud and dogged character, not used to failure and reluctant to admit it, seems ready to hang up his boots, undone by a lack of success on the pitch but also by his PR image among the club's supporters.'

Very encouraging. If Martin Thorpe thinks Sugar is ready to hang up his boots, things are looking up. In the

Standard Adrian Curtis reported the after-match scenes as staff left the ground. Chris Armstrong was escorted to his car by a steward as a fan called him a 'tosser', and Sugar, Pleat and agent Rune Hauge eventually emerged after the protesters had dispersed. When Sugar was asked if he had any reaction to the match and the demonstration, he said, 'Yes, f*** off.'

Tuesday 25 August

Interviewed on *London Today* TV programme, 1pm. Carlton sent a car to my office. More speculation: Joe Lewis, Murdoch, the usual suspects. New manager to be appointed, Ruud Gullit in the frame. Coming out of my office in the evening I saw a newsstand with the *Standard* and the poster was 'SUGAR SHOCK FOR SPURS'. The seller was a Spurs fan who had a Tottenham cockerel tattooed on his arm. He gave me two copies of that poster.

It was the front page story by Simon Greenberg, Sports Editor, and the headline was 'SUGAR READY TO QUIT SPURS'. The sub-headline was: 'Chairman taunted by fans is willing to sell £60 million club'. Greenberg wrote, 'It is understood that on Sunday night he had discussions with his family at which it was decided he would bring his seven-year reign as the club's chairman to an end when a realistic bidder appeared.'

I did a piece for PA Sport welcoming the news that people apparently wanted to buy the club. I said, 'If Mr Sugar is indeed selling, he should be applauded and commended for turning the business of Tottenham Hotspur plc around and leaving it in the healthy financial state it is in. We are deeply disappointed that his fine performance off the field has not been mirrored on it, and he should be thanked wholeheartedly by supporters for everything he has achieved.

'We must now look to the future and hope that potential suitors are able to lead the club from its current plight and ensure it returns to its rightful place, where it competes not only nationally but globally, and where Tottenham are seen as trendsetters in order that the glory days may return to our great club.'

———————————

Wednesday 26 August

Russell Kempson has a story in *The Times* headlined 'GROSS STILL FACES AN UNCERTAIN FUTURE'. I think that clubs who panic in August, and sack the manager in August, look like the worst-run clubs in football. Do Manchester United or Arsenal or even Aston Villa ever generate these stories in August? Panic in August sends out one loud signal: the chairman does not know what he is doing. The chairman realises he has made a mistake and now he wants to correct it, even though it is too late. Come to think of it, Arsenal did sack Bruce Rioch in August, but at least David Dein had the bottle to do it before the first Premiership match.

Spurs fans reading Kempson's story must have been angry and embarrassed: 'Tottenham Hotspur, a club in crisis with its team in turmoil, emerged no healthier yesterday after a day of rumour, counter-rumour and steadfast denials. The futures of Alan Sugar, the chairman, and Christian Gross, the head coach, remain unclear, but it is believed that Sugar is willing to sell control of the club once he has resolved the problem of who will manage the side.

'After two successive defeats at the start of the FA Carling Premiership season, Gross was reported to have been given one match to turn around the team's fortunes. However, it is more likely that he will be given at least a fortnight to produce an improvement. If none is forthcoming, he will be dismissed after less than a year in charge. Only then – and after a replacement head coach has been found – will Sugar explore the option of selling his 40 per cent shareholding. Reports yesterday indicated that Rupert Murdoch, chairman and chief executive of The News Corporation, parent company of The Times, and Joe Lewis, the billionaire backer of the English National Investment Company, had held separate discussions with Tottenham representatives. "It's just not true," a spokeswoman for The News Corporation said.'

The story also said that David Pleat is believed to have made a £5 million offer for Jean-Paul van Gastel, a Feyenoord midfield player. Jean-Paul who? Never heard of him! A few weeks ago we were linked with Kluivert. The last Dutchman Pleat signed for us was Johnny Metgod, who only started five games.

A story in the *Express* said Sugar will only sell the club if he can find the right owner, and quoted a spokesman as saying that neither Murdoch nor Joe Lewis of ENIC have had any talks with Sugar about buying Spurs. The spokesman, presumably Hewer, said, 'Alan has had enough of the personal abuse he has already received after the team lost their first two games of the new season – and who can blame him? He now feels that, no matter what he does for Tottenham Hotspur, he will always be blamed if they are not performing well, and he finds this scenario incredible.'

But wait, the best bit is yet to come. The spokesman added the following amazing words: 'As far as Alan is concerned, he has delivered all he promised to deliver. He has put everything in place for the club to progress into the next millennium. But he is not the one who picks the team and tells them how to play, so he cannot understand why he is the target for such abuse.'

Astonishing stuff! Sugar had been thinking about employing a director of football for some time. He may have told Gross that he was looking for two men, not one, and that a director of football would be hired after he (Gross) started work. But did Sugar consult his manager about this appointment? It may be argued that an English director of football would undermine a foreign manager. The fact that Pleat was a former Tottenham manager obviously had the potential to undermine Gross still further. If a player took his problems to Pleat, and not to Gross, Pleat's presence would be divisive.

Last season, as relegation became a real danger, Sugar decided to re-sign Jürgen Klinsmann, who demanded a clause in his contract saying he could not be dropped. Sugar agreed to that clause. No self-respecting manager would allow such a clause, so Gross was undermined again, even though Jürgen's second coming saved us from the drop.

Now, after losing our first two games 3-0 and 3-1, everyone can see that the once proud and stylish Spurs have a mediocre team. But Sugar's spokesman is claiming that the chairman has delivered all he has promised to deliver. I don't think so!

Thursday 27 August

Glenn Hoddle picks his squad today for the game in Sweden on Saturday, 5 September. David Beckham will miss this game through suspension. The Premiership programme will be interrupted by England playing on the fourth Saturday of the season. The tabloids are making a big stink about Hoddle's faith healer Eileen Drewery being paid £75 a session for healing work with Darren Anderton *et al*. Chelsea's chairman Ken Bates has demanded an FA inquiry into a possible conflict of interest.

Friday 28 August

The Times reports that Sugar visited Gross at the training ground yesterday and has promised to drop in every week. I bet the coaches and players are really looking forward to that. Gross said, 'Alan said that our position was very serious, which everybody knows. When you lose your first two games, including your first home game, that is normal. It was not 3½ hours of crisis talks, it was a short analysis of the situation. We are going to do that every week, with me telling him how I saw the games and why we won or lost.'

Poor old Gross. He knows better than anybody that the situation is very serious, and he does not need a grumpy millionaire dropping in to ask why we did not win last Saturday.

Kenny Dalglish was sacked by Newcastle yesterday, and Ruud Gullit replaced him. The king is dead, long live the new king! Gullit apparently signed his two-year contract at the Wembley hotel where Glenn Hoddle was announcing his England squad in the next room. Newcastle finished 13th last season and reached the FA Cup Final under Kenny, who spent £35 million on players but won only 11 of his last 40 Premiership matches. Newcastle have fallen apart since Sir John Hall and Kevin Keegan left. Thousands of Geordies may have thought finishing second was failure, but Newcastle played exciting football under Keegan. The Geordies are desperate for their first major trophy in 40 years. And Tottenham fans think we have problems!

Gullit's agent Jon Smith said, 'Ruud is absolutely delighted by his new appointment.' I'll bet he is. He's 35 and needs a job after being sacked by Ken Bates seven months ago. He was offered to Tottenham in the summer, and punted all round Europe with no takers. Well, not no takers. Jon Smith said Ruud had turned down five jobs. Which five jobs, Jon?

Saturday 29 August
Everton (a)

William Hill have Everton 11-10 on to win this relegation battle. Gross makes crucial team changes. He drops Walker and brings in Baardsen. He drops Armstrong and plays Ginola up front with Ferdinand, and he puts Calderwood in central midfield, moving Nielsen over to the left wing. After five minutes Ginola hits a high corner to the far post and Ferdinand scores with a power header. Baardsen makes five good saves, including a tipover of a Dacourt free-kick and two Duncan Ferguson headers. We hang on to win 1-0. There are two penalty incidents. Ginola, who had earlier been booked for diving, is refused a penalty by referee Peter Jones when Unsworth brings him down, so he throws a massive tantrum. And Materazi, a clumsy Italian centre back, is tripped by Anderton but no penalty is given for that either. Gross now has nine victories in 26 FA Carling Premiership games since he took over in November 1997.

In this morning's *Telegraph* Mihir Bose says that Klinsmann may come back as coach, and that Daniel

Sugar, the chairman's son, is meeting Andy Gross, Klinsmann's lawyer.

Sunday 30 August

Joe Lovejoy writes a two-page feature in *The Sunday Times* which summarises the last three years at Tottenham. The article, obviously prepared in anticipation of another defeat, has been tweaked to include mention of the victory at Goodison. Lovejoy grew up on the Double team and treasures one item in particular among his club memorabilia: a programme from our 13-2 annihilation of Crewe in 1960.

The headline is 'SUGAR AND SPITE', and Lovejoy says Alan Sugar is the root cause of the unrest at Tottenham and should take his share of the criticism. He says that the hiring of David Pleat and the re-signing of Jürgen Klinsmann undermined Gross's authority last December.

Lovejoy also points out that the current situation is a repeat of August 1995, when Sugar said, 'I'm sick of all the aggravation. I'm not going to stand the abuse any longer. I've worked my nuts off for Tottenham and what do I get for it? Abuse from all these ratbags. Give me back the money I'm owed, purchase my shares and I'll be off for the good of the club.'

He says that Sugar is capricious and that U-turns have become his trademark: 'In August 1995 *The Sun*'s back-page headline 'SPURS FOR SALE' was followed the very next day by 'SUGAR: I STAY'. He waved good riddance to Jürgen Klinsmann, saying he wouldn't wash his car with his shirt, then welcomed him back.'

CHRISTIAN GROSS STRUGGLES

Monday 31 August

John Ley, in the *Telegraph*, compares Christian Gross's position to that of Brian Little before he was replaced by John Gregory:

'Once again, we have a decent man's future questioned not necessarily because of his capabilities but because of the indolent approach of his players. Remember Aston Villa last season? Brian Little left, in came a new manager, and those same players took Villa into Europe and now sit at the head of the Premiership. Managers do make a difference. A breath of fresh air can lift confidence and morale. But too often, players escape the finger of blame.'

There is never much hard news in international weeks so the papers love to gossip. Today it is all Newcastle gossip. They were hammered 4-1 at St James's Park yesterday by Liverpool. Michael Owen scored a hat-trick. And now people are asking whether Gullit will cash in on Alan Shearer, who is 28 and past his best. Shearer has been a goal-machine but he has not scored in Newcastle's first three games. The club allowed Dalglish to spend £15 million in the summer and then sacked him after two games. What an own-goal by the directors! Gullit really needs that £15 million to build his own team.

Tuesday 1 September

Glenn Hoddle is now raving about Owen, who is still only 18. He said: 'Michael was sensational against Newcastle. He could have had five goals in the first-half alone. His finishing at the moment is second to none in the country. The way he has performed since the World Cup, he's done everything right. He is the top striker in

51

the country at the moment.' We all told you that in June, Glenn, but you stubbornly started Teddy Sheringham in the first two World Cup games!

Wednesday 2 September

We are reported to be lining up a £12 million bid for Chris Sutton and Tim Sherwood, Blackburn are said to want £3m for Sherwood and £9m for Sutton. We have also been linked with Charlton right back Danny Mills and Wimbledon centre back Chris Perry. Pleat has said, 'We made an offer for Sherwood at the end of last week but it was rejected. We will wait for developments. We haven't made an offer for Sutton, we haven't shown an interest in Mills and although I was at the Wimbledon-Leeds match on Saturday, I wasn't particularly watching Perry.'

Thursday 3 September

The FA want Glenn Hoddle to sign a new contract till 2002, taking in the next World Cup. But Glenn is stalling. There are rumours that he has his eye on Tottenham, and fancies the job if Gross gets the chop. Glenn is a Tottenham legend, but has always felt reluctant to come back because he did not want to spoil the memory of what he did for us as a player. He is very highly regarded by the fans because he could do things with a football that none of us have seen since. Or maybe Glenn felt he was still too young for the job. The responsibility of managing Tottenham, to him, would seem much bigger than the responsibility of managing Chelsea.

CHRISTIAN GROSS STRUGGLES

Friday 4 September

England's preparations for their Euro 2000 Qualifier in Stockholm have been ruined by a huge furore over Glenn's World Cup diary, which betrayed the secrets of the squad and infuriated reporters who felt Hoddle was keeping information back to sell in his book, which was serialised in *The Sun*. Alan Shearer is peeved with all the talk about Hoddle's book, and Tony Adams's book, in which he criticises Hoddle. Shearer says we should get back to talking about football.

The last time we played Sweden was in 1995 when Darren Anderton scored twice in a 3-3 draw at Elland Road. Anderton is in Sweden and saying he is back to his best again after a good World Cup and a good pre-season. After three seasons of 'pure hell', Dazza reckons his confidence is sky-high again.

He said, 'The last three years have been an absolute nightmare. At the beginning of the World Cup people in and out of the game were asking questions about whether I should even be in the squad, yet alone the team. The negative vibes did create a bit of self-doubt and I suppose Glenn was taking a bit of a gamble in taking me because of the history of my injuries. I'd come back loads of times and kept breaking down.

'Then I played in the first game of the World Cup against Tunisia and felt I did OK, only to once again get slaughtered afterwards in some quarters. But Glenn had a lot of faith in me and made me believe in myself as a player. It makes a hell of a difference if you've got someone like that in charge and you've then got the confidence to play your normal game.'

———————

Saturday 5 September

At about 4 o'clock Carlton TV News said that Christian Gross 'had resigned'. That's how it originally broke, that he had resigned. Then I flicked up Teletext to find out what had happened. Tried to make some phone inquiries and spoke to a couple of journos. Was Gross pushed? There were rumours that he would be pushed after the Everton game anyway, even if we won.

But why does it happen on the day of an England-Sweden international? Because this was seen by Sugar as an opportunity to sack Gross with a minimum of fuss. All the top reporters are in Stockholm. Part of Sugar's thinking must have been to keep coverage of Gross's sacking to a minimum.

Sweden v England is the main sports event of the weekend. So Tottenham sacking Gross will be bottom of the page. Sugar has had five days to sack Gross. He could have done it last Sunday or Monday or Tuesday or any day this week. And it would have been a back-page lead. He could have done it after the Everton game, even though we won 1-0, just as we won the West Ham game before he sacked Ossie Ardiles in 1995. He should have replaced Gross at the end of last season.

Gerry Francis probably tendered his resignation after half a dozen games of last season and the crucial factor was that Sugar did not want to go to the shareholders' meeting with Francis in charge because he would have been lynched. And once again we have a situation with a shareholders' meeting coming up again, probably in November, and attention focused on the club, so Sugar again feels he wants a new manager in place. Maybe he is licking his lips at the prospect of getting Hoddle. That would be an appeasement exercise, just like Ossie was after Venables was kicked out. But would Hoddle, or any manager worth his salt, come and work for this board of directors? Or come with David Pleat as Director of Football above him? Probably not.

Sol Campbell wants to improve, wants to win things, and he is not going to learn anything from Gross. If you look at Sol's performances for England in the World Cup, and then this season for Tottenham, his level of play has fallen. By all accounts he made the point to Sugar, who was alleged to have said, 'If you feel like that, say it.'

———————————————

Sunday 6 September

This morning I went out to get a paper. Then had a phone call from Carlton TV asking me to do an interview. There is a press conference at the training ground, could we meet there? Despite what Mr Sugar may say, I don't necessarily jump at the opportunity of being on TV, but someone has to do it. Someone has to make a stand and argue. You cannot continue with the directors controlling the media from their side. The media will use people, will use quotes, as they use everybody. But that is the only forum, apart from an AGM. And we all know that Sugar does not listen at AGMs. Last year he did not say anything, and yet the following day he opened his mouth at the Oxford University Union. There is no alternative. The only alternative is not to go any more, not to support Tottenham any more, to lose faith. But Tottenham is in my blood. So I arranged to go down to Chigwell.

I've read a few papers this morning. John Scales, Ruel Fox, the usual suspects opening their mouths. Clearly, the players were not playing for the manager and wanted him out. The players have pushed Gross out. It seems that Sol

Campbell knew something we didn't because he made some amazing remarks in Stockholm yesterday. Sol said, 'Some games you are disheartened. There are some games where you wonder what is happening. Whoever comes in as manager, I want him to teach me and make me a better player.' Sol was asked the obvious question: Doesn't Christian Gross do that? He replied, 'I'll pass on that.'

Obviously, Gross was the wrong manager. But who appointed the manager? That is the fundamental point. At the shareholders' meeting last year Sugar went on record as saying that Gross was his third choice, after Ottmar Hitzfeld and Leo Beenhaaker.

If you keep appointing a new manager who wants his own players in, your team will always be in a state of transition. Profit warnings are coming out of Tottenham all the time. The half-yearly results are not going to be as good as the end-of-year results. So we might just about break even on a season which was pretty traumatic.

At the Sheffield Wednesday game we saw empty seats, empty boxes. With the lack of activity in the transfer market, and the lack of merchandising, profits for next season will probably be down. We will probably make a loss. So for all Sugar's business acumen, look at the share price. It is almost at an all-time low. Look at the capitalisation value of the club: £60 million, half of what it was a year and a half ago. If you do not get it right on the pitch, you will suffer off the pitch.

At Chigwell I tried to drive in but the guards on the gate asked if I was with a paper. I said, 'No, I'm a Spurs supporter, could I go into the press conference?' They said, 'Press only.' So I turned round and waited outside. I saw a few hacks walk in, and touched base with Carlton TV.

Then I waited, listening to the radio to see whether there was any news.

The press conference started at about 2.30 and finished about 15 minutes later. Gross came speeding out in a bottle-green Mercedes. I tried speaking to him but he just shook his head and drove straight off. A couple of minutes later Daniel Sugar left in his silver-grey Porsche Boxter. I didn't bother trying to flag him down.

Then Alan Sugar came out in a black BMW S83. He saw me. I didn't want to speak to him. I just wanted to look at him, just stare him out, let him know I was watching over him, like he does with other people. Not to say anything. When he stopped I thought: what's he stopped for? He's obviously stopped to have a go. He wound his window down.

He said, 'Don't worry, your chance will come in a few minutes when all the press come out with the microphones, so you'll get your bit on the box later today, no doubt.'

He said, 'You are the cause of all this. Tottenham fans should realise it was people like you who have caused all of this. You're a very dangerous man. You shouldn't talk to the press because they are all leeches. You should be careful what you say when you open your mouth.'

I said, 'Look, Mr Sugar, I respect you for what you've done, and what you've achieved. All I want is five minutes of your time to sit down and talk about strategy, the future, etc.'

'You don't deserve it,' he said. 'You've caused a lot of trouble at the club. You don't have the right to speak to any of the board of directors, or the right to be put through to them.'

When he said his piece about the press, I didn't know whether he was giving me advice about being used, or trying to discourage me from speaking to the press because of what I would say. The truth hurts, Alan. The truth hurts. And if I felt for one moment that I was wrong, I would not continue.

Then he threatened me. He said, 'I'll put your picture up on the big screens at the Blackburn game on Wednesday. I'll put your face up the screen and find out how much support you have.'

Sugar drove off leaving me somewhat stunned. And worried by what he might say about me. Nigel Clarke had written an article in the *Daily Mail* on the Saturday morning about the Solskjaer deal, so before the home game against Sheffield Wednesday Sugar put his name on the screen and said his story was totally false. So I might be this week's Nigel Clarke.

But what can he do? Put up: 'WANTED – Do you know this man? Do you like him or me?' Are we back in Roman times, asking the crowd to give a gladiator the thumbs up or the thumbs down? Is that is what it has come down to? If it is, then Sugar has completely lost the plot! It is not only me. It is thousands of Tottenham supporters. It is not about one person, it's about Tottenham fans demanding the best.

For seven years the club has been in a state of decline and turmoil, ever since he took over. Sugar corrected the ship at the very start, but having got it on an even keel, he has been unable to take it forward. Spurs is now a rudderless institution.

Now that he has sacked the manager will he still proceed against David Mellor, who said Spurs should not have appointed Gross in the first place? If Sugar bans me, so what? I can go to away matches. I can still watch the games on the box and speak to people. But he won't ban me. It would be one of the own-goals of the century.

Tottenham-Blackburn isn't live on Sky but the Middlesborough game is on Sunday. So maybe Sugar will do it for that game as well. Maybe he'll do an interview for Sky beforehand, and put my picture up on the screen and say: 'This is the person who has caused all your trouble and strife. Blame him! Get your bagels here to throw at him!' I would be *persona non grata*. That would be great. Fame at last, what I've always wanted – not! It's pathetic.

I just want the best for the club. It's about the name of Tottenham Hotspur. And as I said to Carlton, the name of Tottenham Hotspur has been brought into disrepute. The name of Tottenham Hotspur, to people of my age and older, evokes memories of good times. A lot of good times in the Fifties, Sixties, Seventies and Eighties. Recently, it's been bad times. So much controversy, turmoil, bickering and in-fighting, so many accusations and court cases.

I have visions of Tottenham playing in front of a few hospitality boxes. You can drive straight in, no crowd, no atmosphere, loud pop music blaring over the PA, bottle of Chablis in the fridge, nice hors d'ouevres, petits fours, vol-au-vents, a few poor waitresses and stewards, guests decked out in dinner jackets, women in long dresses. The lights are on but no-one's home.

Bring on the entertainment! Bring on the gladiators! Eleven men in white shirts come out and kick a ball around and get thrashed. And the people watching do not know what is going on, and are not really interested, except that they are returning someone a favour by allowing themselves to be corporately entertained.

It is just business. What can you say if someone picks up the phone to you and says: 'Would you like to come to Tottenham, have a bite to eat and watch the game?' You have to be polite to the people you're in business with. And we were one of the innovators in executive boxes when Irving Scholar was chairman.

But, then again, if someone's trying to get you into a box at Tottenham, a declining football club which has obviously lost the plot, would you want to do business with those people? You just had to see the empty seats and empty boxes two weeks ago to realise that there is something drastically wrong.

A few of us stood up and said we wanted what was best for the club.

And we could have easily been placated if Sugar had listened and communicated. Those are two fundamental factors. If Sugar steps down the new directors must take that on board. There must be regular meetings with the fans and with the shareholders and the institutions. They need to know what is going on because ultimately the fate of our club will be decided in the City dealing rooms.

Monday 7 September

Yesterday's sensational news is confirmed: BSkyB is involved in talks to take over Manchester United! Murdoch has offered £575 million for the club. I am very worried about what this will mean for us in the long term. And in the short term. This is a signal that Man Utd want to go out on their own and become a brand leader, a world leader, and to hell with the Premiership. For £575 million you could buy four or five English clubs. You could certainly buy ten Tottenhams for that.

How will this affect any bid for Tottenham? Manchester United's share price was up 57p at 216p at noon, while BSkyB's shares were up 20p to 482p. Aston Villa's share price jumped 40p to 602.5p, and our shares rose 3.25p to 63.75p. *The Financial Times* says ENIC is ready to match BSkyB's offer. United have announced plans to extend the capacity of Old Trafford to almost 70,000. Putting in 12,000 more seats would cost £30 million.

Chapter Two

DAVID PLEAT IS CARETAKER

Tuesday 8 September

David Pleat press conference, no real news. He is the caretaker manager. He will do the job. He feels that he is capable of doing it, but he does not want to commit himself as his head will be on the chopping block. Spurs are paying Pleat £250,000 to be Director of Football. No manager worth his salt will take on the job with an overlord like David Pleat.

George Graham, the jury is out. Some people say his track record is second to none. But he is an Arsenal man who plays boring football, plus he was sacked by Arsenal for taking two bungs from Norwegian agent Rune Hauge, and suspended from the game for a year. Glenn Hoddle, the time may not be right. Hoddle has not really failed with England, but has not succeeded either, so this is not a good time for him to become manager of Tottenham.

Joe Kinnear has kept Wimbledon afloat but has a barrow-boy image. We have one barrow boy in the board room. Do we need another in the dug-out? Jürgen Klinsman, maybe he's taking this year out. But Berti Vogts has just resigned from the national job, so Klinsmann may end up coaching Germany. Raddy Antic might be Pleat's choice as he played under Pleat at Luton and scored the famous goal which sent Manchester City down in 1983. Antic did well for a while at Atletico Madrid but had bust-ups with star players including Italy's best centre forward, Christian Vieri. Kenny Dalglish has just been kicked out of

Newcastle. Kenny is dour and highly unlikely to move to his family to London.

Looking at that list, it's unpromising. Pleat could be running the team for quite a while. Maybe Sugar could manage as well as direct. Maybe he envies Ron Noades, the tracksuit chairman, who has just won the Manager of the Month Award.

We are playing Brentford next Tuesday night in the League Cup, and maybe Sugar wants to sit on the bench.

Prediction for tomorrow's Blackburn game? I really have no idea. Who will captain the side? Fox, Ferdinand, Vega, Calderwood? Who cares? Will victory mean everything in the garden is rosy? Defeat will probably hasten the end of Alan Sugar. Realistically, a boring 0-0. Like the game I went to tonight: QPR 0 Walsall 0. It was the first-round first leg of the Worthington Cup. And we thought we had problems!

———————————

Wednesday 9 September
Blackburn (h)

Had a funny dream last night. Raddy Antic is given a three-year contract as manager. Some dreams do come true, but not this one, I hope! Tonight there will be no Sol, no Dazza. Vega and Calderwood facing Sutton, Gallagher and Davies. Blackburn rested skipper Sherwood, who is 'mentally unfit'. Why has it taken Roy Hodgson so long to realise that Sherwood is mentally unfit? He is unfit because of all the bids by Spurs for him. Sherwood is a Gooner, a big Arsenal supporter.

Perhaps Sugar is trying to turn Tottenham into Arsenal? George Graham, Theo Foley, sign Sherwood. What next? A bid for Merson? Of course George hasn't signed yet but I wouldn't put anything past Sugar.

I was informed today by one of the partners at work that another party was in talks with Alan Sugar regarding the sale of the club. Don't know who yet, don't know how much. Very surprised no news has been leaked. Will try to find out more.

We went a goal down after about ten minutes. Sutton crossed, Flitcroft headed down to Gallacher, who scored. But we got a goal back after Kenna had fouled Ginola, whose free-kick was headed in by Ferdinand. Baardsen made a brilliant pointblank save against Wilcox to keep it 1-1 at half-time. Ginola laid on the winner for Nielsen to head in after 50 minutes, and later went off to a standing ovation, after suffering a hamstring strain.

———————————

Thursday 10 September

Only 28,000 people saw our win over Blackburn compared to the 32,000 who saw the Sheffield Wednesday fiasco. Are fans voting with their feet? Or did Wednesday bring 4,000 more fans than Blackburn? A much better performance, though the opposition was poor. Left the game a bit deflated. Don't know what I should be feeling.

The friend who went with me disappeared into the vice-presidents' suite to hob-nob with all and sundry. I'm beginning not to trust these people. Am I just being used as the battering ram to have a go at Sugar in the press and on television and radio? Then, if he sells, other people move in to take control of the club. It is now reported that Carlton are in talks with Arsenal. Obviously Tottenham weren't big enough for Carlton. I feel totally deflated.

Pleat described Ginola's role last night as being lazy. That was an understatement. At one point I thought

Hughton was going to bring on Ginola's pipe and slippers. People just cannot see Ginola for what he is, an individualistic glory-hunter. Last year's débâcle was partly down to his selfishness, his refusal to play for the team. When he opens his mouth and says Tottenham fans have lost heart, it's outrageous. Jürgen was right. Ginola's best role is on the wing, getting the ball in early. The bickering between those two was a problem at the end of last season.

Eventually Jürgen got his way, Ginola was stuck on the wing, and Jürgen scored the goals that kept us up. Ginola supplies crosses. He is the only one creating in this team. So why have teams not wised up to us? Man-mark Ginola and you eliminate most of the threat from Spurs. How many shots off-target and failed dribbles does Ginola produce? Do the Carling OPTA stats never lie? Was Ginola really the top attacking midfield player last season? No, but he was the most selfish, the most individualistic.

4.40pm. Harry Harris phones to ask: 'Who is in the market to buy the club?' I said, 'Does Sugar want to sell?' He said yes. I said, 'OK, what price? How much does he want? He's got 40%? How much per share, Harry? At 55p a share he'd walk away with £22 million.' He will speak to Sugar and call me back. I won't hold my breath! I think Harry is just fishing around to find about any potential bidders and let Sugar know, so Sugar can exterminate them. Or was he genuinely looking to find out if buyers were serious?

Friday 11 September

Return the club to the people! Tottenham fans could lead the way. People power. Supporters have the power, but they've sold out to big business. Corporations need to be put in their place. They feed on the game. They owe their existence to football. Without Premiership football, where would Sky be? Where would cable TV be?

Football clubs have sold out, pulled the ladder up and ignored the grass roots. They have said: we don't want lager lout fans, we would rather entertain the Pimms princesses. We have a golden opportunity at Tottenham Hotspur to return to real football, not the fantasy that has gripped the game for the last couple of years.

Share price up this week from 60p to 66.5p. Other shares in the sector have moved up by a greater percentage – Leeds, Villa, Arsenal, United, all on the back of the BSkyBs bid for United. Reports that Sugar values the club at £140m. Is he living in cloud-cuckoo land? But we have affluent supporters. Despite Sugar's period of tenure we still have a world name and a stylish image, one that is probably still second best in UK, despite the recent years of decline.

So maybe Sugar would walk away if somebody offered him four times his original investment of £5m. I hope so. £20-25m values the shares at about 55p. But he won't take that. Reports that George Graham wants Darren Anderton at Leeds for £6 million. Or is he just using this as a tool against the Leeds board? Is this what will make or break George's future at Leeds? If they don't give him the money to buy Anderton, will he walk out on Leeds, saying he has taken them as far as he can?

Interesting lunch at Justin's, Marylebone Lane, with a couple of accountants and Irving Scholar. Two words were used quite often: humility and glory. Found out that Barry Townsley, the brother-in-law or ex-brother-in-law of Michael Green (Carlton), is believed to be putting a bid together for Tottenham. Have not heard that name before.

ENIC are now interested, apparently. Have investment will travel. We concluded the lunch by agreeing that the key decision of a board is the choice of manager to ensure that you get it right on the pitch. But the bottom line is: will Sugar sell?

After lunch I received another call from Harry Harris. Sugar wants 80p. Joe Lewis of ENIC offered 60p. Where do we go from here? I have had a number of meetings with potential investors. David Buchler was approached by a wealthy Canadian who was prepared to put in £20 million. Buchler is an insolvency practitioner at accountants Buchler Phillips. He was a director of Barnet last year. Buchler was brought on to the board in 1990-91 by Nat Solomon when Tottenham was in intensive care and the Midland Bank pulled the strings. He knows Tottenham from the inside and has good connections. I was constantly being told, 'Don't worry, the money's there, just deliver Sugar. We can't buy something that isn't for sale.' I've delivered my part of the bargain, as have the fans. We want Sugar out now.

But I'm pissed off at being kept in the dark. I've got Sugar on the retreat, on the back foot, but I'm worried about this consortium. If someone is putting in £10 million or £20 million they will want a say, a piece of the action, a bit of power. Reports that ENIC have bid £80million, but Sugar is now not interested. I can't believe it. Maybe Irving Scholar knew all along. All those phone calls during lunch now seem a bit suspicious. But Scholar calls me after lunch: Sugar has turned down 80p. He now wants £2! Typical Tottenham Hotspur. Nothing is straightforward with our club.

Then I hear on the grapevine that LWT are in the market. What next? Walt Disney? Sugar is obviously getting greedy. I have a poster on my wall, an *Evening*

Standard headline 'SUGAR SHOCK FOR SPURS'. That was when he wanted to sell, after the Simon Greenberg story. The only shock for me is that he is still there. I've been led a dance by everyone. The fans should know that they have been sold down the river. I did what I thought was right in the interests if the club, the name, the heritage, the institution. I feel totally deflated. Looks like I will have to turn my attention to something else now. Never mind. It was exciting while it lasted. Better to have loved and lost than never to have loved at all. These characters from various consortiums haven't phoned. They get what they deserve. Feel totally let down, sick. Scholar was an interesting character. He had it and let it slip through his hands.

Yet again circumstances – BSkyB's takeover of United, Carlton and Arsenal – have conspired to prevent a takeover. So near and yet so far. David Buchler tells me not to worry, to relax, the ENIC base is covered. He likes using sporting parlance, don't think he knows what it all means. Believe it? No way. I should be there. I've done the donkey work. But we are no further forward. I don't think Buchler is clued-in to strategy, and that goes for all of them.

Saturday 12 September

We are ready for three wins in a row. We play Middlesbrough at home tomorrow. A piece of cake. We had the best year of Gazza, 1990-91. Who could forget that Cup run? Blackpool away, lays on the free-kick for Paul Stewart to score, Oxford at home, Notts County at home, Portsmouth away, and a certain semi-final against Arsenal at Wembley. 'Is Gascoigne gonna have a crack? He is, you know!' A 25-yard screamer past Seaman! It still sends a shiver down my spine. That's what football's about. The guy is a genius who has been ruined by various factors. A brilliant player, terrific with kids, but needs someone to keep him on the straight and narrow. But now Gazza is past his sell-by date.

New reports confirm that ENIC have upped their bid to £80 million but Sugar rejects it. More speculation. How many consortiums are there?

Sunday 13 September
Middlesbrough (h)

Hear Richard Littlejohn interviewed on Radio Five Live in the morning. Now he comes out of the woodwork. He goes on record as saying he's willing to buy 29.9% of Sugar's holding and will keep Daniel Sugar on in a role. Littlejohn has the forum and he has used it: his radio show, his *Sun* columns. Littlejohn has spoken to Sugar several times, although not recently. Will he sell or not? He says Sugar spoke to him a year ago and said he'd win the championship in two years or let some other brain surgeon take over.

Indeed, Sugar actually said in an article that if he got close this year, got us into the top three, he'd have to ask the Tottenham Action Group for an extension! It is quite funny and sad to re-read that Sugar interview in *The Mail on Sunday* on 10 August 1997. He told Simon Greenberg that manager Gerry Francis has to deliver this season, and there must be no excuses:

'The chairman believes there are only a handful of truly disenchanted fans and that the views of the self-styled Tottenham Action Group are given undue prominence in the media. But even now Sugar believes that it is time for

Spurs to realise their potential and qualify for Europe for the first time since his reign began in 1991.'

Sugar said: 'I think we are in a position to win the championship in the next two years, barring the sort of injuries that slaughtered us last year. We now have key players back and a tremendous squad. If we are not up there in the top five, I will be very disappointed indeed. I will not rest until we have brought the championship here. That's what I'm going to do, no question of it.

'I hope to do it in this two-year time scale. But if we are third this year and, say, just miss out on the title next, then I will ask the TAG if my sentence can be extended. Certainly, if we finish 10th again or 12th, injury-free, then I have failed. If that happens, it is definitely beyond my comprehension how to do it better and I will stand aside gracefully.'

We finished 10th that season, and we lost 6-1 at Bolton in the Coca Cola Cup fourth round. That would have been a good moment for Alan Sugar to stand aside gracefully.

Meanwhile, back to Middlesbrough in 1998. Vega is dropped. Campbell comes back in. But the game is a disaster. Ricard scores twice in seven minutes in the first half, and Kinder, a sub for Gazza near the end, makes it 3-0 after a Baardsen mistake. Ginola is marked out of the game by Festa. The performance, in a game which is seen on Sky, is an absolute disgrace. Our defence parted like the Red Sea, as usual.

Monday 14 September

I saw a mascot at the ground yesterday, dressed as a cockerel. Have they finally found a role for our Operations Manager? Share price up 14.5p to 86.5.

69

Speculation is obviously causing ripples in the City. Takeovers, media frenzy. I wish all this publicity would stop so that the share price will drop to a normal level.

Call to the Stock Exchange Announcement Department. Ask if there had been an announcement about Tottenham. Yes, there has been: 'Mr Alan Sugar announced today that he received a proposal from ENIC plc on 10 September which would have involved the purchase of his 40.88% shareholding in Tottenham Hotspur and consequently an offer for the entire share capital of THPLC at 80p per share. Mr Sugar rejected the proposal.'

How much longer can supporters, shareholders and sponsors continue to associate themselves with a team which continually under-performs? Enough is enough. I want supporters to let their feelings be known, tell the club what they think about what's going on. We wait for the year-end results so we can judge the performance of the PLC in the light of the continued decline of the football club. All these matters must be raised at the forthcoming AGM, the only forum where shareholders can make their views known.

Capital Radio tried to have a forum with Tottenham but the club have again refused. This malaise cannot continue any longer. We must move on from the Sugar-saved-the-club days of 1991 to here and now, and the future. We no longer come onto the pitch to the sound of *Glory, Glory, Tottenham Hotspur*. Another slice of history which has been cast aside. We are sick of being told that Alan Sugar saved the club, sick of having that rammed down our throats.

I heard today that an offer had been made for 29.9% of Sugar's shares, with an offer for a further 10%. That was Littlejohn's consortium. Contacted ENIC press officer John Bick. He spoke about there being franchises round the globe and said that ENIC have a genuine interest in the future of Tottenham. I put him straight on the use of the word 'franchise'. Is that what we are? I told him not to use it in public for obvious reasons.

Another announcement, this time by ENIC: 'ENIC notes the recent press speculation. ENIC responded to a recent approach from Alan Sugar for it to consider the purchase of some or all of his shareholding at a price of 80p per share. However at the present time Mr Alan Sugar has indicated his desire not to continue with the present transaction. ENIC intended that any offer would be extended to all shareholders on the same terms.'

Surprise, surprise! Sugar approached ENIC. Not the other way round. Sugar approached them! Now the truth comes out. Or does it? Will the Stock Exchange actually investigate the events? I try to stir up a hornets' nest. Made a few calls to the Stock Exchange. They were quite willing to look into it. We are going down a very, very dodgy road at the moment.

I did a piece for PA Sport today: 'PUT UP OR SHUT UP, SUGAR'. I said: 'We are disappointed by what appears to be a U-turn by Mr Sugar. He has said he would like to leave Tottenham with speed and dignity. Given that he put up around £8 million to buy the club seven years ago, and that a couple of weeks ago the share price put its value at £60 million, then a bid of £80 million should have been acceptable to him.

'If the board really cared for the future of the club they would not play business with people's lives. Either Mr Sugar should come out once and for all and say the club is for sale and at what price, or else he should tell us his plans for the future and how he intends to bring the Premiership title to White Hart Lane this season, as he promised to do two years ago.

'The supporters are fed up with the constant games in the boardroom and all the uncertainty is clearly having an effect on the performance of the team. Two recent victories do not mean all is well at White Hart Lane. It simply glosses over the fact that we have not competed for major honours since 1991.'

Then I heard that Alan Mullery had a writ served on him. Called Mullery to give him our support, the support of the Tottenham Action Group, spoke to him briefly about it. At this stage he is defending it. I told him that if there's anything we can do to help, like having people outside the High Court, we will organise it. It would be like 1993, except this time all the fans will be behind Mullery and not divided as they were in the Sugar-Venables battle. Share price is up to 85p on the back of all the takeover speculation.

Tuesday 15 September
Brentford (a)
Worthington Cup, second round, first leg

A *Telegraph* piece by Mihir Bose says Peter Leaver will be chief executive of any new consortium taking over Tottenham. I also hear that one of the consortiums wants the chairman to be Lord MacLaurin, the guru who was responsible for changes in English cricket. And Jeremy Handley, a Tory MP I had never heard of, as a name, a figurehead. The PLC board would be people who were institutionally acceptable like Leaver, Lord M and this Tory MP. The football board would be the football people: Buchler, Berry and, surprise, surprise, they had even said there was a role for me. Read into that what you like! More speculation about Littlejohn who wants to buy 29.9%.

DAVID PLEAT IS CARETAKER

Did someone say we were playing Brentford tonight? Football matches are almost an irrelevance when so much is going on off the field. Tonight's game? We should beat Brentford, but I said that about Middlesbrough. Phoned ENIC at 3pm. Left a message for them to call me back. Things seem to be happening. ENIC may want our involvement, to manage things, with them being passive investors. Don't know how this would work.

Carlton had offered £275 million for Arsenal but the club's board apparently want £450 million. Carlton have bought 2% of their shares. But now I hear that Carlton and Arsenal have fallen out. Arsenal don't want any involvement with a media company. Maybe David Dein was outvoted. Call from Patrick Harverson of the *Financial Times*. Various financial options. He thinks the Littlejohn deal is the one which might happen. But when? And at what price. Found out that a guy called Howard Stanton is chairman of ENIC, though he is not really getting involved, but standing on the periphery. The person at ENIC calling all the shots is Daniel Levy, mid-thirties. He was described to me as the sort of person who, if he wasn't in his uncle's business, would proably be an estate agent in Hampstead, selling houses and flats. Sugar wants at least 125p per share. His starting point is 150p. But who will even go to £1?

We beat Brentford 3-2. Big deal. Reports that we were poor, awful. No news there, then. It was Pleat's third game as caretaker manager. He made five changes: Sinton for Fox, Vega for Calderwood, who played in midfield instead of Nielsen, Rory Allen for Berti, and Armstrong for Ferdinand.

Baardsen got away with two early boobs and Rory Allen missed a couple of headers. Andy Scott scored after a corner was knocked down. But Steve Carr ran on to Allen's lob to equalise. Dominguez, a sub, made it 2-1 after some agricultural defending, and did his backward somersault to celebrate. Then Sinton, who played for Brentford before he joined QPR, gave them an equaliser. He pushed an imbecilic backpass beyond Baardsen and Freeman knocked it into the empty net. But then our foreigners came to the rescue in the final minute. Ginola took a corner and Vega headed the winner.

———————————

Wednesday 16 September

The takeover is not going to happen. Sugar is giving conflicting signals. Will he sell? Won't he sell? Littlejohn not a real goer. So we are left with ENIC and whoever. Predictions? Shareholders' meeting coming up. Big changes must be made by then. Manager and players. Otherwise Sugar will be lynched, or will have to be in negotiations to sell. Maybe he will postpone the shareholders meeting, pending negotiations.

I'd like to organise a meeting on the day of the AGM an hour before at, say, Rudolph's pub, like the one we had a couple of years ago. And all those interested in taking over – ENIC, Littlejohn and others – could be introduced to the fans and shareholders. Give us their pitch, and let people make a decision. And then go into the shareholders' meeting with a sense of euphoria that potential investors actually want the club and are willing to make it great again.

We could walk into the AGM *en masse* with a list of questions and demands. Full and frank answers required, depending on the moodswing of the people. Maybe even make an offer there and then. Someone to stand up, make an offer for the club, and embarrass Sugar, put him on the spot. Then I find out that Carlton aren't interested in Spurs.

DAVID PLEAT IS CARETAKER

Thursday 17 September

I really think our brand name is only second to Manchester United round the globe. Can we resurrect our global image after seven years of decline? We have a name, a history, a heritage. Compare this to Chelsea. Will the short-term investment last over at Stamford Bridge?

It was in 1995 that Sugar needed to invest when we had the Famous Five of Klinsmann, Sheringham, Anderton, Barmby and Dumitrescu, and things were looking up. Not wait until things went wrong. At the start of the 1994-95 season we were docked 12 points, kicked out of the FA Cup and facing relegation, even before a ball was kicked.

Sugar went out, signed Jürgen Klinsmann, Ilie Dumitrescu, and, soon after the season started, Gica Popescu. He challenged the FA, got our points back and got us reinstated in the FA Cup. He took on the establishment and won. Full credit to him for that. The FA acted beyond their powers *ultra vires* and his solicitors Herbert Smith took them apart. The FA did not have the power to impose those punishments. So people then sympathised with Sugar and gave him a pat on the back. They thought he was there for the right reasons.

At the moment people are still quite sympathetic to Sugar. If he had walked away for £80 million after the Sheffield Wednesday débâcle, no-one would have criticised him. He could have left with his head held high. He could have said, 'I gave it a good crack, but unfortunately we didn't succeed. I've left you in good shape financially, and good luck for the future. Just give me a couple of tickets in the West Stand and I'll be on my merry way back to Chigwell.' Now, forget it. Fans think he is being very, very greedy. The tide is turning. More and more fans are turning against him.

Friday 18 September

Why should Sugar sell? No manager, only a few decent players, share price falling, now down to 75.5p. No bidders. Arsenal finish with Carlton. Man Utd and BSkyB making slow progress. The accounts will be published soon. Tough games coming up, we could slip down the table. Prediction No1: he sells below 80p. Prediction No 2: Sol Campbell asks for a transfer. Stand up if you hate Sugar! We want Sugar out! I hope they sing that.

He could have sold last week for £80-90 million and left with a bit of pride. Now he is seen as a money-grabber. Share price down to 74p. Telephone call to ENIC, John Bick, finally caught up with him and his assistant. Arranged a meeting with him on 1 October, two weeks from now. Sugar has dismissed as 'fantasy' a new bid to buy into Tottenham by a consortium headed by Littlejohn. Sugar was quoted in a Bill Pierce PA Sport report: 'Contact has been made but this is a football fan's fantasy dream and has not been given serious attention by the board.' In fact, this was a respectable offer made by the Bank of Luxembourg.

Preparations for the game at Southampton, who have no points in five games. What do I expect and want? We should win. But we could end up being their whipping boys, giving the Saints their first points of the season. News filters through that Littlejohn has upped his offer to 90p a share, and may go to 100p a share. But this is probably only for Sugar's 29.9%. Where is his money coming from? Will we be in hock to the Bank of Luxembourg? So if Littlejohn is struggling to buy 29.9% at 90p, where is the new money for players?

DAVID PLEAT IS CARETAKER

Saturday 19 September
Southampton (a)

Hans Segers played because the other two keepers were injured. Fox controlled a ball from Carr and put us 1-0 up, Ferdinand and Calderwood missed chances, Berti hit the bar with a header from Ginola's corner. The goal we gave away? A Mark Hughes ball over the top to Matt Le Tissier. Who was trying to mark him? Ramon Vega. The ball went over Vega's head and Le Tissier volleyed it in. So it was 1-1 after 65 minutes. Segers saved a Le Tissier free-kick, then stopped a header with his legs at the end. So we could have lost the game. Two more points down the drain.

———————

Sunday 20 September

What a see-saw week for Mr Vega. He scores the winner at Brentford and then costs us the game at Southampton. So Pleat has had four games: a 2-1 home win over Blackburn, a 3-0 home defeat by Middlesbrough, a 3-2 win at Brentford and a 1-1 draw at Southampton.

———————

Monday 21 and Tuesday 22 September

Jewish Rosh Hashanah. No real news except that George Graham is in the frame for the manager's job. Would Sugar dare negotiate with George over the Jewish New Year? Surely not.

———————

Wednesday 23 September
Brentford (h)
Worthington Cup, second round second leg

Cannot believe people are still more interested in what's going on off the field rather than on it. Sugar's probably won. He has defeated us. If the spectre of relegation is still there, who will pay £1.25 a share? Sugar has completely split the club.

Call to someone in the know who says it looks like George Graham. What a U-turn by Sugar! Found out that Steve Kutner was George's agent.

The game against Brentford was crap and had an eerie atmosphere. We were a goal down after a minute. Andy Scott went past Carr and shot just inside the post. Some dissent from the corner of the Shelf and Park Lane: *You can stick George Graham.* I know where I'd like to stick him.

It took us 24 minutes to get the goal back. Ginola played a quick free-kick to Fox on the right. Fox crossed, Armstrong's shot was blocked but the rebound went to Nielsen, who made it 1-1. We scored again just after half-time. A Ginola shot was parried to Campbell who headed in. A short corner, 53 minutes, Clemence crossed, Nielsen's shot came back off the post to Armstrong, who scored his first goal of the season. His first for six months, in fact. But Brentford got a late goal to make it 3-2. So David Pleat has got us through the second round of the Worthington Cup on a 6-4 aggregate against a team three divisions below us.

After the game Pleat admitted that Sugar was 'in dialogue' with the Leeds chairman about George Graham. The fans are divided. Graham had eight 0-0s in his first season with Leeds. Eight goalless draws in the 33 League games played after he took over when Howard

Wilkinson was sacked after five matches. If we have eight 0-0s we will be a laughing stock.

Indications are that the year-end financial results will not make pleasant reading. That is not taking into account the following: Gross pay-off, Graham compensation to Leeds, and his reported wages. So where will the money come from to spend on new players? We now have empty executive boxes. For years there was a waiting list for boxes in the West Stand. Now there are several empty. Presumably the City investors are now taking their money and running. When the share price went to 75p and 80p and 85p they thought Christmas had come early.

Why do we support Tottenham? A style, a swagger, a way of doing things. Glory, that's what football is about. We might not win trophies every season but at least we used to compete for star players who created an exciting brand name.

The proposed appointment of George Graham has completely split the club. What did Sugar say when Arsenal failed to sack Graham as soon as they found out about the bungs from Rune Hauge? He referred to the Arsenal board as being gutless and having no balls. In 1995 Sugar preached a sermon that was holier than thou. But three years later Sugar comes up with the biggest insult in Tottenham's history and the biggest U-turn of his career as a football chairman. Just how much more humble pie is left in the cake tin for Mr Sugar to eat?

And who suffers most of all? The supporters. What voice to do they have? They cannot do anything except vote with their feet and boycott matches and merchandise. But you can't do that because supporting Tottenham is in your blood. Lost my love of Spurs? Never. But will I go back? Not until Sugar leaves. I am disgusted. Goodnight and goodbye.

Thursday 24 September

In a PA Report I said, 'The branding of Tottenham Hotspur has dissipated over a period of time and the appointment of Graham will be viewed as the final nail in the coffin. And an admission that the history, heritage and tradition that is Tottenham Hotspur no longer exists. In the past we have not won trophies every season but we've had star players who have given the team a certain style, and given credence to the brand name of the club and all it stood for. Football is all about emotions, and rivalry plays a big part in those emotions. Mine tell me that I do not want Graham because of his past associations with our biggest rivals.'

Friday 25 September

Financial losses before trading of £1 million. The hypocrisy of Sugar. The club/plc is suing Mullery, but is prepared to hire George Graham. Why Graham? His style of football, his authoritarian handling of players, his bung inquiry. Sugar wanted to rid the game of bungs. Tomorrow's game is against Leeds. What an irony. The papers carried stories about Leeds chairman Peter Ridsdale looking forward to having lunch with Sugar.

PA Sport had a story quoting David Pleat talking about the money which would be available to the new manager. Pleat told Neil Silver, 'We haven't bought players so we have got money available to buy them. For the last seven months we have resisted buying mediocrity and it is a great challenge for somebody. The club needs three quality players, of course we do. If we buy two or three top players for £18 million – that is £6 million apiece – we can become a top-six club again. The new manager will have that money available. He can also generate money by selling. I would hope that George, or whoever takes the reins, could make Tottenham great again.'

Had an e-mail from 'Whiteblood', a fellow fan with whom I have co-written a little sketch. It is a commentary on the club done in the style of Australian DJ Alan 'Fluff' Freeman, the oldest young trendy on radio.

(*Background music: Alan Freeman's Top 10 intro tune*)

'Hello pop pickers – have we got a great chart for you today. It's the Alan Sugar Top 10 U-turns.

'Just before we start, bubbling under the Top 10 this week is **Facilities for the Fans**. Yes folks, having promised more facilities for you West Stand season ticket holders, Mr Sugar took away your coffee lounge. And you ladies out there still have to queue to **Share Three Toilets** at half-time.

'Now for the Big Top 10. And down at 10 this week is **Youth Development Scheme**. Yes, that promising youngster Garry Brady is now rebuilding his career in Newcastle – and all because Spurs wouldn't pay him another £12,000 a year, which is what some of their stars earn in a week.

'Up one fantabulous notch at Number 9 is **No Second-rate Foreign Players** featuring Paolo Tramezzani. In this excellent duet with David Pleat, the Chairman really seems to have lost the plot there.

'**Carlos Kickaball** slips back this week to Number 8. Oh yes, pop pickers, let's not forget that Mr Sugar, having rubbished all foreigners, quickly signed Jose Dominguez, David Ginola and Allan Nielsen.

'Climbing back again at number 7 is **Christian Gross**. That man just won't go away, folks. Mr Sugar scouted the whole of Europe and promised you that Gross was the best available.

'That old favourite *Jürgen Klinsmann's Shirt* is a non-mover at 6. Mr Sugar still hasn't washed his car with it but then he did re-sign the German captain last season. An absolutely megatastic swallowing of humble pie from Alan.

'Now for the Top 5 U-turns. And climbing ever closer to the top spot at 5 is '*I Wouldn't Pay £6 million for Les Ferdinand*. Thankfully, the remixed Newcastle Ferdinand, who was two years older than the QPR Ferdinand, cost Mr Sugar exactly £6 million. Good purchase, eh!

'Falling one place at Number 4 is the longest-standing chart runner *£4 million Pound Ceiling* featuring DJs Ruel Fox and Chris Armstrong. These two favourite panic buys are still on the books at White Hart Lane, reminding Mr Sugar of yet another broken promise.

'The tension's building and down at 3 is *Dennis Bergkamp's Cosmetic Marketing*. Having spent two years at Number 1, Double-winning Dennis falls for the second week in succession. And let's just remember the now classic lyric from our chairman that got him there: "As the season progresses and the fog, ice and cold arrive, his approach could change, especially when someone gives him a good kicking, an elbow in the ribs or a whack in the earhole. Arsenal have taken an almighty risk. There's no way Bergkamp is going to have the same impact as Klinsmann. If he thinks he's going to set the world alight, he can forget it. Clubs weren't exactly queuing up for him were they? Arsenal got him because they needed a bit of cosmetic marketing."

'And, shock of horrors, last week's new entry at Number 1 has already been knocked off the top spot. It's the ever popular *I Intend to Sell Tottenham*, which seems to be falling as quickly as the shares themselves. Well folks, your favourite uncle Alan has told ENIC and Richard

Littlejohn where to go, so it looks like the club will be in his hands for some time yet.

'And yes, you've guessed it pop pickers! I do not have to tell you that *Georgie Graham* is straight in at this week's Number 1. And Georgie Graham will take some beating. Mr Sugar once wanted to cleanse football of its financial irregularities, but now he hires the only manager ever suspended from the game for taking bungs!

'Well that's it, you Spursdicious supporters. But be sure to tune in for next week's Top 10 Alan Sugar U-turns! Watch out for the chart over coming months. Ones to watch include *George, You Can Spend What You Like On Players* followed by a quick tightening of the purse strings. And there's always *I Will Never Sell Sol Campbell* which has a great chance of entering the charts if Liverpool go on leaking goals as they are. Thanks for listening, pop pickers!'

———————————

Saturday 26 September
Leeds (h)

Will Graham be booed by both sets of fans today? The atmosphere outside the ground is strangely neutral. There is no buzz because our fans have such low expectations these days. The game of football is changing, Tottenham is being left behind, and the fans are depressed, resigned and sullen. There is none of the boisterousness, the sense of expectation, the feeling that 30,000 people are about to see some red-blooded sporting entertainment. There is little or no organised resistance to the idea of George Graham taking over.

We draw 3-3 after being 3-1 down. Leeds defended very badly and Ferdinand and Armstrong missed a lot of chances. Ginola was not playing so everyone else had to take responsibility. We played a quicker game, and more of a team game without him. If we are better without Ginola, what future does he have? Will Graham play him? Eerie silence at the ground.

The fans are united in supporting the club but divided on the subject of George Graham. And even more divided on Sugar. A fan ran onto the pitch in front of the directors' box, sticking two fingers up. But Sugar wasn't even there. Later on a second man ran onto the pitch. Sugar was said to be in Los Angeles on business.

————————

Sunday 27 September

It looks like Graham. He says he wants to come back to London for personal reasons. That's a bloody good start! Personal reasons. Not because he admires the club, likes the style of play or wants to work with our players.

An article in *The Observer* by Amy Lawrence: 'George Graham has revealed the main attraction of a move to Tottenham is neither avarice nor avenging his former employers Arsenal, but *amour*. His clan in London is calling. 'I am happy at Leeds but this is personal. I want to get back to a family life again,' he explained. 'I'm engaged to be married, and while [my fiancée] has been very supportive and understanding, if there is a chance of me going back to London she will be ecstatic. My son, daughter and wee grandchild live in London.'

Did he not know where Yorkshire was before he joined Leeds? Maybe he should have approached Sugar after his sabbatical to save us from Francis and Gross.

Graham said, 'I've been living on my own for two years in Harrogate, and I've only got away with it because 80 per cent of my life is my job. Nothing should overtake your family life and mine has suffered – that's why I got divorced. Eventually I will retire and live in London, and it makes sense for me to work in the area where I am going to retire if I have the opportunity. This has nothing to do with money because the contract I have with Leeds is fantastic.' So there we have it. A lonely Londoner in a lonely flat in a small Yorkshire town. He blames football for his divorce, and the move is not about money. It is about marital bliss.

Ever the realist, Graham reminds us that top foreign stars prefer to play for London clubs. 'The class foreigners do not want to go to the North, I've run into Chelsea's Italian boys at restaurants and they love it in London.' Fair enough. You run into Zola, Vialli and Di Matteo on the gourmet circuit. Would you sign a couple of Italian stars to play for Tottenham? Haven't you always said you are dubious about players who take a step down from *Serie A*, which is technically the best league in the world?

Graham said that his ideal team are the current Arsenal side, suggesting you need steel as well as class. So maybe he will sign some quality players like Bergkamp, Overmars, Vieira and Petit. With players of that calibre you can compete, create and finish. As he said, referring to Arsenal, 'If you want power football they can play it, if you want a nice passing game they can play it. I genuinely feel they have a wonderful team.'

Monday 28 September

Pleat states that £18 million is available for new players. Now we're announcing our transfer budget to the world. This is completely contrary to what Sugar said at the shareholders meeting last year. He refused to say what funds were available because he didn't want clubs to put up the prices of their players.

Hasselbaink, Radebe and Nigel Martyn are linked with possible moves to Spurs, following George. The papers always run this type of story when a manager moves. Lazy journalism. I wouldn't even call it journalism. I wouldn't even call it gossip. I might call it pub talk.

The debate goes on. Do we want GG as Spurs manager? A feeling of resignation. We don't want him, but we cannot suggest an alternative. Graham is inevitable. It is going to happen anyway, so we have to get used to the idea. But we must focus attention on the accounts. Sugar's role, post-balance sheet events, Gross compensation, Graham's astronomical salary and compensation to Leeds. We, the shareholders, pay for Sugar's mistakes.

Tuesday 29 September

Richard Littlejohn finally comes out in a hilarious column in *The Sun* attacking Sugar and Graham. He should have written it weeks ago. Headline is 'SPURS DON'T DESERVE THIS GRUESOME TWOSOME'.

Littlejohn is a Spurs season-ticket holder who was given shares in the club as a leaving present when he joined *The Sun* from the *Evening Standard* in 1989. He describes the £85 million bid by his consortium and reminds us that Sugar had appeared on his ITV talk show (8 May 1997) and promised that if he didn't deliver the championship in two years he would stand aside and let 'some other brain surgeon' have a go. Amazingly, Sugar also hinted on air that he had been speaking to Littlejohn's bosses before the programme started, saying,

'At the moment, talking from the backroom, I'm your best pal.'

By mid-afternoon the pugnacious tycoon was fighting back under the Teletext headline 'SUGAR HITS BACK AGAINST LITTLEJOHN'. Sugar said, 'If and when Tottenham needs a new owner, it would have to be a big corporation with deep pockets. Not, with respect, a group of passionate fans with a sarcastic, career-enhancing media mouthpiece as their spokesman.' As usual Sugar had been drawn into a slanging match which a sensible chairman would have ignored.

Will Sugar postpone Graham's appointment until after the results are announced so that the post-balance sheet events are not published, the huge cost of changing managers. Where will this mythical £18 million come from?

Wednesday 30 September

Yom Kippur. Day of Atonement. Have a good one, Al.

Chapter Three

GEORGE GRAHAM TAKES OVER

Thursday 1 October

Had a meeting with John Bick of ENIC. It would seem that the issue now is not George Graham. The club made an announcement to the Stock Exchange at 8.30am confirming his appointment. There is a news conference at White Hart Lane at 4 pm today. He is going to be our manager and there is nothing we can do about it.

We must continue to get behind the team. As supporters of Tottenham Hotspur we have been around a lot longer than Sugar and Graham, and will still be around long after they've gone. The issue is the name of the club, the brand, what it means to supporters and football people generally. There has been a decline in performance on the pitch and off it. As far as we know, pre-player trading profits are substantially down on last year. And the current financial year's figures will show three major items: Gross pay-off, compensation to Leeds and Graham's new contract.

I was interviewed on the phone by BBC Essex. I said the fans should just get behind the team because that is what matters most. And I said George Graham is the last throw of the dice by the chairman.

Today is a unique day in Tottenham's history, so maybe it is just as well that we now have 24-hour rolling news on satellite and cable. Sky Sports is pretty tabloidy and showbizzy. Sky is about stars, and Sky News is star-driven. So the caption on the bottom of the screen did not say, 'TOTTENHAM HOTSPUR PRESS CONFERENCE'.

The caption said, 'Coming up: 'LIVE TO GEORGE GRAHAM PRESS CONFERENCE AS NEW MANAGER OF SPURS'. He has not even started work yet and already the Gooner is bigger than our club.

The star's limousine has arrived at White Hart Lane and our fans can see, as it happens, an incredible Double Whammy, an event few had ever contemplated until recent weeks, an event which seemed impossible and unthinkable: Tottenham betrays its heritage by hiring an Arsenal manager and an Arsenal manager betrays his heritage by joining Spurs.

George Graham gets out, an elegant hard man in a navy blue suit, mid-blue shirt and a two-tone blue tie. He makes the most of his entrance, milking the moment like a pro celebrity. The moving TV camera catches the moment when Graham, an accomplished actor, freezes his big grin for the still photographers.

The grin says: I'm here, and I'm loving it. I'm the King of the Gooners and the enemy have had to hire me! I'm the £10 Million Man! I'm the charismatic messiah who will lead you out of the wilderness and into the promised land. There are security men in blazers. David Pleat, waiting by the door in shirt sleeves, poses briefly with Graham for the cameras. Back in 1987 Pleat and Graham were in opposite dug-outs here for a pulsating Littlewoods Cup semi-final replay which Arsenal won. Neither man could have imagined that 12 years later they would be working together.

Pleat's reign as caretaker is almost over. He must be relieved that he will not have to do the dangerous job any more. Pleat would probably agree with former Leeds boss Jimmy Armfield, who once said, 'The three hardest jobs in the world are football management, lion-taming and mountain rescue, in that order.'

But Graham is in charge now. The circus has hired a new ringmaster, a new lion-tamer. Graham will crack the whip. Graham will put his head in the lion's mouth twice a week while thousands watch in wonder. Graham will decide who comes and who goes and who plays. Graham has proved he can build a winning team. That's why he is so expensive. That's why he is the £10 Million Man.

Sky cut back for some more studio chat as Pleat whisks the new manager through unfamiliar corridors to the stage where he sits on the chairman's right. Pleat sits on Sugar's left in a grey suit. Sugar, who wears a black suit, has an abrupt manner at the best of times, but here we see the body language of self-disgust. Today looks like a trauma for him. His manner says: I don't want to be here, I can barely believe what I'm doing, and I don't want to admit it has come to this. The ultimate climbdown. The ultimate U-turn. The ultimate compromise.

Sugar's introduction of the £10 Million Man is neutral and minimal. His mood as he introduces Graham seems, oddly enough, the same as it was four weeks ago when he sacked Christian Gross. He looks as if he regrets one as much as the other. Chairmen invest huge hopes in each manager they hire. Each failure damages them. Each sacking is a kind of funeral.

Sugar simply says, 'Thank you, ladies and gentlemen, for attending this afternoon. The purpose of the press conference is obvious. I think the easiest thing is to throw the meeting open to the floor, to ask whatever questions you wish.'

Any other chairman would have said something like, 'I'm delighted to welcome one of the finest coaches in football, Mr George Graham. George has agreed to be our manager for the next four years.'

But Sugar apparently cannot bring himself to mention

the name of the man he has just hired. The name must taste like poison. Those contract negotiations must have been rough! Then the questions begin:

George, can you tell Sky News why you came to Spurs?

'Mainly to come back down south again. To come to one of the major clubs, not only in London but in England and hope to resurrect it again and push it back up where it was ten years ago.'

Do you have any regrets about leaving Leeds?

'Yes. I had two very, very happy years at Leeds. Not only happy but I think successful. It was a very rewarding time.'

Was it a difficult decision, George, in the end?

'Yes, it was a difficult decision. It was an important decision. It was also a personal decision as well.'

George, you're not associated with the sort of football that Spurs fans traditionally like. Do you think you can bring a bit more style, a bit more flair?

Graham smiled, but he clearly considered this an ignorant question, and perhaps a rude one:

'I think you're asking the wrong question there. To the wrong person. The first thing we've got to do here is to get them back up the League in a challenging position. Hopefully, maybe within the next two years, get them in the top six. That would be Phase One. And if we can get them there, hopefully then we can compete with the big boys. As I said, when I was manager at the other North London club, Spurs were up there with us. What's happened in recent years is they've got further up the successful tree, and Spurs have just started drifting a little bit.'

But Spurs fans do like a bit of style don't they?

'Yeah. But let's have a winning style.'

George, you saw the team play last week. What did you think of them?

'I thought their passion and their commitment was first class. And if I can get that reaction from them on a weekly basis I'll be delighted.' Graham said he would meet the players tomorrow morning and explain his management style. 'I'll probably have a very short conversation with them. Outlining my managerial beliefs and my managerial strategy. How I work. I'm not gonna change. Some of them may have to change a little bit. And probably they'll be delighted to do so.

'Because I don't care how good or bad a player you are, we all want to be successful. And all good players, and outstanding players, of which there are some here at Spurs, they want to be successful, they want to play in a successful team, they want to be up there challenging. If I can convince them that my way, my way to do it, can put us up there challenging, I think they'll perform and they'll be delighted.'

Do you expect to be busy in the transfer market sooner rather than later?

'No. I would say that in most of the jobs I've had, or the few jobs that I've had, I always gave everybody an opportunity to prove themselves to me. I love passion in my teams, and I love passion in my individual players. I think we're working in a profession now that's a very rewarding profession. The only thing I'll be asking for is a return on the type of contracts they're on.'

You want to be in the top six in two years. In this day and age do you think you'll get that amount of time?

'I think so. In the previous clubs I've been involved with, Millwall, I remember, when I took over, were third bottom of the league. Within six weeks we went bottom. And after that we resurrected the club and went on to promotion. Similar thing happened at Arsenal. We were seventh twice before I joined. Then we went on to win things. I think the Chairman's a much more astute businessman than I am. He'll be able to tell, fairly quickly, if I'm on the right lines. And if I'm on the right lines, I'm sure I'll be given my head to carry on like I have done at my previous clubs.'

Do you think the Leeds fans will be unhappy about you moving?

'That's understandable. I think the job's been done there. The club's been turned around. And I think I've left them in a very healthy position. I think the playing staff is a vast improvement. And I think with two or three players at Leeds they could be challenging for honours. So I'm proud of what's been left there, and I think we should be thinking about the positive things that's happened in the past two years rather than the negative things. It's understandable, a few fans being upset.'

What would you say to the Tottenham fans who are dubious about you?

'I would say, if I was a Tottenham fan, I would be wanting a winning Tottenham team. I don't care who the manager is. They're just coming along to see the team on the pitch on a Saturday. If I can get a winning team playing with a little bit of style, who the manager is I think is immaterial.'

What would you say to the Arsenal fans?

"I would say: we're gonna be after you! Hopefully, as quickly as possible. And I think they know that, anyway.'

How much catching up have Spurs got to do to get to the level of, say, Leeds, let alone Arsenal?

'I think, with the talent that's at Spurs at the present time, they should be further up the league.'

So why aren't they?

'Well, I don't know. I've just joined the club. I don't know yet, but I'll soon sort it out.'

Was part of the attraction of coming here that you're gonna go head to head with Arsenal and Arsène Wenger?

'No, no. Each club I go to I put myself under pressure. I don't need added pressure of competitions from different clubs, I don't need any more pressure from the media. I put enough pressure on myself. So if I come here and get it right, it's immaterial what other clubs do.'

George, how are you gonna preach loyalty to your players when you've left Leeds at the drop of a hat?

'Well, that's not true is it? You've not done your research. It took a few weeks, and I think both chairmen and myself handled it with a bit of diplomacy. Went through the right channels. My contract was bought out. And I thought the way it was handled was a credit to football.'

Mr Sugar, you've tried several managers at this club and none has been able to bring the consistent success that you want. Does George Graham represent your last throw of the dice?

'I wouldn't put it as last throw of the dice. What I would say is that in the past few months we've reconstructed the board of directors at Tottenham, and included David Pleat and others, Martin Peters for example, with a view to having more people on the board that have more knowledge of football. The choice of the previous managers have in the past been board decisions. They've been unanimous board decisions.

'The first manager that I appointed was Ossie, and that was done on the recommendation of a couple of the board members. And the second manager that was appointed, Gerry Francis, again was done on the recommendation of the board. On this particular occasion, having had three managers, I put it to the board, on three different occasions, for them to draw up a shortlist of candidates. Of who should be our next coach. And George was on top of that list. And unanimously everybody in the board decided that he should be the one that we should go for.'

Sugar was then asked a question about the fans which was partially inaudible due to the amplified clicks of nearby camera shutters.

He said, 'I think I've passed my sell-by date in the eyes of the fans, quite frankly. The appointment of George is to get this football club in shape and get it to start performing in the manner in which it should be, and what's its expected to be, and what its status deserves. And that's why he's been appointed. As what we consider to be, one of, if not the top, manager in British football.'

Graham was asked about his backroom staff. He said that no decisions had been made yet. He said that while many new managers like to take down the pictures and memorabilia of former triumphs by the club, he was the opposite. He said he enjoyed the challenge of trying to emulate those feats.

Are you going to be getting rid of some of the memorabilia in your own home?

'Yes,' he said, smiling.

Mr Sugar, you said there would be extra cash resources?

'We've had money available for player purchases for ages. One of the first matters that was discussed with George, so that he knew, before he considered taking this position, was the amount of money available, and the financial position. So he was fully signed on to what that is. There's always been money available which I, regretfully, were unable to spend during the summer.'

George, how important do you think it is to win the fans over as quickly as possible?

'I've always been a bit suspicious actually, in any business, in any walk of life, of overnight success. If you look at my track record, at each club I've been with, I've always done a building process. I'm a great believer in lasting success and I think that's been proved in the two years at Leeds, and the previous years at Arsenal and Millwall.

'So I'd be a fool if I think I could just go out there and win the first six games, and thinking the fans are gonna be on my side. I think the view here is that once we get up there, further up the League, it's gonna be a continuing thing. And that's gonna take a little bit of time. I'm gonna say: be patient. Because we don't wanna go up there and win one cup, we wanna go up there and compete on a regular basis every season.'

Are you prepared for a reaction from some members of the crowd?

'Yeah, it's understandable. Some of the fans are real diehards who dislike other clubs. That's gonna come out. I still say that if we can get on the winning trail they won't worry who is the manager.'

Then Paul Hayward of *The Daily Telegraph* asked Sugar: *Does this mean you now won't be listening to any bids for the club? Because it could be argued that by spending £9 million, you've put £40 million or £50 million on the value of the club.*

Sugar said, 'I've not commented on this at all. With all due respect, it's been raised by the media, starting after the Sheffield Wednesday game a few weeks ago. We've seen Manchester United, and all that type of stuff going on. There's been a company that's been talking to me for a very, very long time about purchasing Tottenham. And I'm not in the frame of mind of doing so. It's as simple as that.

'Having said that, there is a limit to the thickness of the rhinoceros skin. And I normally like to work in an environment where there is a goal at the end of the rainbow, or at least your efforts are appreciated. I will not put up with any abuse from any fans. Because that, to me, is not worth it, quite frankly. So that's my position, really.'

Is there any truth in the rumour that you may be inviting Richard Littlejohn to join the board?

Sugar smiled at this impertinence and said nothing. People laughed and they went back to the studio soon after that.

Basically, Sugar was Sugar and Graham was Graham. Sugar said he was being asked to sell the company, but he did not want to sell. But he suggested he might go if the fans failed to appreciate his efforts.

Graham came over as a highly-defined character who takes himself very seriously. He is decisive. He is emphatic. He has confidence and steely charm. He is a winner. For Graham, winning means never having to say you're sorry. Graham is not in the football business, he is in the results business. He thinks that winning makes him bionic. Winning makes him untouchable. And he always uses the same buzzwords, the same phrases. 'Passion. I'll soon sort it out. I turned it round at Leeds. My way. Being given my head.' On Day One, Graham is already talking about the chairman giving him his head, letting him run the show, as he is accustomed to doing.

Tonight I am still struggling to comprehend the events of the day. It has happened. It is a fact. On 1 October 1998, George Graham became manager of Tottenham Hotspur. And the first public appearance of the chairman with his new manager was bizarre.

The Amstrad tycoon has brought the disgraced exile back to London from his rehab club in Yorkshire, rescued him from his lonely gulag in Harrogate. Are they the Odd Couple, or what? A tycoon who is abrupt and abrasive, a manager who is cool and smooth. A stubbly geezer from

Essex who likens himself to a rhinoceros, and a tall, handsome Scot who lives in Hampstead.

Do Sugar and Graham have anything in common? Well, they are both self-made millionaires with a lot of front. Their toughness means they are more likely to be respected than loved. Sugar admits that the fans consider him past his sell-by date, and Graham says the fans won't care who the manager is if he gives them a winning team.

A uniquely weird starting situation, but does this unholy alliance have its own strange, perverted logic? Because, despite what has been said today, they both want to be loved. The bottom line is that Sugar and Graham are both self-made millionaires who want to be loved.

Friday 2 October

I hear on the grapevine that George had a three-minute meeting with the players this morning. He told them, 'The only thing that matters is winning.'

GQ editor James Brown, who also edits the fanzine *Leeds Leeds Leeds*, wrote a piece for *Football 365*, the online magazine. He said, 'When you look at it, he hasn't won anything for four or five years and that's a disgrace. I think the media goes overboard about him when you look at that record. There's no doubt Leeds are more consistent and better to watch now but he bought a lot of mediocre players so I'm happy to see him go.'

Brown said that Graham had spent more money than Arsène Wenger. He reckoned a lot of Leeds fans wanted the new manager to be O'Leary or Strachan. Interestingly, he only credited Graham with one good signing: 'The best players at the club – obviously with the exception of Jimmy Floyd Hasselbaink – were here already when

George arrived. Nigel Martyn, Lee Bowyer, Lucas Radebe and Harry Kewell all played under Howard Wilkinson. Most of the players George bought in are not as good as those they replaced. Basically, he created a mediocre squad. He got rid of some very talented players and, OK, some of them may not have been great team players but Tony Yeboah and Tony Dorigo in particular were treated very badly.'

Will George change his style of football now he has joined us? Most managers have just one box of tricks. They stick to what they know, what has worked for them in the past. So how do we feel now after all those years of suffering Arsenal's power football, last-minute winners, boring football, offsides, hands in the air, grinding teams down, solid defence, set-pieces, send the big men up, goalmouth scrambles. Welcome to the Tottenham Hotspur of 1998.

The Sky Sports Friday night talk show, *Hold The Back Page*, is hosted by Brian Woolnough of *The Sun*. His guests this week are Joe Melling of *The Mail on Sunday*, Rob Shepherd of *The Express* and Henry Winter of *The Daily Telegraph*. Woolnough asked them: is Graham the right manager for the job?

Melling said, 'Definitely. No question about it. The right man for Tottenham at this time, without question. I just thought it was interesting yesterday to watch and observe Alan Sugar. Because he looked a deflated and beaten man. He sat there, slumped down, virtually sat there saying: I can't believe I've done this, I can't believe I've appointed George Graham.'

Woolnough said, 'At one stage he actually said, "I can't do any more. Here he is: we've got you the best manager in the country, or one of the best." '

Melling said, 'It was almost a flop resignation speech. I'm not saying he's gonna resign, because he's not. But it was almost: that's me finished now. Here's a guy I'm having to appoint whom I castigated more than anyone. I started the bungs inquiry, this is the one who was caught in the net, the only who was caught in the net, and here I am appointing him! If I'm doing the right thing for Tottenham as a football club to get results, I've had to do it. And I think he has had to do it.'

Henry Winter said, 'Expediency rules in football. And what Tottenham need is a manager like George Graham who will come in and sort out the defence, which we saw last weekend. Apart from Sol Campbell, who you can't criticise about anything, he's a terrific footballer, that defence needs a good two months of George Graham drilling on the training ground. And then I think towards the end of the season, or certainly the season afterwards, they could be pushing for Europe. He will build from the back, there probably won't be too much flair. Tottenham traditionalists, and I can sympathise with their position, will be disappointed there isn't any glory, glory stuff. But he's gotta sort out the defence.'

Shepherd said, 'It's interesting you say that because George was a talking at length in the press conference yesterday about the real glory, glory team. That side had three or four internationals, and the rest were hard working. There's a bit of a myth. The last European trophy they won, in 1984, their two centre halves were Paul Miller and Graham Roberts. They were hardly flair players were they? Steve Perryman was the right back. They had some graft in that side. There's a kind of myth grown up about Tottenham, that they've always played stylish football.'

———————————

Saturday 3 October
Derby (a)

David Pleat picked the team for this game, and ran the show from the bench. George has not taken over the reins yet. He will take his first training session on Monday. He sat in the directors box at Pride Park (see cover pic) and watched us score an early goal when Sol sprinted forward to head in a quickly taken free-kick by Ginola. Armstrong came on for Ginola with 20 minutes left, and hit the post with a shot at the death. Ginola has obviously not regained full match fitness yet. Baardsen made some saves in the second half, but George must have been reasonably pleased with the performance. He likes winning 1-0. He loves keeping a clean sheet. George will want to see a lot more clean sheets from now on. Sol Campbell was questioned by police about an incident with a Derby steward which took place after the game in the players' tunnel.

Sunday 4 – Sunday 18 October

I spent a week on holiday in Turkey and a week moving house. Nothing much happened while I was away. International duty for several players.

Monday 19 October
Leicester (a)

What will his team be? Baardsen, Carr, Vega, Campbell, Edinburgh (or Tramezzani), Fox, Anderton, Calderwood, Clemence (if no Nielsen), Ginola and Ferdinand up front.

101

The team probably picks itself. Though I would rather see Iversen instead of Ferdinand, and no Vega.

The match is on Sky, so a large audience will see George Graham's first game in charge. What do I expect? The city of Leicester is in turmoil because Martin O'Neill is linked with the Leeds job, so we should get a draw at least. We need a point as there are some tough games coming up. No movement in the share price, still 70p. Will the result make a difference to the share price?

Leicester fans wave hundreds of banners begging Martin O'Neill to stay. We create the first opening when Ginola finds Clemence, who turns inside Frank Sinclair, but Robbie Savage clears. Then we go 1-0 up after 13 minutes. Fox puts Anderton away down the right and his low cross gives Ferdinand a tap-in.

Leicester do not put any decent moves together. Matt Elliott just hoofs long balls into our half. Referee Mike Riley speaks to Sol after he flattens Heskey near the touchline but he is not booked. Lennon plays the ball to Heskey on the edge of our box. Heskey turns away from Vega and smashes it into the top corner. It is 1-1 at half-time. The game gets fractious after the equaliser and Fox is booked for verbals with Guppy.

Half-time. O'Neill takes off Taggart and switches to a flat back four with Ullathorne going to left back. Stuart Campbell comes on and almost scores when Cottee picks him out at the far post. It is all Leicester as Guppy lets fly from 25 yards. Vega blocks a shot by Savage, Ginola is booked for throwing the ball away after a free-kick goes against him, Stevie Carr has a shot just over.

Then Muzzy Izzet scores the winner after 85 minutes. Ferdinand clears the ball to the edge of the box and Izzet hammers a sensational volley past Baardsen. Martin O'Neill walks on the pitch as the crowd cheer. But nobody could tell whether his wave meant 'I love you, I'm staying' or 'Goodbye, thanks for everything!'

Tuesday 20 October

So we went a goal up at Leicester but lost 2-1. If we dump Ramon Vega we might survive. How many more goals will he give away? Leeds, he cost us two points. Leicester, he missed a tackle on Heskey and costs us two points. Southampton, beaten by Le Tissier, another two points. That's six points already. Did George Graham really try to sign Vega when he was at Leeds? I'm told he did. He also tried to sign John Scales at Leeds. And we ended up with both of them! If O'Neill leaves Leicester, they will go down. Even if George Graham does succeed there will inevitably be a stain. Will the fans be 100% behind him, singing *Georgie Graham's Blue and White Army*? Probably not.

In the short term, Graham has to give a massive injection of confidence to the players. Some will respond, some may be anti. He urgently needs a centre half, and a central midfield ball-winner to play with Anderton. Anderton was our best player yesterday. He is finally getting fit. How long will it last? So will Graham go for a short-term fix and buy players he has worked with? Will he raid Leeds? Bowyer and Radebe perhaps? Graham now has several days to get it right for Newcastle. Sexy football versus boring, boring Spurs. Should Alan Sugar have gone for Ruud Gullit?

Wednesday 21 October

Graham's reaction to defeat. He says a strong core is needed. Where is this coming from, George? Prediction? Graham and Sugar are on a collision course. When will that happen? Where? How?

A piece in *Football 365* says that Graham has told his players that it will take two months to sort out our defence. Chris Armstrong, for one, was gobsmacked. He said, 'We expected to have a heavy defensive training session when George took his first session. But when he said it would be the same drill for the next two months, well, I was quite shocked.' After working with Graham for three weeks, Les Ferdinand has been impressed. Said Les, 'I haven't seen many managers with George Graham's confidence. He knows exactly what he wants and when you look at his track record, he gets results. It's all about respect. The players want to achieve success at this club and I think there is no doubt that he's the man to bring it here.'

Arsenal are playing in the European Champions League against Dynamo Kiev at Wembley tonight. Leeds played last night against Roma, who were poor. Leeds played well, but their defending was dodgy at times and they lost 1-0. Radebe made a dreadful mistake for the goal.

Thursday 22 October

Reflections. Too many twists in this tale. Who will Graham bring in? He surely cannot think that Vega or Scales can do a good job for him.

Results now published. A £1million loss. So Sugar has failed off the pitch as well. And the accounts do not include the £3 million compensation to Leeds, the £500,000 pay-off to Gross, or Graham's £1.25 million annual salary for the next four years. So where is the £18 million coming from? Sugar's philosophy seems to be stop, start. Invest big one year, maybe one year in five, not incrementally.

In a statement to the Stock Exchange, Sugar said, 'With the goodwill of the clubs devoted supporters, I am confident that we can reinstate Spurs as one of the big clubs again.'

He also admitted, 'Last season was uncomfortable for everyone connected with Spurs. From the very start of the season we were struggling. Having won only three of our first 14 games, Gerry Francis resigned. After a search and some excellent references we appointed Christian Gross as first-team coach. Over the close season, Christian worked very hard with the players at his disposal. However, it became apparent, especially on the return of the internationals, that continued negative media reporting had resulted in a breakdown of confidence throughout the club. The situation became irreconcilable and the board had no alternative but to dismiss Christian Gross. In George Graham we have a manager with a superb record and one who we believe can bring the success that this club and its supporters deserve.'

So there we have it. Our failures have been caused by a negative press! Sugar wants the media to put a positive spin on his signing of Les Ferdinand for £6 million, Ruel Fox for £4.5 million and the hiring of an almost-unknown Swiss manager.

AGM now announced for the Wednesday 25 November, four days after our home game against Forest. Irving Scholar can really put one over us then! Arsenal were held 1-1 by Dynamo Kiev, a very skilful side.

Friday 23 October

I expect to win against Newcastle. What team will George pick? Same as Monday I expect, except Nielsen for Clemence. Will he be brave and drop Vega for Scales?

Saturday 24 October
Newcastle (h)

Lo and behold, he drops Vega and Fox. He makes three changes, Nielsen coming in for Clemence, Scales for Vega, Calderwood for Fox. Two of the problem areas have been identified. This makes up for his mistake on Monday night with Sol not man-marking Heskey for the whole game. It's 4-4-2 with two wingers, Anderton and Ginola. He has Ferdinand and Armstrong back up front, and two screens in front of the back four, Calderwood and Nielsen. The match itself is dreadful, spoiled by referee Graham Barber. Ferdinand goes off early, injured, Iversen comes on. We then look more balanced, with a better shape, more drive, more commitment. But the frailties are still there.

If we think we have problems, Newcastle are worse. We out-battle them and win 2-0. Iversen took his goals well against poor defending. First goal after 39 minutes, loose ball after Stuart Pearce tackles Anderton. Second, 76 minutes, a backpass from young full back Andy Griffin. Our defending is, for once, unpunished. Baardsen has to pull off a couple of excellent saves from Solano and Shearer. Near the end, when it is too late to matter, Calderwood is sent off, a second yellow for a foul on Solano.

Ginola is substituted again. Not one of his best games. How long will George keep picking him? Yet another booking for Ginola, his sixth of the season. He will be suspended. George says he doesn't want Baardsen to be our man of the match. Iversen must have been thrilled to hear that his manager had described him as an 'outstanding prospect'.

Graham said, 'When you're a new manager, Ruud Gullit and myself, you've got to formulate certain plans in your playing staff, who's going to leave, who's going to be retained, who's going to come in, and you've got to look at the total picture. But while you're doing that, you've got to be picking up results.'

Where next for Graham? I feel now is the time to spend. Show your intent, be bold! Spurs are back, beating Newcastle 2-0, moving forward, signing talent. Now is the time to buy. Sign a gutsy, wholehearted centre half. And a good midfield player. Not Sherwood, but perhaps Ince. Maybe look at Chris Perry of Wimbledon, one of the best uncapped defenders in the Premiership.

He must also start unloading players like Sinton, Wilson, Edinburgh, Berti, Fox, Vega. Create a strong spine: centre half, centre midfield, centre forward. I'm sure George knows what he needs and who he wants. Let's just hope he has the funds to go out and buy them. Hope he doesn't sign bit-part players like Haaland and Molenaar. Be brave. You're at Tottenham now, George!

———————————

Sunday 25 October

George will tighten things up. He already has. But I don't know if he has the ability to take us one stage further than he took Leeds, and compete at the top level. He won't be able to do that with the players we've got. He has ten days till the next league game, Charlton at home. He has to make a signing quickly, make a statement of intent, give us a signal. He says he has the money but the accounts tell a different story.

Does he buy a centre back? Or a defensive midfield player? Certainly not Sherwood on his performance today against Arsenal, who win 2-1 at Blackburn. Chris Sutton is sent off. Arsenal move up to third, Blackburn are fourth bottom.

Blackburn boss Roy Hodgson said: 'I was very disappointed to see Sutton sent off and I can't justify the tackle. It was a bad foul. It was a reckless challenge but he had just had his nose broken. Tim Sherwood also needed five stitches in his shin.' But Arsenal manager Arsène Wenger said: 'The sending-off was a fair decision. I also think Sherwood should have been sent off for his tackle on Vieira.'

Sherwood is over-rated. A better choice might be Ince, an East Londoner who would be happy living in Hornchurch or Romford and training at Chigwell every day, especially as Mrs Ince is an Essex girl. That would be a good short-term buy. Liverpool might sell Ince. But they might say OK, but we want Sol Campbell. And no Tottenham manager can sell Sol, who is the captain of the club and a current first choice for England.

Look at the players Graham signed for Leeds: Molenaar, Hopkin, Haaland, Hasselbaink, Wijnhard. They are not top-class players, except for Hasselbaink. They are B internationals and guys who get into the Dutch squad but don't get a game, Hasselbaink only started one game in the World Cup and was taken off.

Ginola still does not realise that he should beat his man and get the ball in early. Ferdinand, Armstrong and Iversen all thrive on that early delivery. What they don't thrive on is the big, high, floated cross where they have to go up with the centre half.

When Ginola did get to the byeline he tried a shot and scuffed it when he could have crossed to Armstrong at the near post. That was selfish and George will not stand for that. He wants his players to shoot as often as possible, not but not from such narrow angles. Maybe Sinton might come into his own under George. He will have soon some very unhappy players. Berti, by all reports, does not put himself about in reserve matches, although Clive Wilson does. George does not know the good from the bad from the ugly yet.

I was very surprised that he dropped Vega and Fox on the same day.

Anderton had his best game of the season playing centre midfield at Leicester, but he is at his most effective playing wide, as he was against Newcastle. He tucked in as well, which is fine because George likes his wide players to come inside when the ball is on the other side of the field, as Marwood, Rocastle and Limpar did.

But I can't see Sugar and Graham getting on. It's only a matter of time before they clash over something. And Graham is used to having a lot of power. The directors were scared of him at Arsenal, and he was Mr Big at Leeds, where he earned more than Alex Ferguson did at Manchester United.

Sugar now says he will take a back seat and concentrate on commercial activities, rather than the football side. Excuse me, but was he involved in the football management side of the club? Why? By his own admission he knows nothing about the game. It will be fun trying to anticipate where Sugar's next U-turn will come. It will be like following a London cabbie!

We kept a clean sheet against Newcastle but we were lucky that our mistakes were not punished. Edinburgh missed one cross but Shearer had a powder-puff shot.

Another went over the head of Scales, and Shearer scuffed his shot again. Calderwood was sent off for two yellow cards. The first one he grabbed Batty round the body, a definite yellow card. The second one I felt he was a bit unlucky. The referee should have made allowances for the wet slippery conditions, and given players the benefit of the doubt.

Monday 26 October

All quiet on the Spurs front. A pleasing performance on Saturday. Discover that proceedings have been issued against Littlejohn. Is it for *The Sun* article? Hardly surprising if it was. Littlejohn threw down the gauntlet, but it was not taken up. So he had a go in print. And Sugar reverts to type. Share price down half a penny to 67p.

Tuesday 27 October
Northampton (a)
Worthington Cup, third round

What team will George pick? Same as Saturday with Iversen starting for Ferdinand. We are now linked with Matt Elliott, the Leicester centre half. But this story has been rubbished by Martin O'Neill. Surely we don't want Elliott. He was awful against us. Now it is reported that our foreign legion will leave: Berti, Vega, Tramezzani. Who will want them? And at what price?

Drove up to Northampton in wind and rain, a two-and-a-half-hour journey. Drenched. Team as expected. Referee Graham Poll passed the ground playable an hour before kick-off. Ideal conditions for a Cup upset: rain, gales, mud and puddles. We go a goal down after half an hour when a Nielsen backpass does not reach the 'keeper in the mud. Baardsen rushes out and boots it to midfielder Sean Parrish, who chips him. Shock horror on a monsoon night at the Sixfield Stadium. We are 1-0 down to a team 56 places below us in the pyramid of mediocrity that is English football.

But help is soon at hand. A defender miskicks Armstrong's cross straight to the feet of Iversen. The 'keeper saves his shot but the rebound breaks for Armstrong to make it 1-1. Sol puts us ahead just after the break. Ginola's corner on the right skids through a packed goalmouth and Sol knocks it in off the post. Yet again the skipper scores at a vital moment. Sol's fourth goal in six games. George loved his defenders scoring from set-pieces at Arsenal.

Ginola goes down in the box, the Northampton defenders claim a dive, Poll gives a penalty, Ginola takes it, a feeble effort which is saved. Armstrong heads another goal from Anderton's cross. Northampton play with a lot of spirit and Sol and Calderwood kick shots off the line at the end. We win 3-1. We are in the last 16 of the Worthington Cup.

A gritty performance on a wet night, and Armstrong's best game in years. He has a good understanding with Iversen, so it looks as if Ferdinand will not get his place back. Scales looks better, but it was against Division Two opposition. Ginola substituted for third game running. Drive home takes an hour and a half.

———————

Wednesday 28 October

Share price down to 66p. Draw for the fourth round of the Worthington Cup. We get Liverpool away. We avoided

Arsenal. Maybe we will meet them in the semi-final like 1987, George's first year in charge at Arsenal. Pleat's one-season wonder seems a long time ago right now. What a semi-final that was. We were ahead in the whole tie except for the last eight minutes of the replay. Even the replay was at home, although we all wished for an away match. Clive Allen, what a season!

We are now linked with Chris Sutton at £8 million. George tried to sign Sutton from Norwich while he was at Arsenal, but Blackburn offered him higher wages. If we sign Sutton maybe we will get some money back for Ferdinand. But who would buy Les and pay his wages? A couple more people join the Tottenham Action Group via the website.

Thursday 29 October

George played his strongest team against Northampton while Villa, Arsenal, Manchester United and Chelsea all played their reserves. George can't go wrong in the next round because we will not be expected to win at Anfield. But he has a good record against Liverpool. He won the 1989 title there in the last game of the season.

This will be another test of character for the team. We have Charlton at home on Monday night, a Sky game. No Ginola, suspended, so Clemence might come in. But Sinton may come into George's plans. He is workmanlike, George's type of player, like Brian Marwood, who was at Arsenal in his first season. George tried to sign Sinton from QPR when Limpar went off the boil. Sinton had a choice between going to Arsenal and going to Sheffield Wednesday – and he chose Sheffield!

The share price has not regained its pre-takeover speculation level. Even the arrival of Graham has not arrested that decline. A hostile takeover must be an option which ENIC are considering. All quiet from Littlejohn. Has Sugar banned him from the ground? Writs have been issued against Mullery and Littlejohn, but who is paying for it? Tottenham Hotspur PLC? Now there's a question for the AGM. Share price is now 65p.

Friday 30 October

Player power is big news at the moment. Dion Dublin on his way from Coventry to Blackburn? Brian Laudrup, a £1 million signing-on fee after a free transfer from Rangers to Chelsea. Van Hooijdonk returns to Forest after walking out. This all seems to happen on the same day. But will the managers take a stand? When George Graham was at Arsenal everyone owed their careers to him. A state of dependency. He could not sneeze without people bringing him a box of tissues. He had all the power at Arsenal. If George had given the money back, apologised, cried on camera like Merson, he'd probably still be there. He is thrifty, so he suits Sugar.

George's style of football at Arsenal was based on organisation, organisation, organisation. It was power football, a style which generated a lot of momentum. Arsenal could score, raise the tempo, and score again. It was never especially attractive, but it was effective. He believed that a good team could not always win but could make sure they didn't lose.

Above all, George Graham was single-minded, focused and blinkered. He was also scripted. He made himself a master of the soundbite. He knew what he wanted to say, and said it. He only said what he wanted to say and no more. After a game he did his Clubcall interview. Then he did radio interviews saying exactly the same thing. Then he did TV saying exactly the same thing again. Then he would stick to the same script at his press conference.

He had his own agenda. He was very shrewd and calculating. He did not need a spin-doctor to tell him what to say and what to avoid. He had a deal with Aquascutum, the menswear company. He was slim, well-groomed and vain. Reporters who knew him well said he was the only manager who combed his hair for radio interviews.

Monday 2 November
Charlton (h)

Still no news of signings. Results over the weekend mean we can go fifth if we beat Charlton tonight. What a false position that would be! The various consortiums did not realise how quickly things would move. They were not ready for it. There was a moment when Sugar might have sold the club, but it quickly passed. Sugar is now taking a more active role in running the club. We need to put pressure on him before the AGM, and during it. Results. Why pay a dividend? Institutional investors. Who owns the club? Directors' salaries, share options, further costs. Graham compensation, Gross pay-off, new kit, shirt sponsor. Who will these be? Where is the £18 million coming from? How much can we afford in wages? Is Sugar happy with mid-table? Will he take the plunge? Will he speculate to accumulate?

So what team will Graham play? No Ginola, Sinton or Fox? Surprise, surprise, no Iversen, who is replaced by

Fox. Mistake No 2, George. You changed the system. Why not keep 4-4-2, Rory Allen for Iversen? We start brightly, loads of pressure, but no creativity, apart from Anderton. Charlton are mediocre. We appeal for a lot of offsides, hands in the air. Boring, boring Arsenal! There is no way I will put up with this next season. Edinburgh is clearly not good enough. Vega and Edinburgh are a disaster. How many points are they going to give away? What has Pleat been doing? Does he not have a list of potential players we monitor week by week?

We almost lose a goal through playing the offside, but get away with it. Then we go 1-0 down against the run of play. Mendonca gets through after some atrocious defending, Sol blocks Mendonca's shot but it rebounds to Andy Hunt at the far post. It's 1-0 at half-time. Lots of boos as the players leave the pitch.

Charlton start the second half brightly, but we score two good goals. Anderton plays a great ball into Carr's overlap and Nielsen knocks in his low cross. Then Anderton starts a move on the other flank, Sinton gives it to Edinburgh, cross to the far post, diving header by Armstrong. So after 56 minutes we are 2-1 up. And Richard Rufus, their best defender, has gone off injured before half-time.

But we do not capitalise on our dominance after that. The longer the game goes on the more I feel that we will concede a goal. Sure enough, Edinburgh gets turned by Steve Jones on the wing, and Jones crosses for Hunt to make it 2-2. George screams at ref Mike Reed, claiming a foul by Jones on Edinburgh, which it might have been. But a better left back would have made sure that foul didn't take him out of the game. Sol has a chance near the end but Charlton have the best opportunity to win it when, once again, Edinburgh is turned and one of their strikers shoots wide.

I was disappointed by Charlton. Their manager Alan Curbishley thought it was the worst they'd played this season. George Graham cannot be happy. We didn't have Ginola. Did that make a big difference? Well, for all his faults, Ginola is still far better than Fox or Sinton. You cannot play Armstrong alone up front. His control is simply not good enough. Scales and Campbell do not look good together. George must buy. It may already be too late.

Wednesday 4 November

We are linked with Taricco at £1.75 million. The accounts are released.

Our next three games are Villa away, Liverpool away (Worthington Cup) and Arsenal away. Consider next week's battle of the former greats, Liverpool and Spurs. Both eager to continue their runs in the Worthington Cup. That shows the decline in both clubs.

Thursday 5 November

Talks with Taricco continue. He was in the Tottenham in-tray long before George arrived. Why is it taking so long? And will Taricco send shivers up the opposition's spine? The game is all about confidence, signals, ambition. What does the Taricco signing suggest? That Spurs have settled for a Nationwide full back who has been playing for Ipswich for the last three years? We have needed a left back since Chris Hughton retired.

But there are other priorities. The spine, George. You need a strong spine. You need a dominant centre half, a ball-winning No 4 and a star striker. That would have signalled our intent. As it is, we go to Villa on Saturday with no Iversen, no Ferdinand. Ginola will be back. Share price down to 65p during the day, half a penny down, but closes at 67.5p. Someone's been buying.

———————————

Friday 6 November

Share price is up to 69.5p. We play Aston Villa away tomorrow. Villa are top of the table and unbeaten in their first ten games. They bought Dion Dublin today from Coventry for £5.75 million. He signed a five and a half year contract and says he was offered higher wages by Blackburn and Leeds. Dublin lives in Stratford and obviously did not want to move from the Midlands. It feels ominous. We lost 4-1 at Villa last season.

———————————

Saturday 7 November
Aston Villa (a)

Ginola is back after suspension and Iversen has recovered from a knee injury, but Ferdinand is still crocked. Alan Wright took a corner, we couldn't clear it, and Dublin knocked in a sitter from close range. Four minutes later Anderton and Scales contrived an amazing misunderstanding where they left the ball for each other. The kind of bungle you simply never see in professional football. Dublin took the ball, cruised into the box, slipped it past Baardsen. A gift, but a cool and tidy finish. Dublin also had a third goal disallowed for offside, wrongly, as TV proved.

Half-time, we are 2-0 down. Vega and Sinton came on for Edinburgh and Fox but Collymore was given acres of

117

space to put Villa 3-0 up after 48 minutes. Anderton hit the bar, then scored from a penalty after Ehiogu had brought down Ginola. Anderton then took a corner which Scales flicked on and Vega made it 3-2. Villa are unbeaten in 11 League matches. Their best start for 65 years.

Sunday 8 November

At half-time yesterday George went with three centre halves. He switched from 4-4-2 to 5-3-2. We thought we had seen the last of Vega, but he came on and scored. How long will Armstrong and Ferdinand be out for? Will they be back for Tuesday's Worthington Cup fourth-round game at Liverpool?

Share price up to 70p. Honeymoon period for Graham is in full swing. Will he make big changes now during his honeymoon. Nobody can complain about him yet. It's too soon. So he can do what he likes at the moment. He can kick players out, maybe make some mistakes, but no-one will question him yet.

Joe Lovejoy has a massive interview with George Graham in *The Sunday Times,* previewing the Arsenal game at Highbury next Saturday. In a paper notorious for its long, magaziney football features, this is a marathon feature. It will take me the rest of the week to read it:

'He says he does not want the occasion to be all about him, which is a bit like Pavarotti asking the audience to concentrate on the orchestra. All eyes will be on George Graham, no question, when the sergeant-major whom both sets of players will be tempted to call "Boss" takes his new Tottenham charges back to his old parade ground to play Arsenal next Saturday. *Match of the Day* will not have to look far for their "man of the day".

'We met, appropriately enough, on 5 November and a bonfire of the vanities was soon alight. Graham has no time for prima donnas, and less than six weeks into his spit-and-polish regime at Spurs those all-important first impressions have been formed, and he is already talking of the need for "a complete revamp" of the club's playing staff and methods.

'Standards had been allowed to slide, he said, and he had found "sloppiness" wherever he turned. The discipline for which he is renowned was a prerequisite of instilling what he calls "a winning mentality" in an underachieving team. Egos will be bruised and relationships fractured – in some cases irreparably – in the cause of the greater good. Those whose appetite for the work ethic fall short of his own would have to go.'

Lovejoy asked Graham how he found the place, and George's reply was as modest as usual: 'The club needed a proper sense of direction. It needed somebody strong. Yes, it needed somebody just like me.' The messiah explained how he had miraculously cured the injured. 'I make them have treatment three times a day. Once in the morning, once at lunchtime and again at 4 o'clock, which gets them out of here just in time for rush hour on the M25. It's amazing how quickly they're all improving.'

George said the club had done nothing in the league for 30 years, but that if he gets it right we will need an even bigger stadium. He said that Bill Nicholson's Double side were by far the best team in the country, but since then we have drifted downwards.

'Spurs have kept the fans happy by giving them a star or two, but have not fulfilled their potential. Give them a couple of big names, finish in the top 10, win a cup every 10 years. It's not enough. The reason there has been less opposition to me coming here than I expected is that the fans have been asking themselves, "How can we get back to those heady Bill Nick days and start winning trophies on a consistent basis?" '

Monday 9 November

Ploughed on with the Joe Lovejoy article, where George was still saying some good things, although they are exactly the things you would expect him to say. For instance, the Scottish hard man does not think discipline is old-fashioned.

'I always start training on time, regardless of who is missing, and I fine anyone who is late. In fairness, there's only been one so far. I've banned mobile phones from the team coach and from the canteen. I don't want the distraction. And I've already ordered club blazers. I bumped into an Italian team a couple of weeks ago, and they were immaculate. I think smartness in appearance fosters smartness of mind and helps to build the collective spirit that all successful teams have.'

Graham sounds as autocratic as ever. He said he would not tolerate player-power, which is no surprise. We always figured anybody trying to do a Van Hooijdonk or a Dublin would be out the door so fast their feet would not touch the ground.

George said, 'I don't care how much money a player is on, or what he's worth, a manager has got to be strong. Look at the players Alex Ferguson has got and there's nobody stronger. He has kept his values and maintained his discipline. I'll do it here.'

GEORGE GRAHAM TAKES OVER

Tuesday 10 November
Liverpool (a)
Worthington Cup, fourth round

Share price up again! It is now 71p. Tonight's
Worthington Cup fourth-round tie will be a test of reserve
strength as Liverprool will also be missing a few players. I
think Graham will play it very, very tight. Expect a 5-2-2-1
formation with Baardsen; Carr, Scales, Vega, Campbell,
Wilson/Sinton; Calderwood, Nielsen; Anderton, Ginola;
Iversen up front on his own. Not quite a Christmas tree.
More like a weeping willow.

George has only four points out of 12 from four
matches. Leicester and Villa, both away, were defeats.
Newcastle, home win, Charlton, home draw. We have
fallen back to 14th in the table.

In his column in the *Express*, touted as the column the
players read, Johnny Giles says we need six new players.
He described the Villa game as a débâcle and suggested
that Ginola and Fox should be sold. Plenty of wheeling
and dealing was required, said Giles, to replace six
players. He reckoned David Batty should be a target. 'He
would provide a vital injection of steel,' said Giles.

Liverpool are a team with even more troubles than us.
Redknapp, McManaman and Berger are all missing, so
their midfield is decimated. George Graham, a good
tactician, attacks his opponents at their weakest point.
Liverpool's weak point is central defence. Everyone knows
that weakness, but nobody exploits it more ruthlessly.
George plays three centrebacks, Campbell, Vega and
Scales, against Owen and Fowler. He keeps Calderwood in
midfield, so we really have four centre backs.

We are dodgy at the start. Liverpool hit the woodwork in
the first minute, then we score a fluke goal. Liverpool's

121

back four was their regular one. David James had flu, so Brad Friedel played. With less than two minutes on the clock, Iversen scored, a header from a long diagonal cross by Sol, sailing over the head of the stranded Friedel. Then an Anderton free-kick is blocked and Friedel fails to hold it as Iversen runs in. Scales slides in to score against his old club. With a 2-0 lead we let them pound us. It was still 2-0 at half-time. Riedle came on and sent a header just past the post, then nodded back to Ince who blasted wide. Owen got through once but Sol made a brilliant block on his shot.

Anderton is patchy, but Nielsen is excellent, winning the battle with Ince and producing a cool finish when a good Scales-Iversen move put him clear for a one-on-one against Friedel. Very good finish by the Dane for 3-0. Sinton is a fish out of water at left wing back, but Liverpool are so abysmal it does not matter. Liverpool get a goal back, again from a mistake by us. Baardsen mishit a clearance against Owen's body. Owen reacted sharply, knocking in the rebound, but injured himself. He was substituted.

Wednesday 10 November

Anfield's lowest crowd of the season so far, 20,772, booed their team off. And I don't blame them. This is the worst Liverpool team I have seen since since the immediate post-Souness period. Their defending is atrocious, and Ince does not look an international. Roy Evans and Gerard Houllier might not be joint managers much longer. Evans will go soon, and Houllier will take sole charge, as he should have done in the summer. So there we have it. George Graham's Tottenham can beat poor sides like Liverpool but cannot beat average sides like Leicester.

Wonder who we will get in the next round? Arsenal? We draw Manchester United and the game will be at White Hart Lane on Wednesday 2 December. We are linked with Mark Draper and some Frenchman playing in Turkey, who is homesick!

Thursday 11 November

Struggling to think of book titles. *A Marriage of Convenience? White Hart Pain? Sleeping With The Enemy? The Bitterest Pill? Cheap 'n' Chigwell ? The Odd Couple?*

Friday 13 November

The unlucky day before D-Day. The day before we play Arsenal at Highbury. What do I expect in this game? A 0-0 draw? See, George Graham is already having an effect! Realistically, who knows? No real developments. Share price climbing slowly. What will George Graham's reception be like? Hostile, I imagine. I could never have done what he has done.

Saturday 14 November
Arsenal (a)

Call from Capital Radio who want to do a piece about the reception Graham will get at Highbury. I said the Arsenal crowd would probably be negative, with calls of 'Judas!' and so on. The Arsenal fans fear he might bring success to us. Little do they realise that it will take more than George Graham to do that.

Listened to the game on Capital. Heart palpitations every time the ball was near our area. I find it hard work listening to Jonathan Pearce's commentaries. I remember him doing the England-Germany game in Euro 96. We watched it on TV, switched the sound off and had the radio commentary. When the game went into extra-time and then penalties, the agony of Jonathan Pearce was quite unbearable.

We had one chance to score at Highbury in the whole game and came away with the 0-0 draw that George had obviously planned. His motto is: if it doesn't hurt, it won't work. No pain, no gain. Predictable, really. George's second clean sheet. I suppose it would have been too much to ask for a last-minute winner like all those Arsenal used to get against us. The 1987 semi-final, the odd Ian Wright last-minute winner.

Never mind, I will settle for a point at Arsenal. George thinks: if you do not concede a goal you will not lose. But, of course, if you do not score a goal you will not win. Charlton and Newcastle both drew at home, so we have not lost ground on them. We are at the bottom of the mid-table teams, with a slight cushion on the relegation-haunted clubs. We are battling to achieve mid-table mediocrity. Nothing new there, then.

Sunday 15 November

We had no game in the morning due to a waterlogged pitch. Did not watch highlights on *Match of the Day* last night. Read George Graham's book, *The Glory and the Grief*. Dare not read it in public. It is bad enough him being in charge. Some of George's signings were pathetic. When you list them you wonder why he is in charge at Tottenham: Colin Pates, Siggy Johnson, Jensen, Kiwomya, Helder.

But Arsenal have a distinct identity which George knew all about because he was a player there. Arsenal traditionally play a methodical game, working hard, keeping to a pattern, with a bit of flair here and there. They like to produce their own players, who grow up in the system. They sign a few skilful guys from time to time, but they were never as ambitious in the transfer market as Liverpool, Tottenham or Manchester United. They were the Gunners, a club with a military team spirit, a team without stars. That was their DNA. That was what won them the double in 1971.

Alan Hansen famously said, 'You'll win nothing with kids.' But that was rubbish. Hansen played for Liverpool, and that is a Liverpool comment. Liverpool were a chequebook team. They always signed star names and paid top wages. That worked very well for them in the Seventies and Eighties. Sammy Lee and Phil Thompson came up through the ranks, but who else?

Liverpool were gritty and methodical under Bill Shankly. After Shankly they always promoted from within, from the legendary Boot Room, so there was a continuity of ideas. They gave the manager's job to Bob Paisley, Joe Fagan and Kenny Dalglish, and those three built classy teams by signing quality players. Liverpool was Britain's most successful club because it was Britain's best-run club. They always had the best Scottish and Irish players and always managed to stay relentlessly focused on winning the next match.

Liverpool's DNA was Shankly, the Kop singing *You'll Never Walk Alone*, and the Boot Room, just as Manchester United's DNA was Matt Busby, the Munich air crash and the dream of the European Cup.

George did brilliantly at Arsenal because he knew how to build on the healthy situation he inherited. He had a crop of talented kids coming through: Adams, Rocastle, Thomas, Merson and Quinn. Even Martin Hayes gave him one good season. Kevin Campbell did well for a while before Ian Wright was signed from Palace. Paul Davis was still there, another very good player from their youth system. Davis was a skinny 18 year-old when he made his début against us at White Hart Lane. Arsenal had enough faith to throw Davis into a red-hot atmosphere. He did well, and was in the first team for the next ten years.

We produce very few kids as good as that. In the late Seventies/early Eighties we had Hoddle, Hazard, Hughton, Perryman, Miller, homegrown talent with a passion to play for Tottenham. You need a balance between homegrown players and those you buy.

Chelsea, like Tottenham, were a stylish team who could turn on a Cup run and beat almost anybody, but lacked consistency. Chelsea today have nine foreign mercenaries in their side at the moment. But they have good kids coming through. There was a gap to fill, so they went out and signed Gullit, Vialli, Di Matteo, De Gooey and others and won four trophies in two years. Their ambition created a buzz, the buzz created momentum and the momentum created success. So Chelsea were able to attract Marcel Desailly, a World Cup winner. So when Jody Morris gets a game he is playing in a winning environment, just as Ray Parlour was when he broke into the Arsenal team. You need to speculate to accumulate. You can't take it with you, Mr Sugar.

Monday 16 November

It is a workmanlike, methodical team that George Graham always produces. There are no stars, no style, no charisma. When will the fans realise what is happening? And will George change his principles?

He was a striker at Chelsea, but he became a midfielder with Arsenal, and was one of the players who added a bit of flair to their strict pattern. The team won the double in 1971 and he saw then what was needed to win the League: efficient defending, great leadership from Frank McLintock, a supply of good crosses from little Georgie Armstrong, big powerful strikers, a bit of flair from Charlie George, Eddie Kelly, and George himself.

International week coming up, England v Czech Republic. Called up: Sol and Dazza. With Shearer, Owen and Sheringham out, Ferdinand would probably have played but he is still unfit. Ian Wright is called up. We have Forest on Saturday. Return of our former chairman Irving Scholar. Will he turn up?

Tuesday 17 November

Taricco has still not signed. Apparently he plays right back, not left back. Surely George is not thinking of replacing Carr?

Received a couple of e-mails to the TAG website about style and glory. Andrew Martin says, 'I have been a true Spurs supporter for over 17 years. The glory days must return but we must win in the Spurs way. Winning is nothing if it is not done in style.' Colin Hammond says, 'George Graham, a hero or a headache? I have mixed views on his appointment. Although I want the glory days to return I also very much want to watch a team with style and flair. Already Graham has dropped Ginola. Is this the shape of things to come? The thought of our opponents chanting *Boring, Boring Tottenham,* as the Gooners were on Saturday, sends shivers down my spine.'

Call to Chelsea ticket office. How many Spurs tickets were allocated? We took only took 1,411 tickets. Half our possible allocation of about 3,000. Call to Tottenham ticket office. They say Chelsea are redeveloping their ground, so we could not get our full quota of tickets. But they are showing the game on the big screen at the Lane.

Spoke to Karen Murphy at the Tottenham ticket office. She said Chelsea sent a letter about their development in August, and that we could not have our full allocation. Spoke to Gavin, supervisor at the Chelsea ticket office, who knows nothing about this. Chelsea always offer 1,411 tickets immediately on a sale-or-return basis. Then other clubs have six weeks in which to take a further 1,576 tickets. They have to pay for all of those, even if they only sell one ticket. I am sure we could sell 3,000 tickets, but Spurs apparently prefer to take 1,411 and show the game on the Jumbotron. This is a story which should be brought into the public domain. Spoke to Adrian Curtis at the *Standard*. He sounded very interested and said he would speak to his sports editor, Simon Greenberg. Share price is now 72p and relatively stable.

Wednesday 18 November

Sol captained England against the Czech Republic, and Anderton scored the first goal in a 3-0 win. Both played OK, Anderton as a wing back, not his best role. He is much better wide in a 4-4-2 with a right back behind him. That allows him to push forward and roam inside.

Thursday 19 November

Share price up to 75.5p. Man United shareholders have a meeting re BSkyB takeover. There is also a Liverpool shareholders meeting.

Friday 20 November

The *Standard* did not want the story, so I gave it to Hugh Southon on *The News of the World*. Graham tells the press that he is unlikely to sign any new players for at least four months. 'There's money to spend but this a bad time of the season to be searching. February is a good time because a lot more teams are willing to sell because they've been knocked out of the FA Cup and the League Cup by then. You don't get many players leaving now.' But will they not be cup-tied?

Manchester United PLC had reported a profit of £29.6m from a turnover of £87.9m for the year up to 31 July, which makes United the biggest and most profitable football club in the world. But reports from the AGM at Old Trafford all said that United shareholders were furious and rained abuse on Martin Edwards and the board for three hours! The anti-takeover campaign is working. I would have loved to have been there among the 1000 people, whose hostility was almost total, apparently. They made it abundantly clear that they do not want Manchester United FC to become a subsidiary of BSkyB. Is this a signal for fans at other clubs to realise their power?

This issue has certainly galvanised supporters. The AGM became a big rally for people who want the club to keep its independence, and a lot of organising was done by people like Michael Crick of Shareholders United Against Murdoch, and Andy Walsh, chairman of the Independent Supporters' Association.

The first speaker said, 'Most people are against the takeover, and it's about time we elected to the board people who reflect the majority view.' There were calls for Edwards to resign and PLC Chairman Sir Roland Smith, was described as 'not fit to hold office in this company or any other company'. Andy Walsh said, 'Without the supporters the club is nothing. Players, managers and even members of the board come and go, but supporters stay for life, and I think they deserve the respect to be consulted.' Absolutely right! When will more supporters realise they should not be so passive?

Saturday 21 November
Nottingham Forest (h)

One of the worst matches I have ever seen. Boring, boring, boring. Steve Stone is marking Ginola and it is a good duel until Stone picks up a second yellow card a minute after half-time and is sent off. Armstrong soon scores from a low cross by Ginola. Then Scott Gemmill wrestles Ginola to the ground and is booked. Anderton takes the free-kick, Nielsen glances it in and we win 2-0.

I recall taking my Dad to the Forest game a couple of years ago. It was his first game in years and within 15 minutes he was dozing off. By the end Dad was asking why I had taken him. I said, 'So you can suffer like I've been suffering over the last few years. It was you that first brought me here.'

When Dad was a teenager, and football was affordable, he used to go to Spurs one week and Arsenal the next. In the early Seventies I stood on the terraces below the Shelf and dreamed of the day when I would be big enough to stand up on the Shelf with my cousin. I remember the European nights, walking towards the ground from Stamford Hill, seeing the floodlights in the distance. If I was away at camp, and missed the first home game of the season, Dad would go to the ground and buy me a match programme.

On the way home we hear that Roy Hodgson has been sacked as Blackburn manager. Blackburn lost 2-0 at home to Southampton and dropped to bottom of the table. Spoke to Richard Littlejohn about the offer.

Sunday 22 November

The News of the World runs the Chelsea ticket story on the back page: 'FANS' FURY AT SPURS RIP-OFF – Exclusive by Hugh Southon'.

'Tottenham were last night accused of ripping off their own fans after the club rejected an offer of extra tickets for next month's sell-out London derby at Stamford Bridge. Amazingly, White Hart Lane officials turned down Chelsea's offer of 1,600 tickets because they didn't believe they could sell them. But that hasn't stopped Spurs going ahead with plans to show the 19 December Premiership clash on giant screens at the club and charging £8 for adults and £4 for juniors for the privilege of watching it.'

Monday 23 November

The Times headline is 'FOREST NOMINATE GINOLA FOR BEST ACTOR AWARD'. The report noted that Van Hooijdonk and Gemmill were both booked for fouls on

Ginola. It also said that Crossley, the Forest substitute goalkeeper, was screaming abuse at Ginola after the final whistle. Dave Bassett revealed that his players were 'fuming'.

A guy e-mailed me to say: 'TAG has made strong stance against all the lacklustreness and made a few points very clear. Also helped in the resignation of Gerry Francis and the sacking of Christian Gross. Therefore I feel it is quite appropriate to join and become one voice behind Tottenham Hotspur, our true love.'

We learned today that Sugar has banned the press from the AGM.

Share price up to 88p. Big Al, you can call me Mr Sugar, says he asked the other board members who they would like as manager and they said Graham. I think he's just covering his arse in case it all goes wrong and he can blame them. But if it works out well it will be an inspired appointment by his humble self. Somebody with his ego, and vast amounts of money tied up in the club, will not give up the right to appoint the manager of his business.

Tuesday 24 November

Hugh Southon phones to tell me he has received a call from Nick Hewer, Alan Sugar's PR man.

'Hugh, I'm disappointed you didn't ring me to check it was true,' says Hewer.

'But it is true, Nick,' says Hugh.

Hewer asked where Hugh got the story but Hugh decided not to answer that question. So Hewer said, 'Oh, you got it from Mark Jacob. I hear he has been touting the story around London.'

I was quoted in the original version of the story Hugh wrote. But I was not quoted or mentioned in the short version of the story that was actually published. So how did Hewer know I was involved? I only gave the story to Hugh and Adrian Curtis at the *Standard*.

Curtis did nothing with it. Did he tell his sports editor Simon Greenberg?

Journalism in Europe's biggest city is just too cosy. How hard is it to suck up to millionaire chairmen? What about the fans? What about the readers? Aren't they being short-changed? The *Standard* is a local paper, not a national paper, as some suppose. Their reporters depend on access to the managers of Arsenal, Chelsea, Tottenham and West Ham. They have to be able to talk to Arsène, Luca, George and Harry. Don't rock the boat! We all make a living out of this boat! Don't bite the hand that feeds you!

Incredibly, Duncan Ferguson is sold today from Everton to Newcastle for £7.5 million. This must mean Alan Shearer is on his way. It is rumoured that Shearer has been taking Italian lessons for 18 months. So it must be Chelsea!

Richard Littlejohn phoned me back. He probably won't be at the AGM. He has been told by the BBC's lawyers not to say anything. He said George Graham met the board of Spurs before Leeds had given him permission to talk to them. Which we always suspected.

We discuss various other aspects of the George Graham appointment. Role of Steve Kutner quite interesting. Littlejohn said it was an ignorant and aggressive response to the Bank of Luxembourg's offer, which was a *bona fide* offer. Why was his offer a fantasy? Who is paying for Tottenham's litigation against Littlejohn?

Chapter Four

THE AGM

Wednesday 25 November

The *Daily Mail* backpage lead is 'SPURS LINE UP £8 MILLION LAMPARD'. So we want West Ham's England Under-21 captain, Frank Lampard junior, a strong, useful player who is improving all the time. But his father is Harry Redknapp's assistant and neither of them will want to let him go, especially to another London club. And, of course, Harry is his uncle.

Thoughts before the AGM? I feel concerned that Sugar has something up his sleeve. Perhaps a writ for me? Should I ask any questions? Go for it? Or just look and listen? There are so many questions that need to be raised. The events of the summer. ENIC, Littlejohn, sacking of Gross, compensation, Graham, what does he mean by 'brand' in the shareholders' report. Seven years of torment. Litigation! Why are we suing fellow-shareholders? Why is the PLC taking action, using our money?

I get a call from a friend who says he is ill and cannot attend the AGM. So I'm on my own. Sugar is now due to take a hands-on approach with Claude Littner taking a step down to non-executive director. Heaven help us!

The AGM starts at 2.30pm. Top table consists of Chisholm, Sandy, Pleat, Sugar, Littner, Sedgwick, Ireland. The legal and accountants team are on one side. On the other side, Graham, Martin Peters and Igal Yawetz, who are joined, later on, by Bill Nicholson.

We are told that Sam Chisholm has been appointed as an advisor to the Premier League so he will have to stand down in his director's role at Tottenham, probably becoming a non-executive director or consultant.

In his introduction Sugar says he wants the first part of the meeting to be questions in respect of the various resolutions. Sugar sounds depressed. Does he have a cold? Bernie Kingsley asks a question. He is introduced by Sugar as 'the self-appointed supporters' spokesman'. Kingsley asks what is being done to reduce overheads. Sugar passes the buck to Graham, saying it is his decision who is bought and sold. Sugar says, 'We're going to have to speculate to accumulate.' Where have I heard that line before?

Some time is spent discussing replica kits, the stock market being down, and things like that. A question is asked about Hodram Inc, who have the beneficial ownership of 3% of Tottenham shares. Any connection with the Sugar clan? No. Crédit Suisse are advised on 24 February 1998 that Hodram holds more than 3%. Apparently they are a Greek family behind the Easyjet travel organisation.

First resolution passed, second resolution, regarding the dividend, passed. Why, if we are making losses, are we paying dividends? I vote against this. Third resolution, appointment and re-election of Sam Chisholm passed, blah blah blah. Auditors' Report passed.

There is a surreal feeling around the room. A tacit acceptance of the position of the board. Little or no dissent. Eighth and ninth resolutions, a bit more detailed. Do people really know what they are voting for?

The 10th resolution will give the board the right to buy its own shares. Where is the ambition? If the company is using its money to buy its own shares, where is the money coming from to buy players? Sugar explains that he and his company or family cannot buy shares without making a formal offer for the whole of the company. So this will enable the minor purchase of shares by Sugar and members of his family, or by the company.

Quote from Sugar: 'The company has no intention of spending £8 million to buy the company's shares, but it may be needed to increase earnings per share.' If the company needs to support its share price, it may need to buy shares. This is a ploy used by PLCs to bolster their share price, and is traditionally done before they find a suitable buyer for the company. Boost the share price, get more money for it. A cosmetic exercise. Sugar says, 'I merely ask you to trust me.' Yeah, right! He talks about paying massive fees to advisors. Yet why is the company bringing actions against Littlejohn and Mullery?

Then a guy asks a question about one of the resolutions which he didn't quite understand. Sugar replies, 'I'll explain it to you in joined-up writing.' An insult which sums our chairman up. When it comes to resolutions 10 and 11, why are we not intending to spending the £8m or £10m on players? Predictably, both are passed.

At this point Sugar asks, 'Does Mark Jacob speak for any fans?' Some people say no. Nobody says yes. But these are shareholders, not supporters. Sugar says, 'This particular gentleman says he speaks for all Tottenham Hotspur football supporters.' That's rubbish! I have never said that. Sugar complains about the general feeling of the fans. Negative love of the club. It backfires in the club's face.

Then he speaks out about the Chelsea tickets. He says that a *Watchdog* programme is going to be screened about that. *Watchdog* interviewed shareholders outside the gates of White Hart Lane, as they were going in to the meeting, to find out whether they wanted to go to Stamford Bridge. And nine out of ten people said they would if they had the chance to buy tickets.

Sugar then told us that every club has to offer 10% of the ground capacity on a sale-or-return basis. But Chelsea do not do this. They gave us only 1,400 on sale-or-return, in breach of the Premier League rules. If we want more we have to take a further 1,600 and pay for the whole lot.

If Chelsea are in breach of the rules, why doesn't Sugar take it up with the Premier League? And get something done about it. Sugar says that the club is not prepared to buy another 1,600 in case it gets left with unsold tickets. Sugar claims that I said that we are restricting fans access to the game. But of course the club then advertised the fact that Chelsea v Tottenham would be shown on the Jumbotron. This would generate income for the club.

Sugar is then congratulated on his brave appointment of George Graham.

Someone says, 'The future is bright, the future's Graham!' Why does the team not run out to *Glory Glory Hallelujah* any more? Sugar doesn't know.

I'm wondering about what Sugar has said about me. Should I rise to the bait? I decide to wait. George Graham says he has been impressed with the response of the players. The club has under-achieved and his job is to put Tottenham back where it should be. He assures us he will do his best, but says it will not happen overnight. The youth academy needs to play a role, but that will take time.

Someone else congratulates the club for getting Pleat here! We are told the East Stand poles are finally going to be removed. But these will only be taken down if the team is successful, forcing the expansion of the stand.

Should I get up and say something? Will I be shouted down? I ask to speak. Sugar refuses. I say that it is a public shareholders meeting. He says: 'No, the business has been closed, and you are not allowed to speak.' I say,

'Well, you've criticised me openly in front of everyone here, so I think I have the right of reply.'

So eventually Sugar lets me speak. We then have a debate over something he claims I said. He reckons that I said that the appointment of George Graham was the 'final nail in the coffin'. But he quoted six words out of context, and didn't look at the whole quote. He even decided to send someone out of the meeting to see if he could find the exact quote so he could read it out.

What had I said? It was a line from a PA report on 24 September where I had said, 'The branding of Tottenham Hotspur has dissipated over a period of time and the appointment of Graham will be viewed as the final nail in the coffin. And an admission that the history, heritage and tradition that is Tottenham Hotspur no longer exists. In the past we have not won trophies every season but we've had star players who have given the team a certain style, and given credence to the brand name of the club and all it stood for. Football is all about emotions, and rivalry plays a big part in those emotions. Mine tell me that I do not want Graham because of his past associations with our biggest rivals.'

So Sugar has saved this story up for two months in order to bring it out at the AGM! He has picked out five words which have offended him, rather that repeat the whole quote. But I'm not gonna take umbrage at that.

Then someone stands up and talks about the Tottenham Action Group. The guy has respect for me. He says I do get the Spurs supporter's view across in the papers. And to redress the situation we need more information, so we don't have to wait for someone to expose the Chelsea ticket saga.

The way to counter people like myself and other supporters' organisations is to expand the Media Monitor apparatus which they have now established. This is a non-profit hotline where fans can phone up every day. If there is speculation in the press the club then comment about it. The line is basically there to deny misleading comments in the newspapers. Even the press phones it, Sugar says. Would he have set up a Media Monitor without fans like us?

Sugar says he has no objection to any fan stating things and talking to the media. Unfortunately, newspapers want to increase circulation. He then goes on to acknowledge that I am a dedicated and committed supporter of the club, but says that the press take a couple of words out of context.

In the summer, with all the speculation, Sugar brought Martin Peters on board to try and bridge the gap between the board and supporters. Sugar is asking Martin Peters to look into other aspects, such as meetings with the fans. This is precisely what we've been asking for two years! Where did you hear it first?

I then ask Sugar about the litigation against Littlejohn and Mullery. He says, 'I can't comment about the litigation. I don't know what you are talking about.' Someone then spoke about Chisholm's role. *Spurs TV*, when is it going to happen? Chisholm said that football is a rapidly developing sport. He has seen what has happened in the Premier League and he has experience in the broadcasting/communications revolution in which sport will play an integral part, and he wants to make Spurs a part of that. Are the board considering a TV channel? They do not really answer that question.

A man asked about the Chelsea tickets, and in effect asked why we bought 1,400, not the full 3,000. This brings applause. So, finally, the penny has dropped with my fellow-shareholders.

Someone even comments that surely George Graham would rather go to Stamford Bridge with 3,000 supporters rather than 1,400? And Graham agrees. Are we saying that we couldn't sell 3,000 tickets for a match against another London club? We take more than that to Liverpool and Aston Villa.

Have we made an offer for Frank Lampard? No reply. Graham does not confirm or deny this. Question: 'What is the latest position with regard to Taricco?' George says, 'Who?' Pleat answers that the deal was done with Ipswich but they wanted him to play a couple of matches prior to the sale. The guy got injured. The deal has been agreed, subject to a medical.

Someone asked for assurances that Sol Campbell would not be sold. In complete contrast to last year, when he said that Campbell would never be sold, Sugar said, 'I do not make that decision. It is the manager's decision.' Pass the buck, Alan.

Wednesday evening. Reflections on what Sugar said. It was an unprecedented attack on me. I have never seen him have a go at a supporter before. At last ! He has realised the power of supporters. I've won. I've finally made him see that the supporters are important and must have a voice. Looking back on it, Sugar did say that he knows I love Tottenham. That I am a lifelong supporter trying to act in the best interests of the club. He has changed. He has acknowledged things: brand, speculate to accumulate, stuff like that.

What do I think now? Speak to Littlejohn. He said Sugar's just a bully. I feel OK, relieved. Sugar has accepted that I'm right. I should continue to act as a check and balance against him and the board. Lost my love of Spurs? Never! Lost my love of Sugar? Afraid so!

What next? Should I write to Sugar saying that I'm

disappointed by his reaction. He's acknowledged the power of the TAG and supporters. Perhaps now he wants to enter into dialogue? Maybe I should remind him of the background, my support for him against Venables.

ITV are getting some good games in the Champions League. Man United v Barcelona is fantasy football, an exciting, spectacular 3-3 draw.

Call to Steven Harris who is writing a book about Sugar. He approached me after the shareholders' meeting. Discussed things with him. He wants to meet.

Thursday 26 November

I asked *Watchdog* to write to the club pointing out that I had not given them the tickets story. This was their fax.

British Broadcasting Corporation
White City
201 Wood Lane
London W12 7TS

Press Office
TottenhamHotspurFC
748 High Road
London N17 OAP
26 November 1998

Dear Sirs,

Re: Mark Jacob
I write today to confirm that we have been today contacted by Mark Jacob. I would like to inform you that this has been the first and only contact between Watchdog and Mr Jacob in any form

whatsoever. Should you wish to discuss this matter any further please do not hesitate to contact me at the above address.

Yours sincerely,
Helen O'Rahilly
Editor

Perhaps, *Watchdog* saw the story in *The News of the World* and decided that there was an issue that needed to be addressed. The BBC did not contact me and I did not contact them.

PA release a story headlined: 'TOTTENHAM STAND FIRM IN TICKET ROW'. The club have defended their decision. They say that last season they only sold 1,600 tickets for the Chelsea match and they did not want to get stuck with unsold tickets again. But we were in relegation trouble when we played at Stamford Bridge on 11 April. We were 16th in the league. I'm not surprised fans did not want to go to an end-of-season game at Chelsea. We had had enough by then.

Friday 27 November

Further reflections on the AGM. Who was it did a U-turn over Graham? Who called the Arsenal board gutless and spineless? Perhaps I should have said this in response. Would have probably been shouted down. All those U-turns and broken promises. Alan Sugar said, on ITV, to an audience of millions: *Championship in two years or some other brain surgeon can take over.*

There were about 500 shareholders at the meeting, not 500 supporters. Out of how many? Shareholders will go with the flow. How many season-ticket holders who attend regularly have shares? What have Sugar's seven years brought? Europe? Cups? Success? No. Since Sugar has been chairman we have had turmoil and relegation battles. But it is impossible to think these thoughts while having a microphone stuck in your face, knowing that it can be switched off at any time, knowing that he has the floor and is sitting at the top table. People who live in glass houses shouldn't throw stones.

Share price down to 72p. Probably because people realise Sugar is taking a hands-on approach! *Watchdog* is broadcast. Baardsen has been negotiating a new contract, even though he has 18 months to go on his present deal. He has been playing well.

Saturday 28 November
West Ham (a)

We went to Upton Park with a depleted team which included Luke Young, 19, making his début at centre back. Baardsen fumbled a Frank Lampard shot to give Trevor Sinclair a simple goal from five yards. That was after 38 minutes. Then Sinclair made it 2-0 from a Paul Kitson pass after 46 and Armstrong got one back with a header from Ginola's corner after 73. Young had a superb 25-yard shot which Hislop tipped onto the bar. So we lost 2-1. Reports said we played OK but missed chances.

Trevor Sinclair, playing as a right wing back, was turned inside out all afternoon by Ginola. West Ham are now second in the Premiership! That won't last long. Manager Harry Redknapp rubbished talk of Lampard junior being sold. 'That's cobblers. Frank isn't going anywhere.' But last week the Hammers sold Andy Impey to Leicester City against his wishes.

George Graham said, 'I thought Ginola was tremendous. He was tormenting them the whole game. I am not going to blame him for the goals, because it was not his job to defend.'

Ginola is much brighter and more charming than most footballers, and his comments were remarkably diplomatic. He said, 'Since I have been at Spurs, I have played for four managers and I think George Graham is the one the club deserves. He will take the club back to the top. People think I am frustrated, but I am not. He has given me the freedom of the left side and I am really grateful for that.' One of the best quotes of the season. He is saying he is grateful to George Graham for insisting he hugs the touchline! That is what Ginola fought with Klinsmann about last season. A wonderful quote:*He has given me the freedom of the left side*. I love it! What a diplomat! What a star! What a soundbite!

Sunday 29 November

We learn that Graham was in Germany on Friday, apparently watching a midfielder.

Monday 30 November

Trevor Sinclair was quoted: 'The two goals and a great win were a big bonus. But stopping Ginola? How do you do that? I still don't know. The man has so much ability and he really hurt us out there. How he is not in the French international squad I just can't believe. I just had to get his shirt afterwards and he was good enough to autograph it for me. The guy is something special and although we won the game the biggest thing I'll remember is the performance he put in.'

Graham said: 'We deserved something from the game. At times we outplayed West Ham and I'm very happy with our performance apart from in the last third of the pitch. We played better than we did when we beat Nottingham Forest last week. Our finishing was below standard and that goes for Ginola, too. It has got to improve, but otherwise he was tremendous. He has been inconsistent in the past but in the last few games has been outstanding at getting down the line and getting crosses in. It's a pity we haven't made more of them.'

Everton chairman Peter Johnson resigns after a fall-out with his manager Walter Smith. Smith says: it's him or me. Can we really see Graham standing up to Sugar? I admire Smith's principles. Will Sugar heed the warning?

Chapter Five

MANCHESTER UNITED

Tuesday 1 December

Preparation for the Manchester United game in the Worthington Cup. How many reserves will Fergie put out?

_____

Wednesday 2 December
Manchester United (h)
Worthington Cup, fifth round

United field a reserve side because they have Aston Villa away on Saturday in the Premiership, and a Champions League game against Bayern Munich next Wednesday. Ryan Giggs is back after a foot injury, and Solskjaer, Ronny Johnsen and Teddy Sheringham are playing.

I go to the game with Nigel Williams, a pal from the Nationwide Building Society. We arrive on a cold night to find that George has dropped Baardsen to bring in Ian Walker. Baardsen fumbled Frank Lampard's shot to give Sinclair the first goal at West Ham on Saturday, but I did not expect him to be dropped. Ferdinand and Fox are on the bench. New full back Taricco is introduced to the crowd before the game.

We play attrition football in the first half; fast and fierce, grinding United down. Early on Ginola fizzes in a cross which Raimond van der Gouw grabs as two white shirts race in, Anderton has a 30-yarder over the bar, and Calderwood blazes ten yards wide after Nielsen has been blocked in the box. Solskjaer makes a good run and hits a low shot just past the post. Right winger Greening comes infield and has a good low shot which Walker holds well.

Half-time is a relief. Nice to have 15 minutes of not watching fightball. For the second half George takes off Calderwood, who is injured, puts Fox on the right wing, and brings Anderton inside alongside Nielsen. Immediately, Armstrong scores the first goal. Nielsen crosses from the left, Fox jumps to flick on neatly, and Armstrong places his header in the top corner.

Solksjkaer replies with a shot that goes two feet wide. Our fans are singing, *Que Sera, Sera.* Our second goal is one against which there is no defence, if the move is properly executed. Ginola shuffles past Greening, a novice, and whips in a perfect cross to the near post. Armstrong's header gives the keeper no chance from five yards. Ginola turns immediately to the television cameras. Is he playing for us or the cameras?

Sol trips Nicky Butt 25 yards out. A free kick Beckham could score from, but he is on the bench. Ryan Giggs hits the wall. When Carr chips forward, Armstrong heads wide from near the penalty spot. What a hat-trick that would have been. Sheringham crosses to give Solskjaer a header which goes wide. It is not over yet because United are still making chances. We should wrap it up when a Ginola chip goes over Armstrong and a defender, and Iversen, running in, stabs it just past the post.

Then United score from a seven-pass move starting with the 'keeper rolling the ball out. Phil Neville makes a bright run down the left, crosses and Teddy, making a smart run to the near post, flicks his header down and inside the far post. A typically clever Sheringham header, nobody does it better. He had to score against his old club. Predictable chant of *Oh Teddy Teddy, went to Man United and you won **** all.* Sheringham is bitter. Loves

147

the club, but does he love the chairman? Charlie, his son, and Nicola, his girlfriend, are at the game.

Then Ginola finishes it in the 85th minute from centrefield. He picks up a square pass from Anderton, cruises forward and hits a left-foot screamer, a fabulous shot which never rises more than four feet above the ground and flashes past the diving 'keeper. It has been a good second half with four goals: three headers and a 25-yard thunderbolt.

Walker made a convincing comeback, although he did not have much to do. Nielsen was a dynamo as usual, but his touch let him down when he got into the box. Anderton worked effectively, hitting 30-yard passes in the first half without doing much that caught the eye. Luke Young is on a steep learning curve, and will not face players as cute as Solskjaer and Sheringham every week. So we beat Manchester United's reserves 3-1 with a typical George Graham game-plan.

It could have been interesting if Les Ferdinand had been on for longer than his five minute sub appearance. He did not get a chance to tackle Ryan Giggs, who has also dated Danni Behr, the blonde TV presenter. But maybe Les had a word with him as they walked off the pitch. 'How was it for you, Ryan? Did the earth move?'

Even when we were 3-1 up, nobody sang *Georgie Graham's Blue and White Army*. We beat Manchester United but we can't sing his name.

Thursday 3 December

Reflections on last night's draw for the semi-final. Wimbledon's first team will give us two harder games. Maybe Sugar has the buzz now with a semi-final against

Wimbledon coming up. Maybe it's been scripted that way. The man who should be king, Kinnear, versus the man who is King, Graham. The mother of all artillery battles. Those two nights will not be games for the faint-hearted. Maybe Sugar will remember me confronting him outside Selhurst Park. How I believed in you, Alan.

George is working with what he's got. He is pragmatic. He can improve defenders and improve defending by the whole team, and he does not need outstanding defenders to do that. The football we played last night was not pretty. But, in a cup- tie, winning is what matters. George did not want to lose at home to Manchester United reserves, so he set about winning the game in the best way he knew how. And it worked. The first half was horrible, but the second half was fun. And a lot of cup-ties are like that.

Are we better than the three teams left in the Worthington Cup? Are we better than Sunderland, Leicester and Wimbledon? We will soon find out. We now play Wimbledon in the semi-final first leg at WHL on 27 January with the second leg on 16 February at Selhurst Park. Wimbledon beat Chelsea's second team on Tuesday night. If our finishing is as sharp as it was last night we will be at Wembley on 21 March. The bookmakers now make us 7-4 favourites for the Worthington Cup.

'Wembley has been good to me, especially in this competition,' said George in this morning's paper. 'But you never know, Wimbledon have a knack of knocking down favourites. But getting to the semi-finals is a bonus. It's come so quickly and it's wonderful.' George praised Ginola. 'He really excites me when he plays like that. But David has to keep it simple. We must make the entertainer an effective entertainer. Some of his early crossing was superb.'

I will say one thing for George: you know where you stand with him. He hates slackers. He hates complacency.

He loves hard work. He insists that his players earn their money. He likes to see good players running their socks off. He says, 'It is the basic requirement, because footballers get fantastic rewards for what they do.'

Friday 4 December

Sam Chisholm has resigned as a director of the club and the PLC. Obviously a potential conflict of interest in broadcasting negotiations. But Sugar made it clear in a statement to the Stock Exchange that Tottenham will continue to utilise Chisholm's TV expertise. The statement said: 'Under the Premier League's constitution, no employee of, nor consultant to, the Premier League can be a director of a Premier League club. Accordingly, Tottenham has agreed to allow Mr Chisholm to resign so that the Premier League can benefit from his experience. However, that will still remain available to Tottenham through Mr Chisholm, who will now act as consultant, thereby contributing exactly the same as he was doing as a director.' This last sentence is typical Sugar. Pugnacious as ever, he is saying: don't tell me what to do! Don't tell me who to employ!

Brian Kidd, Alex Ferguson's No 2 at Manchester United, takes the Blackburn job. A good coach, and someone the players will like more than they liked Roy Hodgson.

Kidd will get a big pay rise, and money to spend. Blackburn should stay up.

Saturday 5 December
Liverpool (h)

We go ahead in the 26th minute when Ruel Fox's shot takes a deflection off Robbie Fowler. Sadly, Iversen collides with keeper David James after heading the ball into the net after 33 minutes. Iversen suffers a serious facial injury. And the goal is disallowed for offside.

We score again early the second half when Jamie Carragher, under pressure from Ferdinand, prods the ball into his own net. Then, as usual, we make things difficult for ourselves. Robbie Fowler is brought down on the edge of the area and Patrik Berger curls a free-kick into the top corner to set up a tight finish. It is Armstrong's best game for a long, long time. Luke Young gives a solid performance against Owen and Fowler. Scales is on the bench against the team that unloaded him. Good choice by George. I agree with his decision to play the speedy Young ahead of Scales.

We had a very unusual line-up today. We had four wingers, if you count Anderton as a winger, which I do. Our 3-5-2 formation was: Walker; Carr, Young, Campbell; Sinton, Fox, Anderton, Nielsen, Ginola; Iversen (Ferdinand, 33min), Armstrong. Liverpool played 4-4-2: James; Carragher, Staunton, Babb, Heggem; Gerrard (Thompson, 55), Ince, Berger, Bjornebye (Murphy, 75); Fowler, Owen.

George Graham said: 'I'm surprised when people ask me what I've done to get players working hard. Whatever club you are in players know they have to work hard for what they get.'

The overall message from Graham is the usual one: my players have to earn their wages. Those who fail to do that will be replaced. He said, 'There will be changes, probably a lot of changes, within the next year. I'm looking to buy many more quality players because the squad is not anywhere near as big as I would like. It was always my intention to give everybody here the chance to impress me. So far their response has been fantastic, and I love it when my job is made easy by people who give everything they have.'

Sunday 6 December

Iversen had an operation on his broken jaw in Oslo today. He will have to wear a protective plate for two weeks. This is bad news. Iversen is our best striker, younger and more skilful than Armstrong and Ferdinand. We cannot afford to be without him for long. We should consider signing Jamie Redknapp from Liverpool. He could do a job in front of the back four. We really need a holding player who can pass the ball from deep positions, who can start our attacks. Redknapp is a London boy whose girlfriend Louise, the pop singer, lives in Chelsea. He should be playing for a London club.

Monday 7 December

Iversen will be out for six weeks, and Baardsen has rejected his new five-year contract offer. Baardsen said: 'What's happened has changed the entire world for me. I'm not going to sign now. After I was dropped for the United game I went to speak to the manager to ask what had happened. He just told me to be patient but I don't want to be patient. I broke the negotiations off. I've proved I'm good enough for the first-team.'

Surely, George, you drop him *after* he signs his new contract, not while you're negotiating. Who is his agent?

Rune Hauge! Has George made his first big mistake? Baardsen has asked for a transfer, but George says he will have to stay and fight for a first-team place.

———————————

Tuesday 8 December

George Graham's Tottenham? It still doesn't sound right, does it? But maybe, in time, it will. George has shown that he can organise a team, tighten it up, motivate it, win matches, create confidence and momentum. The atmosphere has improved 500% in the 10 games since George took over. Everyone is happier, prouder, more positive. Players, fans, staff, everybody. People, including myself, who have been moaning and grumbling for years are now coming to the game in a different frame of mind, knowing we will not lose.

Already Tottenham seems more like George Graham's club than Alan Sugar's. The 36,000 punters, the 110 executive boxes, the 99 players and football administrative staff, the 41 administrative staff, the 31 retail and distribution staff, the 482 temporary match-day staff, it all belongs to George now. He has transformed the club by turning lethargy into energy and gloom into optimism. Every goal, every point and every victory adds to his reputation.

———————————

Wednesday 9 December

Our next visitors are Manchester United, who drew with Bayern Munich at Old Trafford tonight. It was the sixth and final group game in the Champions League and a draw suited both sides. Near the end you could see that both teams had settled for 1-1. Both clubs will go through to the quarter-finals. But Dwight Yorke was injured and may not play against us on Saturday.

Thursday 10 December

George's biggest achievement so far has been the improvement in Ginola. He has done something much harder than dropping the Frenchman. He has, incredibly, persuaded Ginola to play for the team. I did not think it was possible for anybody to stop Ginola shooting over the bar from 30 yards eight times in a match. But George has done it. The idol of the fans now does the right things and says the right things.

It will be interesting to see how Ginola does against Manchester United on Saturday.

Friday 11 December

Whether George can take it one stage further, and create a stylish winning team, we do not know. It all depends on whether Sugar forks out for those elusive 'quality players' that George is always talking about. Or maybe George Graham is just a Mr Fixit. You hire the hatchet-man to come in and chop out the dead wood, rebuild the foundations, and get the vehicle pointing in the right direction. Maybe George is a drill sergeant and a structural engineer who teaches the basics and builds foundations. Then he moves on to do a Mr Fixit job somewhere else. And then you hire an Irishman like O'Leary or a Frenchman like Wenger to loosen it up and give it a bit of flair.

MANCHESTER UNITED

Saturday 12 December
Manchester United (h)

Alex Ferguson started Sheringham and Solskjaer, with Cole on the bench. United's first goal was sensational and the second was very good. On the first, after 12 minutes, they were defending a free-kick at one end and broke with electric pace. Giggs put Beckham away down the right wing and raced in for a diving header which Walker blocked. Solskjaer tucked home the rebound. Almost immediately United scored again from a similar move. A perfect cross from Beckham, and Solskjaer got across Sol Campbell to sidefoot past Walker.

That was 2-0 to United and the only question was: how many more will they get? Solskjaer almost scored again from another Beckham cross, and then Gary Neville was sent off for holding Ginola's arm as they ran together on the left wing. Roy Keane marked Ginola until half-time.

I thought United would win even with ten men. They had matched us for pace and power, and Stam was winning everything in the air. For the second half Fergie took Solskjaer off, brought on Henning Berg, and switched Ronny Johnsen to right back, where he struggled to contain Ginola. A tackle by Beckham flattened Sinton, who was furious and soon exacted his revenge in a totally obvious and stupid manner. Keane grabbed Sinton by the shirt front and referee Uriah Rennie was struggling to maintain control.

Then Anderton took a free-kick and Sol scored with a powerhouse header. We were back in the game with 20 minutes to go. Nielsen missed with a header, but Sol rose again to head in another free-kick by Anderton in injury time. It finished 2-2.

155

A tremendous fightback against the best team in the country. United were furious at conceding such a late goal and having Neville sent off. Their players crowded round Rennie after the final whistle. Ferguson allegedly refused Graham's handshake after the game and failed to appear for the press conference.

Sunday 13 December

Ginola has given an interview to Joe Lovejoy of *The Sunday Times* over lunch at the training ground. Lovejoy, who has more of an edge than many broadsheet scribes, noted that, far from being the first casualty of the new regime, Ginola is working harder than ever in training and enjoying life with his tough new taskmaster. Or so the French ace would have us believe:

'Sounding suspiciously like his master's voice, he said: "All skilful players have to be really fit, physically, to put their skills to maximum use for the benefit of the team. It is very important to me to feel I am in good shape, which is how I feel now." Credit, Ginola felt, should be apportioned fifty-fifty, between motivational management and his own professionalism. Training had changed for the better since Graham replaced the unlamented Christian Gross. There was no shirking: "It is much more intense now. We give more of ourselves."

'Graham enjoys (some would say cultivates) a reputation as a disciplinarian, but Ginola, like the man himself, believes the sergeant-major image is exaggerated, and said the players' improved attitude to training had more to do with respect than fear: 'If you play for George, yes, you know you have got to listen and work hard, but it's about more than that. If you respect your manager, in terms of his ideas on football and his views generally, you will give him the best you can." '

Ginola said that the team now plays as a unit, that he can do what he wants in the last third, but that George wants him to supply early crosses. 'The best thing in football is winning. When you win, the spirit within the squad starts to get better. Now, we are confident in our ability.' His master's voice indeed!

He said he always tells Chris Hughton that he is happy during the warm-up; he likes the nice pitch, the stadium, the big atmosphere, the chance to show what he can do. 'I played well at Newcastle for one season, and I had three good seasons at PSG. What I'm really pleased about at Tottenham is that I've achieved some consistency. Before, I played every game, but went a long time without performing. Now, I'm doing it regularly. There's more to my game.'

Amazingly, Ginola reckons he still might play for France again. This really is dreamland, but he said, 'I know that the new coach, Roger Lemerre, hasn't given up on me. It could happen.'

Monday 14 December

While Lovejoy was at the training ground to talk to Ginola, George told him he was delighted with the Frenchman's attitude. The manager said Ginola had worked hard, had not missed a day's training, and had played very well the last four or five games. He also said that Ginola had not thrown a tantrum when he was left out at Highbury. 'People said I wouldn't like his temperament, but when I dropped him for the Arsenal match he didn't say a word. I could tell he had the hump, but there were no complaints. He just got on with it.'

What's the Story? BORING GLORY

Tuesday 15 December

We have played pretty well in our last three games. It has been an important fortnight. We have won two and drawn the third. But all three games were at home, and we may pay a price for those efforts. Our next two games are away. We are at Chelsea on Saturday and they are playing well, showing the kind of class we should have.

———————————

Wednesday 16 December

Chelsea are doing well despite having three player-managers in a row. Glenn Hoddle came from Swindon, where he was player-manager, signed Ruud Gullit, left to coach England, and Ruud got the job. He signed Vialli, and when Ruud was sacked Vialli then became player-manager, a difficult double job at this level. I would not like to see Tottenham with a player-manager, although if Klinsmann had stayed a second year he might be our manager now.

———————————

Thursday 17 December

Chelsea have not lost a game since they went down at Coventry on the first day of the season. But they will expect a battle when we go there on Saturday. The last time a George Graham team played at Stamford Bridge was on 13 December 1997. Two Leeds players were sent off in the first half but Leeds still got a 0-0 draw with nine men. Luckily, Dennis Wise will not be playing, as he starts a three-match suspension.

Friday 18 December

An interview with Ginola by Donald McCrae in *The Guardian*. He recalled sharing a stadium with a rugby team who had a rough, tough coach. He admitted that George had bawled out the team at half-time on Saturday: 'Against Manchester United last week, we were 2-0 down at half-time. But in the dressing-room he really shout at us. We showed the right reaction in the second half. We got the draw. Sometimes you need a manager to show that spirit.'

Saturday 19 December
Chelsea (a)

A fierce game with the physios busy early on and seven yellow cards. We had Chris Armstrong booked for dissent in the first half and sent off by Graham Poll in the 61st minute for bringing down Ferrer. We held out for 80 minutes, then Vialli crossed and Poyet's shot went in off the post. Flo had come on for Zola. Petrescu crossed to the far post in injury time and Flo headed in for 2-0. So Chelsea go top for the first time in nine years. But they are only top on goal difference. Their last title was in 1955.

Sunday 20 December

I did not expect to beat Chelsea anyway. They have been drawing a few games, and maybe we might have battled through and got a draw, as we did at Highbury. It was always going to be a containment exercise, but we could only contain them for 80 minutes.

The Sunday Telegraph's Patrick Barclay, a romantic who has never been a George Graham fan, thought Chris Armstrong's red card was a bit unlucky, but was obviously quite pleased to see Chelsea leading the Premiership. He wrote:

'They will not otherwise wish to dwell on a match notable for a plethora of ugly incidents, one of which culminated in the dismissal of Tottenham's Chris Armstrong. In the context of events, Armstrong's offences were mild. He saw the yellow card in the first half for dissent and, on the hour, tripped Albert Ferrer, whose spinning fall prompted a dozen players to gather, air views and, in some cases, jostle. Now Graham Poll showed Armstrong two colours. Ferrer continued, apparently none the worse.'

Monday 21 December

George did not argue with the decision to send Armstrong off, but reckoned it had cost us the match. He said, 'I felt we could have got something out of the game if we hadn't gone down to ten. I was pleased with the way we played. Chelsea are a very good side. I just wish I had their squad. It must be a pleasure to walk into the dressing-room.'

Tuesday 22 December

Hewlett-Packard announced that they are not renewing their sponsorship. Apparently Holsten are back in the frame. George is still enjoying his honeymoon period, but his honeymoon period is different to that of any other manager because there is a reluctance to give him the benefit of the doubt. We have already played against Arsenal under his leadership. We went there and ground out a 0-0. We went to Chelsea and ground out a 0-0 for 80 minutes and then conceded two late goals because we were down to ten men.

It boils down to foundations and parameters. George's baseline seems to be: if you don't concede a goal, you don't lose the game. And even during his honeymoon period George cannot afford to lose games. He came here carrying unique extra baggage. If he lost games people would have criticised him quicker than you can say, 'FA bung inquiry'. If he had lost games people would have said: 'Look, his Gooner methods are not working! George Graham is giving us the worst of both worlds. It's a mechanical team and a losing team!'

Wednesday 23 December

We are linked with Steffen Freund, a German midfielder who played in Euro 96. He played against England but injured his knee ligaments and missed the final against the Czech Republic. Freund has 21 caps and his most recent international appearance was in a 0-0 draw with Finland in May '98.

Thursday 24 December

Steffen Freund signs, costing £750,000. A cheap deal as he is going out of contract and Borussia Dortmund want to get some money for him.

It turns out that on Friday 27 November, George Graham was in Germany. The match was Dortmund v

161

Eintracht Frankfurt and Dortmund won 3-1. Freund was substituted in the 69th minute. He was born on 19 January 1970 in Brandenburg, in former East Germany. He has made 170 Bundesliga appearances and scored nine goals. This season he has played 13 out of a 18 possible games for Dortmund.

Saturday 26 December: Boxing Day
Coventry City (a)

We scored the first goal when Anderton's corner was flicked on by Ferdinand and Sol knocked it in from close range. So were 1-0 up after 17 minutes and in control. But Coventry's new striker John Aloisi, just signed from Portsmouth for £600,000, came on as a sub and soon went past Carr and Young to score with a left foot shot. That was ten minutes from the end and it stayed 1-1 after Walker made good saves from Froggatt and Whelan.

Sunday 27 December

After the game George said that he does not want Walker to be our best player. He should be protected. That was always his philosophy at Arsenal. If Dave Seaman had to make a lot of saves, it was because the other ten players were not doing their jobs properly.

Monday 28 December
Everton (h)

Armstrong hits a hat-trick in our 4-1 win but the scoreline flatters us in a game where Everton came looking for a draw. Armstrong headed a Ginola cross over the bar in the first five minutes. Then, after another Ginola cross, the ball rebounded off Bilic and Ferdinand was first onto the loose ball, hooking it back into the net while the defenders stood like dummies. By then Everton had lost Craig Short through injury but Don Hutchinson then crossed to give Bakayoko a free header, the kind of simple goal which must infuriate George Graham. It was 1-1 at half-time. Walker made a good save from Barmby which would have put us 2-1 down.

Armstrong then scored a hat-trick in 20 minutes. The first came after 63 minutes, Anderton chipped down the middle, keeper Myre came out, hesitated, and Armstrong lobbed him. Replays later showed that Myre stopped because of a hand- ball, which the referee Graham Poll and his linesman did not see. Ferdinand then broke away to set up his second, and Anderton laid on his third. The best player on the field was Everton's French midfielder Olivier Dacourt. He should be in London, not Merseyside. If they go down, we should sign him.

—————————————

Tuesday 29 December.

Yesterday was our biggest home win since Gerry's boys beat Manchester United 4-1 On New Year's Day 1996. But Everton boss Walter Smith was probably right when he said the turning point was the Armstrong hand-ball before our second goal. Smith said, 'It was a clear handball and that's why our goalkeeper Thomas Myre hesitated in going for it. How the linesman didn't flag for it from a few yards away I just don't know. The 'keeper shouldn't have stopped but it was so blatant the referee should have seen it as well.'

Wednesday 30 December

Share price steady at 73p.

Thursday 31 December

What will 1999 bring? Another Cup run? A good team? Some decent strikers? Or just a slightly different midfield?

Friday 1 January

George will play Freund in front of the back four, with Nielsen in front of him. I would rather see someone like Lee Bowyer in Nielsen's position. Many of the goals we have conceded have come down our left side because Ginola creates an imbalance. Our left full back is exposed because there are times when Ginola doesn't track back. So one of the central midfield players has to tuck in on the left to help protect the left back. And if that happens then the opposition's central midfield players have more space.

So the whole issue of Ginola is crucial to the club. He is pivotal. Yes, he is a great player. He gives us a dimension that few other clubs have. But he is only intermittently productive. Ultimately, if Ginola is not making goals or scoring goals, he is a passenger, a luxury player.

This will probably be addressed, one way or the other, in the summer. If you play Taricco at left back, he is a very attack-minded full back. It would be OK if you had a left back who was strong and dominant and would just defend. Someone like van den Hauwe perhaps, who would not cross the halfway line. He just defended for Everton, behind Kevin Sheedy.

That was one of the secrets of Howard Kendall's 4-4-2 system: Trevor Steven and Kevin Sheedy worked back so well and covered their full backs, so it was very difficult to get in good crosses against them. Kendall won the title twice doing that and George copied him at Arsenal. Brian Marwood was a left winger who was a good defender. Rocastle made so many tackles in front of Lee Dixon that Dixon got into the England team. Years before, at Forest, Martin O'Neill made Viv Anderson look good in the same way, allowing him to catch the eye. It took an Irishman to get a black Englishman capped for the first time in 1979.

———————————

Saturday 2nd January
Watford (h)
FA Cup third round

We win 5-2 after going a goal down in the first minute. We still have defensive frailties especially down the left side: Sinton and Ginola. Will Taricco fit in here? Iversen returned. Anderton had a better game. Ferdinand still looks as if he's going through the motions. We have two quality crossers in Anderton and Ginola. The strikers should think it is Christmas every Saturday. But are our strikers up to the job?

In the morning papers George had come out in favour of a winter break and a transfer window. He said, 'I would like to see us start the season two weeks earlier and finish two weeks later and I would like to have the month of January off. If I had my way the first half of the season would finish on 31 December and the League Cup would be completed by then. The second half of the season would commence on 1 February and would comprise the FA Cup and the second half of the League.'

'I would have a shorter break in the summer because I think in the modern game that break is too long. We could span the games out longer and there would be no need for three games in five or six days like we have at times. You could play the majority of games on Saturdays, with the occasional Wednesday game.

'With the pace and commitment of today's game I think it would be good for everybody to have that month off. The players can have two and a half weeks off and then start training ten days before the season restarts. There would be no friendly matches, which means no lucrative games in, say, the Middle or Far East – the FA have the power to veto those.

'The way the game is going, I don't think we need two months off in the summer. Instead we need to give the players a month off to recharge their batteries. The game already spans ten months so let's use that time and spread it out so there is not such a great pressure on the players physically. This works abroad. We are one of the few countries not to have a break at this time of year. The game has got to go forward and I hope the football authorities take the opportunity to improve the quality of the game.'

George also said: 'I wouldn't like any transfers in a season, except during that month break. And I wouldn't like to see any manager get the sack. Clubs would know their manager and set of players for the next six months and would have to stick with them. It would stop some richer clubs trying to buy their way out of trouble.'

Good ideas! A transfer window would be a sign that English clubs were at last taking the game as seriously as Italian clubs. It would favour good coaches and terrify all the bluffers, cowboys and commentator-managers. It would also frighten the tabloids, who might have to start watching the matches carefully and analysing them rather than surviving on quotes and unreliable information from greedy agents seeking to profit from destabilising teams.

Is this the shape of things to come? Are Tottenham now envious of the richer clubs? Are we now a medium-sized club with modest aspirations?

———————

Sunday 3 January

Draw for the Fourth Round of the FA Cup. Who will we get? It has to be Arsenal or Leeds. Third choice? Wimbledon. Surprise, surprise: we get Wimbledon away. Well, Joe Kinnear can really sock it to us this time. Within a couple of weeks the man who perhaps should be manager against the tainted man who is manager. The barrow boy versus the mercenary!

———————

Monday 4 January

FA Chairman Keith Wiseman finally resigned today after giving his side of the 'cash-for-votes' story to the full FA Council of 91 members. The Council is so old-fashioned it makes the House of Lords look modern. It has members for Cambridge University and New Zealand. Yes, New Zealand! Ipswich chairman David Sheepshanks is the favourite for the job. Big executive vacuum at Lancaster Gate these days with Graham Kelly having resigned immediately last month after that unauthorised grant to the Welsh FA was revealed.

Tuesday 5 January

Back in October 1997 Sugar gave the Oxford Union the benefit of his views on the state of football, and, especially, the FA. This was the famous 'Madame Tussauds' speech. He said, 'The FA is like Madame Tussauds. It's hard to tell the difference between the dummies and the real thing. When they come to our place we tell them to keep walking so we can see which are alive and which are not. The FA are totally out of their depth. They haven't a clue about how the outside world works.

'They are more interested in their jackets, their badges, their tickets on match days and going out to Italy on junkets. What we really need is reform at that level. They are totally out to lunch, that lot. The way the FA is run, it takes about 900 people to decide whether to change referees' shirts from green to brown – I'm not kidding.'

Sugar further referred to the 1994 decision to kick us out of the FA Cup, and deduct 12 league points for financial irregularities under a previous regime. 'We won because the wallies at Lancaster Gate didn't even know their own rules. They had never been taken to court before, and when we stood up they ran to FIFA and asked, "What do we do now?" FIFA ruled independent arbitration should decide. We forced that to happen

168

before the FA Cup third round draw and won.' Good knockabout stuff, eh?

———————

Wednesday 6 January

Leeds winger Harry Kewell has told *Football 365* he thinks Ginola is marvellous. Kewell admitted his job is harder this season now everybody knows about him, just as they now know about Michael Owen and Nicolas Anelka. He says young stars have to keep improving. 'You have to go up a couple of levels. Then, the third time around, you have to show them you can do even more. Next season, a defender will be thinking: "Last time he did this, the time before he did that." You always have to come up with something new to beat defenders. The best player I've ever seen do that is David Ginola. I could watch him all day. He's just brilliant. When he gets the ball, people are just so scared of him. I'd love to put that fear in defenders – for them to be that scared of me.'

———————

Thursday 7 January

We play Sheffield Wednesday at Hillsborough on Saturday, but the prospect does not seem very exciting compared to our cup games. But we do not want to lose. Being hammered 3-0 by Wednesday at home was bad enough. Losing twice would be hard to swallow.

———————

Friday 8 January

The Mirror have an interview with Darren Anderton who says, 'I have only 18 months to run on my contract, but the club have not tried too hard to get me to sign a new one yet, which is a bit ... well, strange. Hopefully we will sort something out because I love London, I love Tottenham and I don't want to leave, especially as it looks like things are turning around. My fitness is going really well, George Graham is encouraging people to give me the ball and I don't mind playing out on the right wing as long as I'm involved in the game.' Maybe Anderton will do a McManaman, sitting out the last season of his contract and going abroad on a free transfer.

Saturday 9 January
Sheffield Wednesday (a)

The Mirror has been talking to Andy Hinchcliffe, the Wednesday player who almost joined us a year ago. He now says he was victim of a deliberate smokescreen that could have ruined his career. He is sure that Tottenham exaggerated the extent of his Achilles tendon injury to give Sugar an excuse to pull out of his transfer from Everton. He says Sugar did not want to let Christian Gross spend another £3 million. Incredibly, we also sent Hinchcliffe a bill for the medical he 'failed', although we later claimed this was an administrative error. Hinchcliffe admits he had a minor Achilles injury at the time, but will be making his 37th appearance for Sheffield Wednesday against us today. He has not missed a game through injury since Ron Atkinson signed him.

Wednesday boss Danny Wilson said: 'Spurs will be a different proposition from the side we beat 3-0 at the start of the season. George Graham's influence is there for all to see. He has a well-organised team and players who you don't expect to be working off the ball, but who are doing exactly that, like David Ginola. He must be enjoying his game because he has been named player of the month. He is a fantastic player.'

We draw the game 0-0. Is this the shape of things to come? Freund played very deep. Ferdinand collided with Nielsen, ran into him. Still, we've had six consecutive games from Ferdinand, which is unusual. More worryingly, Anderton went off injured.

Sunday 10 January

Kick around further ideas for the book title. I still like *Cheap 'n' Chigwell*. Or maybe, corrupting the Oasis album, *(What's the Story) Morning Glory*?

Monday 11 January

Anderton injury news confirmed. He has a calf strain. But is this a George Graham smokescreen?

Tuesday 12 January

Ron Atkinson becomes manager of Nottingham Forest, replacing Dave Bassett, who has wasted millions on unproven players like Nigel Quashie and Neil Shipperley. Big Ron is Red Adair, the troubleshooter, the Sir John

Harvey-Jones of football. He saved Sheffield Wednesday from relegation last season, replacing David Pleat, our very own Director of Football, so Irving Scholar thinks he can do the same for Forest a year later.

Wednesday 13 January

I decide to research George Graham's Arsenal record against Wimbledon over eight and a half seasons:

	Home	Away
86-87	3-1	2-1
87-88	3-0	1-3
88-89	2-2	5-1
89-90	0-0	0-1
90-91	2-2	3-0
91-92	1-1	3-1
92-93	0-1	2-3
93-94	1-1	3-0
94-95	–	3-1

The missing game was three months after Graham was sacked. Stewart Houston's team lost 1-0 at Highbury. So George Graham's Arsenal had only four defeats in 17 games against Wimbledon. Eight wins and five draws. A very good record. If anybody knows how to play against Wimbledon, it is George Graham.

Thursday 14 January

George has been talking frankly to the *Standard* about his managerial apprenticeship at Millwall, when he operated on a much smaller budget.

'We would call the club we were playing and ask for the phone number of the nearest chip shop to the ground. Then we would order fish and chips for 16 to be collected an hour after the game. We couldn't afford overnight stays in decent hotels on Friday nights. So if we had a game in the Midlands or up North, I would contact Loughborough College. The students would be away for the weekend and we would get decent rooms really cheap and be able to eat in the canteen. That saved us a lot and allowed us to prepare for the game properly.

'Every summer the old Millwall ground, Cold Blow Lane, needed painting but we couldn't afford to have workmen come in and do it. So I used to go down to Greenwich barracks and see the officer in charge. He would let me have about a dozen soldiers who were on jankers to come down and do it for nothing.' Hope Sugar does not read this article. He will want to know why we can't eat fish and chips, and have the ground painted for free.

Chapter Six

WIMBLEDON: LOADA DIVING

Friday 15 January

Wimbledon signed John Hartson today for £7.5 million. Incredible! The deal, apparently is £3 million now, £3 million at the end of the season, and the rest on appearances. I know West Ham are strapped for cash, but surely Joe Kinnear has enough strikers? Hartson is cuptied and cannot play against us in the Worthington or FA Cups.

Wimbledon's previous transfer record was £2 million for Andy Roberts from Palace and £2 million for Mark Kennedy from Liverpool. So Hartson has cost more than Les Ferdinand, our record signing for £6 million. How can Wimbledon buy more expensive players than us when their average crowds are 17,000 compared to our 33,000? Wimbledon normally sell players for that kind of money, but now they are buying a centre forward for over £7 million!

And Hartson is clearly overweight. How can a serious professional footballer be overweight in January? Is this desperation by Wimbledon? Or is it a signal saying: we are no longer a selling club? We can afford to take a chance on a belligerent Welsh carthorse who may have ability but needs licking into shape.

For years Wimbledon have been the underdogs whose bite was as loud as their bark. Wimbledon have a very distinct identity because they are historically and financially different to any other football club in England. Their attitude is: we are small, we sign rough diamonds, we try harder, we have tremendous team spirit, we have a laugh, we are the Crazy Gang. That is their DNA.

Wimbledon have done well buying bargain basement players from the lower leagues. Kinnear and their scouts have uncovered many gems. Back in 1991 Robbie Earle from Port Vale was their record signing for £775,000. Warren Barton from Maidstone United, John Scales from Bristol Rovers, Andy Clarke from Barnet, plus a load of guys from Millwall and Charlton.

Are we now saying that Wimbledon can sign players from their competitors and, indeed, sign their better players? Suddenly, Wimbledon have gone from buying Carl Leaburn from Charlton to signing John Hartson, an international, from West Ham. Is this a good idea? Or is it a betrayal of their DNA? Only time will tell.

Compare the ambition of the Hartson purchase to what has been happening at Tottenham. We have been buying other people's reserves. Fox and Ginola were being kept out of the Newcastle team by other people. The players we've been buying over the last few years have not been from top clubs, and have not necessarily been their top players. Chris Armstrong was at Palace. If we'd wanted Newcastle's top player we should have bought Alan Shearer, not Les Ferdinand. Once again we were reacting to events rather than anticipating them

So it sets a tone. If you can't buy the best, how can you expect to challenge the best? If we are always buying their cast-offs and squad players? Class is permanent, form is temporary. That is crucial to football.

Graham has said that there is nobody available in mid-season, we can't sign anybody because teams won't let them go. That is not true. Dion Dublin was the club captain at Coventry. He was Coventry's best player, but he was sold to Aston Villa. If Graham wanted a proven striker, Dublin was available. He had a clause in his contract saying he could talk to clubs who offered more than £5 million.

Chris Sutton has a poor disciplinary record, and his injury record is not particularly good either. But Sutton is a target man that George has always fancied. But how much would Sutton cost? If Hartson was £7 million, Sutton would be £10 million. And remember it was George who signed Hartson from Luton. People said he was worth about £1.5 million, and that George had panicked and paid £2.5 million to take him to Arsenal as they started slipping into relegation trouble. Then Wenger off-loaded Hartson to West Ham for £4 million.

So Wimbledon have come out of the shadows and joined the big time. They have lower gates than Tottenham but earned similar TV money last season because they finished on 44 points, the same as us. We were 14th, they were 15th. There must be money coming in from the Norwegian owners who have invested in the club. And good luck to them.

Now we have tomorrow's game to worry about. Will Anderton play? Will Ferdinand play? They both went off injured. There are whispers about Luke Young, our defender. He's not as big as some of the defenders we have, and he's probably not as strong, so it may be a good idea for him to miss this game. Against Wimbledon you need someone big and tough, especially if Hartson is playing. He might play Scales, or Calderwood. Our squad is threadbare and we need to play our top eleven. If we get a couple of injuries in key positions we are in trouble. If Campbell, Ginola or Anderton are injured, we struggle.

Kinnear will probably learn more from this game than Graham. We know what to expect from Wimbledon, whatever side they put out. They will be fighting for every ball, even if it's a 60-40 ball for us. They never know when they're beaten. So we have to make the most of our skill and make sure that neutralises their brawn. We have to use our brains. That's why it always comes back to class. If you have class, you can beat anybody. Brains are important in football.

The game itself? There's a certain anticipation, but it's not the big one. It's the *hors d'oeuvre* before the main course. Graham has gone on record saying that the Worthington Cup is the best route to Europe, then the FA Cup, then the League. Kinnear hasn't said that because every game is a cup game for them. But they are higher than us in the League and in a position to qualify for Europe by finishing in the top six.

What youngsters have we got coming through? Young looks good, but is Clemence going to develop? When Clemence first played a friendly, I thought he had some potential. But since then I have been very, very disappointed with him. He is basically skilful, with a very good left foot, but he just doesn't have the acceleration, and he's been found out. He doesn't really tackle, so he doesn't really contribute. And if players don't contribute, what are they doing out there ?

Certain players have been dropped by Graham and I wonder why they are still at the club. Graham has been there for three months. There should have been more transfer dealings. Berti has gone, and he is willing to unload Tramezzani. But there are others who are mere passengers, collecting their wages and not contributing anything.

Saturday 16 January.
Wimbledon (h)

I expect a Premiership victory here to make up for losing 3-1 on the first day of the season. We need to retain our bottom-of-mid-table status. Then we need to start climbing the League. Jason Euell is out suspended so the attention is on Hartson and Ginola. How will Hartson do on his début? And how will Wimbledon contain Ginola? Kinnear knows that if Wimbledon counter the threat of Ginola they will reduce most of our attacking options. When Ginola plays we are very, very dependent on him.

Freund makes his home début, and Taricco is on the bench. Why has it taken so long to get Taricco fit? And what is Freund going to give to Spurs? He does not really tackle. He's a good link man who will get the ball and give it. Good positional sense and decent distribution. Freund is Popescu with less skill, but more bite. We'll see.

Hartson put himself about as always. His first foul comes after six seconds, an elbow on Calderwood. He should have been sent off for a crude, over-the-top tackle on Sinton after 13 minutes. The referee Mr Riley is in a no-win situation. If he sends off Hartson in his first game, he will be accused of doing it because Hartson has just been sold for £7million and has a bad boy reputation. If Riley doesn't send him off, the slow-motion pundits on *Match of the Day* will say he bottled it.

After the Hartson booking Mr Riley loses a lot of control. A lot of niggly fouls, and not only from Wimbledon. There are a few elbows being used by our players as well. And it set the tone.

The game is a tepid 0-0 draw. We have a couple of chances and Wimbledon have a couple of chances. The next game might be the complete opposite. It might be a thriller. It could be a 4-4 draw. Who knows? I suspect that Kinnear learned more from the game than Graham. Anderton was certainly missed. He's a very good player and we do not look the same side without him.

The *Match of the Day* slow-motion finds Ginola out, showing that he was usually looking to go down rather than play the ball. So by the time he was tripped by Thatcher just outside the box, and bodychecked by Blackwell as he fell forward into the box, he had dived himself out of a penalty award.

If Ginola had not dived three times, he would have had a free kick on the edge of the box. In a perfect world referees would call each one on its merits, but we don't live in a perfect world. If players in general are putting the referees under intense pressure, it becomes like the boy who cries wolf. If you keep on diving, he won't give a penalty when you *are* fouled in the box. If the dive is so blatant that the player is actually looking round in anticipation of the penalty, and you as a referee know that player is trying to con you, his opponents and the crowd, you should book him for ungentlemanly conduct, regardless of who he is or what part of the pitch it is. So the ref does not have a particularly good game, but he was proved right on the first three Ginola dives.

Sunday 17 January

Wimbledon play George Graham-type power football, pressure football. And Graham has inherited a team that does not play that way and can't play that way. But in the last couple of months we have played that kind of football against teams who are not sophisticated enough against it. Either they are not physically strong enough, or not tactically able to play against it.

Against Wimbledon he came up against the only team which is tactically aware of that, and physical enough to retaliate. You can scrap against Man United but ultimately their skill should prevail. Liverpool have some players who might hide, so you can beat them.

We didn't demonstrate much skill yesterday, apart from Ginola. And that was the problem. Iversen had a very quiet game. Unless Ginola put in a cross to the back post, we had little to offer in attack. The through balls that were being played to Iversen and Armstrong were up in the air, not down the channels to make the defenders turn. And when you do that, you must have the support of midfield players who are athletic enough to get up and down.

And with Freund and Clemence in central midfield rather than Anderton and Nielsen, we lacked that support. If the strikers chase a ball into the corner, they only have one teammate in the box. It's no good having your midfield still on the halfway line, trying to catch up after the ball has gone 60 yards over the top.

Monday 18 January

A helluva lot is going to depend on Anderton next Saturday. Ideally, George would like to play Anderton one side, Ginola the other side and Nielsen in the middle, with Ferdinand and Iversen. That would be his strongest side.

It's not a one-off, because we still have replays in the FA Cup, for the moment. The following Wednesday he has the Worthington Cup game against them at home, which is over two legs. Which is more important? I think they're both important. Winning becomes a habit. If we lose on

Saturday, the semi-final is all or nothing. Our season could come down to one night at the Lane, although you could make up for it in the away leg.

But if it becomes a war of attrition it's very rare that teams beat Wimbledon. You beat Wimbledon by playing skilful football. Look at last year. It was the end of the season and Spurs were scrapping, but we had Klinsmann and Ginola on song and we thrashed them 6-2.

Wimbledon want you to play their game. The crucial factors are whether Anderton, Ferdinand and Nielsen will be back for Selhurst Park. Young has had a virus, but we could afford to lose Young and play Calderwood, or even, at the very worst, Vega. But if it's a battle on Saturday I dread to think what our injury list might be on Wednesday.

Hartson is cup-tied, but Jason Euell will be back. There's talk that Euell will be sold, but he has just signed a five-year contract. I don't expect Euell to be sold. He's getting a good apprenticeship at Wimbledon, and I think he will stay for another two seasons.

Are we saying that Wimbledon are a bigger club than West Ham now? Or just a more ambitious club? Because West Ham have always signed second-echelon players. They have never signed world-class players like Ossie Ardiles or Paul Gascoigne. You wouldn't say that Trevor Sinclair is a world-class player. The best players they've had are those that the club has produced: Brooking, Devonshire, Cottee, Ince, Rio Ferdinand.

West Ham's identity, their DNA, is based on the idea of the academy, of schooling young players. When they signed a lot of foreigners – Bilic, Dumitrescu, Radiciou, Futre, Boogers – they lost their way. They need the Frank Lampards, the Joe Coles and Rio Ferdinands.

Tuesday 19 January

Sugar announced a three-year kit deal with adidas, the biggest in Spurs history. The new kit will go on sale in July and should be of merchantable quality.

———————

Wednesday 20 January

Let's hope the goals have not dried up. We have two big cup games coming up against Wimbledon. The FA Cup fourth round on Saturday at Selhurst Park and the Worthington semi-final first leg at WHL on Wednesday. And we have stopped scoring. For the first time this season we have had two consecutive 0-0 draws.

The Mirror has an interview with Gary Mabbutt to mark his retirement at 37, after 20 years as a pro. He says that the 1991 FA Cup Final, when we beat Nottingham Forest, was the highlight. 'To walk up those steps and lift the Cup was the biggest moment of my career.'

Mabbutt was diagnosed as diabetic at 17 and told he would never play again. Now surgeons say his knee has to be rebuilt, which will take a year. He plans to take the UEFA coaching course. 'I could have joined a number of clubs around 1987. I know Manchester United came in for me again after that, but I stayed at Spurs. My first salary was £18,000 a year and now players earn that in a week. That shows you how the game has changed.' Mabbutt said he hopes Sol Campbell is not damaged by the court charge for assault in the Derby County tunnel.

———————

WIMBLEDON: LOADA DIVING

Thursday 21 January

Steve Stammers reports in the *Standard* that we have opened talks with Paris St Germain over central defender Alain Goma today: 'The 26-year-old French international has been a target for manager George Graham during the past two months and although the clubs disagree over the player's value – the French club want more than £5 million for Goma while Spurs' offer is closer to £4 million – a compromise is likely to be reached this week.'

He first impressed Graham when playing for Auxerre against Arsenal in the Cup Winners' Cup in 1995. Earlier this season Roy Evans tried to sign Goma, who has fallen out with PSG's Portuguese coach Artur Jorge. So there we have it. We are chasing a French defender who has only one cap. And he might cost us more than Desailly, who was £4.5 million. George's agenda is the same as it was at Arsenal: sign up reliable competitors who won't argue with him. Sign up a bunch of B-internationals who are always striving to get into their national squads: Dixon, Bould, Winterburn, Smith.

───────────────

Friday 22 January

Expectation and anticipation of FA Cup game against Wimbledon. Will Anderton be back for the game? And Ferdinand? Nielsen and Clemence are suspended. George will probably play Young and Campbell, with Freund and Nielsen in midfield and Ginola and Anderton on the wings. Taricco may be at left back. Wimbledon have Euell back. No Ekoku or Gayle, who are on international duty with Nigeria and Jamaica, and no Hartson, who is cup-tied.

183

Saturday 23 January
Wimbledon (a)
FA Cup fourth round

The biggest game of George Graham's Tottenham career so far ends in a 1-1 draw. Robbie Earle scores with a superb overhead kick. Freund is the closest defender. But when the ball is crossed from the right, and headed back across the penalty area, and an overhead kick is as perfectly executed as Earle's, a defender cannot make a tackle or block the shot. Vega is beaten in the air. He was brought in because he's bigger than Young, who had the 'flu anyway. Edinburgh was lucky to stay on the pitch after a crude challenge on Euell which should have earned him a second yellow card. Then Ginola slams in an excellent shot for 1-1. Ginola must keep it up. He must be close to being player of the season this year, and emulating the feats of Jürgen in 1995.

Joe Kinnear said on *Match of the Day* that maybe Ginola got the message and cleaned up his act. He gave Wimbledon credit for telling the Frenchman to stop diving. He asked, 'Why not play like that for the rest of the season? The rest of his career?'

Sunday 24 January

Ossie Ardiles was in the ITV studio at Wembley for the FA Cup draw which was shown after the Wolves-Arsenal game. Ossie and John Bond made the draw, recalling our 1981 final against Manchester City. I said there was a karma: we get Leeds away, if we beat Wimbledon in the replay. After this we will probably get Arsenal in the quarter final!

184

Further thoughts on the replay? Nielsen will be back. Wimbledon will probably have Gayle and Ekoku back for the replay. Euell may be doubtful for the Worthington Cup game after that foul by Edinburgh. The FA Cup has lost some big clubs already. Villa are out. Liverpool are out.

Monday 25 January

Chelsea are outplayed at Oxford but get a last-gasp penalty. Clumsy giant Kevin Francis is unlucky as he tackles Vialli, who was going nowhere. Francis comes in from the side, playing the ball but also catching Vialli's boot. Mike Reed gives the penalty, Leboeuf equalises. Two years ago Mike Reed gave Chelsea an undeserved penalty when Erland Johnsen took a dive in the box against Leicester! Refs now do only Premiership matches, and not Nationwide matches.

Tuesday 26 January

The other Worthington Cup semi-final is Sunderland v Leicester. Excellent performance by Leicester, winning 2-1 away. Two goals by Tony Cottee. Do I fancy playing Leicester in the final? Yes. They are workmanlike, disciplined, but their three centre halves will be exposed by Ginola and Anderton. But Martin O'Neill would certainly have been on my short list to manage us.

Wednesday 27 January
Wimbledon (h)
Worthington Cup, semi-final first leg

I expect Nielsen to come in for Fox, with Anderton moving wide. Is Ferdinand fit? He owes us a performance. Should we start with him? I think George will keep him on the bench.

Our home record is excellent since George took over. We have not lost. I expect more attrition tonight. Wimbledon have disappointed me in our last two encounters. We must match their work-rate in all areas of the pitch. We must dominate and play the game at our tempo.

The match starts with Nielsen in, Anderton on the right wing, and an incredible atmosphere. The place is buzzing. Expectant. A feeling of: this is it! But, as the evening progressed, it became clear that the game would fizzle out into a scoreless draw. The only chance of note came ten seconds from time when Ferdinand had a free header six yards out. An injury to Ginola may keep him out of next Tuesday's FA Cup replay.

Reflections on the 0-0 draw. Boring, boring Tottenham. I think George is happier with a 0-0 than a 1-1. He would not like conceding a goal. He is the master of the one-off game, but just how many more one-off games does he have up his sleeve?

Our tactic was: knock the ball into the corners and play for the set-piece. Try to win the game with a long throw, corner or free-kick. Our only chances came from Anderton. He hit the post with a 25-yard free-kick, and that Ferdinand header from a corner at the death. The focus will now be on how long Ginola's injury will take to heal. In the event that he does not play, Sinton will come in for him and Ferdinand may come in for Armstrong.

Are we more of a unit without Ginola? We may have another chance to find out.

Claude Littner spoke to me in the West Stand shop before the game. 'Hello, Mark. How are you?' It was good to see him recovered, back to health. He confirmed that he will still be around the club as a non-executive director. We then debated the merits of Sugar. Littner said, 'Why don't you drop it all? Support the club. After all, that's what we all want. Success.' I said, 'Why, all of a sudden has Alan Sugar seen the light? It's because of fans' pressure.' Littner disagreed.

Thursday 28 January

Get a call from Nigel Williams, who tells me that Volvo have been taken over by Ford. He was listening to Radio Four this morning and a Ford spokesman commented about the brand DNA of Volvo. If a Swedish car can have a brand DNA, so can a football club. You heard it here first.

Adrian Curtis says in the *Standard* we are planning another swoop for Tim Sherwood after he rejected the Blackburn's new contract offer on Tuesday night. Our original bid of £2.9 million has increased to £4 million. Sherwood missed the 9 September game at White Hart Lane when former boss Roy Hodgson claimed he was not in the right frame of mind to face us.

Curtis wrote: 'Although Graham has splashed out £750,000 on German star Steffen Freund, he is not seen as the answer to Tottenham's ball-winning problems in the centre of midfield.' Oh, I see! After three games George admits Freund isn't up to it?

Sherwood has been at Blackburn six years and made more than 250 appearances. But I would not call him a ball-winner. From what I've seen Sherwood is tidy on the ball and cute off the ball, but he mostly leaves tackling to others.

Blackburn paid Liverpool £4 million for Jason McAteer yesterday. What does that tell us? That Houllier thinks McAteer is not good enough for Liverpool. And that journeymen now cost £4 million.

Friday 29 January

Ginola has collected eight yellow cards and is suspended for the game at Blackburn tomorrow. His hamstring has not repaired itself yet, so he could not play anyway. This is his second one-match ban. Blackburn have Tim Sherwood and Billy McKinley suspended, and half a dozen long- term injuries including their two best strikers, Chris Sutton and Kevin Gallacher. Matt Jansen and Jason McAteer could both make their débuts against us. We won 3-0 there last season.

Saturday 30 January
Blackburn (a)

Matt Jansen scored a fabulous goal, cushioning a high cross from the left to bamboozle Sol, and swivelling to send a left-foot volley into the bottom corner. A wonder-goal. We equalised after an hour when Nielsen crossed from the right. Ferdinand went up with John Filan, the ball popped out to Campbell, Filan parried Sol's header, but it went to Iversen, who headed in. Within a minute Jason Wilcox was sent off for a tackle on Nielsen, but we could not win it against 10 men. It was the third consecutive home game in which Blackburn have had a player sent off. A 1-1 draw.

Sunday 31 January

A huge storm has erupted about a telephone interview Hoddle gave to Matt Dickinson, which appeared in *The Times* yesterday. Amazingly, Hoddle was quoted as saying that disabled people were 'reaping what they had sown' in a previous life. He has to go.

Monday 1 February

Derick Allsop addressed the question of flair players in his report of the Blackburn game in *The Independent*. He gave George the benefit of the doubt on young, gifted strikers like Jansen because they are unproven at Premiership level.

'Even as George Graham lauded Matt Jansen's first goal for Blackburn, the Tottenham manager was inadvertently exposing a deficiency in his own team, and perhaps in his own transfer strategy. No, he confessed, he had not considered bidding for the striker signed from Crystal Palace for £4 million, a self-conscious smirk rippling across his face. He felt Jansen was serving his apprenticeship, one for the future, he reasoned. He may not be alone, in the more immediate future, in regretting his lack of interest in the England Under-21 player.'

George may be right to consider Jansen as merely a promising youngster. We lack quality up front, and he knows this better than anybody. George admitted, 'All the top teams have got world-class players, especially up front. They've got players who can unlock organised defences.'

George gives Ginola 'a good chance' of recovering from his hamstring injury in time for Wimbledon in the FA Cup replay at White Hart Lane. He said: 'He's been having treatment all week, and the injury is not as bad as we first feared. It is a strain rather than a bad pull and he has a good chance of playing.' We still have it all to do against Wimbledon. Three games in 12 days have produced three draws and only two goals. FA Technical Director Howard Wilkinson is said to be on stand-by to take over from Hoddle, who may be sacked tomorrow. Other stories suggest Hoddle may issue a writ against *The Times*.

Tuesday 2 February
Wimbledon (h)
FA Cup fourth round replay

There is a widespread feeling that the three Wimbledon games so far have been like watching two Arsenal teams coached by George Graham slugging out three bore-draws. Graham prevailed in two finals against Sheffield Wednesday in '93, one after a replay, but Wimbledon may be made of sterner stuff. In fact, I have a funny feeling that Joe Kinnear is a better George Graham than George Graham.

Wimbledon are a fierce, focused, never-say-die outfit who will battle right through to the 95th minute. I have seen nothing to suggest that we are a better team than them, but maybe we will get through and play Leeds in the next round. George is becoming the man who goes back to his previous clubs and finds them playing better football than they did when he was there, and making more friends. But at least Radebe has not started criticising George as Tony Adams did last week.

When a change of England managers is imminent it's best to stick with the one or two really experienced reporters who write sensible analysis, like Rob Hughes and David Lacey. Rob Hughes, in *The Times*, discusses a range of candidates who might grasp the poisoned chalice if Hoddle is sacked today. These include Howard Wilkinson, Terry Venables, Roy Hodgson and even the currently unemployed Roy Evans. Hughes also mentions another possibility:

'Another candidate who doubtless could be persuaded is David Pleat. He has the tactical nous, the ability to handle egos, the charm to cope with the mass media and, without question, the character to appeal to men in the shadows of the committee. Pleat long ago overcame the attempts to smear his personal reputation, after his first engagement with Tottenham Hotspur, and won more than half his games as manager at White Hart Lane, a ratio better than all the postwar managers, including Bill Nicholson, and better by far than Venables.' A mind-boggling suggestion, but full marks for originality!

Arriving at White Hart Lane we find that, once again, our game is overshadowed by news elsewhere. The FA have just announced that Hoddle's contract has been terminated.

Ginola is not playing, and not even on the bench. Yesterday's comment from George that Ginola was winning his battle for fitness turned out to be the kind of disinformation he was notorious for at Arsenal. If George had said Ginola was extremely doubtful for the game, he would probably have played. Sinton comes in and is up against former Fulham defender Duncan Jupp, who rarely gets a game and is a centre half anyway. Sinton has a point to prove. He has been offered a one-year extension to his contract, but he is 32 and says one year is no good to him.

Nielsen knocked a good first-time pass to Sinton, who cut inside Jupp, who backed off deep into his own box. Sinton hit his right-foot shot before Blackwell could close him down and it went in. A decent move and a welcome goal after three minutes.

This did not seem like the real Wimbledon. There just wasn't the same intensity and belief. There were no fierce tackles or bad fouls. Having gone a goal down early on the Crazy Gang didn't react as they normally would. Had they had a bet on Spurs?

This is first cup game not covered by season tickets, so regulars had to pay extra. And thousands stayed away. Big sections of blue seats were unsold and the atmosphere was dead. In the circumstances, with the game live on Sky, they should have reduced the ticket prices. The crowd of 24,000 was 12,000 less than the 36,000 crowd for the Worthington Cup bore-draw last week.

Funnily enough, I think that helped us because the atmosphere wasn't that confrontational. It was played at our pace with no late tackles or niggly fouls or theatrical protests to Dermott Gallagher, the referee.

And, amazingly, Gallagher never had to get his book out, except to note the goals.

On balance, we looked better as a unit without Ginola. The movement was quicker because we weren't relying on him and waiting for him to do something. Sinton can play with both feet and deliver the ball early. And that is what Iversen and Ferdinand thrive on. What they do not want is to be static and have to jump. When they're running they can jump higher. And Sinton allowed Freund and Nielsen to concentrate more in the centre. What has tended to happen was that Justin Edinburgh was being constantly exposed to two opponents because Ginola was out of position. So the central midfield player – Anderton, Nielsen or Freund – was having to tuck across on the left side to cover Ginola. Last night that didn't happen. Freund wants to stay in front of the back four because he's virtually a third centre half. On what we have seen so far, Freund is a very average player.

Jupp was taken off at half- time. Carl Cort came on, Ardley moved back to mark Sinton. Our second goal came after a challenge that might have been a foul. Perry hesitated in the box, Ferdinand muscled him off balance, went to the bye-line before crossing low to give Nielsen a tap in. And Wimbledon barely protested! It was almost as if they weren't trying!

Our third goal was a complete farce. Wimbledon had brought on Ceri Hughes for Roberts, thus removing the anchorman in front of their back four. Jason Euell was trying to clear as Nielsen charged in, outside the penalty area, to close him down fiercely. The ball hit Nielsen's knee and rebounded low past Neil Sullivan, beating his dive at the foot of the post. A freak rebound had gone in from 23 yards! I thought: why couldn't we save that up for another day?

Clearly, Joe Kinnear's priority was the second leg next week. He is one match away from his first Wembley appearance as a manager, and he wants to field his strongest team in that game. If he'd won tonight he was still a long way from an FA Cup Final. He would have to travel to Leeds, not the easiest of games. If Wimbledon were not in the Worthington Cup semi-final they might have risked playing Cunningham or Gayle or Ekoku or a combination thereof. And they would have battled in an FA Cup replay, not just gone through the motions.

We were by far the better side, but the 3-0 victory felt hollow. We had not beaten the real Wimbledon. Bizarre that an FA Cup fourth round replay was not a big game and not a sell-out. But the circumstances were strange. And that's something you learn as a fan. The circumstances of each game are slightly different. Even when we play the same team five times, each game is different because the circumstances are different.

Tuesday 3 February

Our win is overshadowed by Hoddle's sacking last night. Howard Wilkinson will be in charge for the England-France friendly next week. First Graham Kelly went and Geoff Thompson became acting chairman. Then Keith Wiseman resigned and David Davies became Acting Chief executive. And now we have an acting England coach. That's a lot of acting. Maybe Sugar was right about the dummies at Lancaster Gate.

The Sun led the witch-hunt against Glenn Hoddle, but it was *The Sun* which serialised his World Cup diary. What hypocrisy! The biggest, richest tabloid is able to have it both ways. They pay Hoddle for his exclusive story, highlighting the bits which make news. They encourage his self-crucifixion. Monday's *Sun* front page was one word: 'GO!' Tony Blair was on the Richard and Judy morning TV show and said that if Hoddle had said what he is reported to have said it would be difficult for him to stay.

So *The Sun* and Tony Blair had already sacked Hoddle before the FA meeting finished last night. The Prime Minister was part of the lynch-mob! Incredible! The guillotine was more humane than putting people through the mincer in public the way they do these days. The media has far too much power. But, of course, Hoddle had to go. It was not just one incident. Glenn scored own-goal after own-goal after own-goal. It got to the point where the FA just could not stand by him any longer.

We go to Leeds on Saturday 13 February for the FA Cup fifth round. Will Ginola play in that game? Will George *want* Ginola to play in that game?

———————

Thursday 4 February

Reports suggest that Tim Sherwood really is about to sign for us. This has become a boring soap opera. Sherwood set a wonderful example to the other players at Blackburn, so much so that Roy Hodgson blamed his captain for getting him the sack. Brian Kidd came, did well at first, so Sherwood liked Kidd. Now, however, Sherwood looks south again. This saga must be over soon. It is so boring!

———————

Friday 5 February

Sherwood signs a four-year contract at a fee of around £4 million. He will probably be in the squad for tomorrow's game against Coventry. George said, 'I'm delighted to get a quality player who will be a tremendous asset to the club. I believe he will form a great partnership in the middle of the park with Allan Nielsen and my other recent signing Steffen Freund.'

The notion that we would play those three together was somewhat radical, begging the question of whether George planned to change from his favoured 4-4-2 system. But he said, 'I'm just trying to get a squad together that can adapt to all systems. You need quality in the middle of the park, and it's what other clubs who are doing well all have. You need a big squad if you are going to succeed in the Premiership or the cup competitions, and it is no secret that certain areas of the team needed to be improved. I don't care if players are expensive or cheap – so long as they have the quality to make us a better side. Tim has won a championship with Blackburn and has great experience, is a quality passer of the ball and an excellent competitor. I believe he is a winner – and will be a great asset for us.'

Saturday 6 February
Coventry (h)

Walking through to the ground from where we usually park, I thought that George would drop Vega and bring back Luke Young, who is quicker and better able to handle Huckerby's pace. The papers said Sherwood would be on the bench. We outplay Coventry in a 0-0 draw. Iversen plays badly, so does Young. Taricco makes his first start and I don't like him. He is neat and tidy but too casual. Our best players are Carr and Anderton, with Nielsen doing OK. Freund has his best game so far.

We murder Coventry but miss about eight chances. Ferdinand misses four and Iversen stabs over from two yards. We often exaggerate when we say, 'It was harder to miss than to score!' But here it is true: the ball comes in from the right to Iversen, two yards out. He sticks out his foot and, incredibly, the ball flashes over the bar. It is a geometrical impossibility for the ball to go over the crossbar. But it goes over the crossbar. Sherwood comes on for the last six minutes but never gets a kick. Good substitution, George! As we walk back to the car we get the results on Zak's little radio. Man Utd have thrashed Forest 8-1 at the City Ground. Solskjaer came on as sub after 80 minutes and scored four goals!

Sunday 7 February

Coventry was our 10th game without defeat, and our seventh draw.

We scored three goals against a Wimbledon team that wasn't trying, four against Everton, five against Watford. The other seven games were draws. Three were 0-0 draws. We should have won yesterday. But our strikers didn't strike. Arsenal went to West Ham and won 4-0. Bergkamp and Overmars got the first two goals. Zola scored Chelsea's only goal from a free kick against Southampton. They are world-class players. We cannot compete with Arsenal and Chelsea unless we have world-class players. Who would have guessed, watching Les Ferdinand yesterday, that he is the second most prolific striker in the first six years of the Premiership? That he scored 112 goals in 214 games?

Watched highlights on *Match of the Day* last night. We play at a pace which is greater than our skill level. That's why we miss so many chances. We are one-paced, and it is a fast pace. We lack a touch player with the finesse of Yorke, Zola, Bergkamp, a classy creative forward. A Berkovic, even. Man Utd carve out openings, then play softer passes and crosses. Their scorers are not always stretching and lunging for half-chances. Their goals are set up, not forced. Yes, they play early balls and long passes and they create dynamic, penetrating moves. But

197

they can slow it down in the last third and set up unmissable chances.

Monday 8 February

George has put Saib, Tramezzani and Dominguez on the transfer list. Christian Gross signed Saib from Auxerre for £2.5 million just under a year ago, and bought Tramezzani from Piacenza for £1.6 million. Saib joined up with Algeria last month for a match against Tunisia even though he had been refused permission by the club, who insisted he was not 100% fit after a back injury.

Tramezzani won a dispute about an Achilles tendon operation, which he had in Belgium after the manager said surgery must take place in England. Dominguez has made a few appearances as a sub this season. George has had him on the bench, but never brought him on.

Tuesday 9 February

Sol Campbell has a stomach virus that will keep him out of England v France, but Darren Anderton will play at Wembley tomorrow night. Caretaker England coach Howard Wilkinson has named a probable team of 13 players! He will finalise his strikers tomorrow but it looks like Shearer and Michael Owen. Lee Dixon was drafted into the squad after the withdrawal of Gary Neville through injury. Dixon, 34, joins Adams and Keown in defence. Probable England team: Seaman; Dixon, Adams, Keown, Le Saux; Beckham, Redknapp, Ince, Anderton; Owen, Shearer.

Wednesday 10 February

England lose 2-0. We are outclassed in the second half. Anelka scores both goals after hitting the underside of the bar with a shot which TV replays showed was over the line. Anderton, playing out of position on the left, is one of our better players.

Thursday 11 February

We are being linked with Rangers' German midfielder Jorg Albertz, but Borussia Dortmund also want him. Albertz is a powerhouse who scores goals with his left foot. Rated at £5 million, he is 27 and has three years left on his contract. But the signing of Hearts left-winger Neil McCann suggests Rangers manager Dick Advocaat might let Albertz go.

Friday 12 February

The most likely score tomorrow is Leeds 0 Tottenham 0. Sol has recovered from his virus. I expect Graham to play a containing game, even though Leeds have lost their last two matches. They went down 3-0 at Southampton, and then lost 1-0 to Newcastle when Solano scored at Elland Road. Ginola has been having treatment for a hamstring strain for the last 17 days. He has missed three games but may be fit now. But I would not be totally surprised if he rested Ginola to keep him fresh for Wimbledon. Ginola said, 'I had to stay in the treatment room until four o'clock every day, and it is very, very boring.' He admitted he had been a bit lazy with his stretches and warm-ups.

Saturday 13 February
Leeds (a)
FA Cup, fifth round

Had to take work home this weekend, so I made an executive decision to miss Elland Road. Listened to the game on Radio Five Live. George got plenty of abuse as he stepped off the bus, and as he walked to the dug-out. He had a police bodyguard at the start of the second half.

Sherwood scored the first goal with a mis-hit shot from Anderton's cross. Sherwood was in the right place at the right time, but the finish was a fluke. The ball looped up and over Nigel Martyn. So we were 1-0 up after 52 minutes. Leeds left back Ian Harte equalised after 73 minutes. A goal which had a touch of class. Harte picked the ball up wide on the left, came inside Anderton and Sherwood, and surprised Walker with a low shot just inside the post. A very good right-footed shot by a left-footed left back, hit from the edge of the penalty area. But lackadaisical defending by Sherwood. The game finished 1-1. The replay is on the 24th.

Sunday 14 February

We are playing at 110mph every game and that worries me. Our style is intense, fast and forceful, and not just in cup-ties. It seems a bit manic. George would argue that we have to play that way because of the lack of quality players. There will come a time when there's no more left in the tank.

Monday 15 February

Alan Smith, writing in *The Daily Telegraph*, thought Sherwood made a good start. As a former striker himself, he appreciated one of Sherwood's early passes:

'The Cup tie at Leeds, with all its managerial overtones, was never going to be an easy place for Sherwood to make his full début. Yet a sharp, first-time reverse ball to Les Ferdinand in the opening minutes, giving the striker a clear sight of goal, demonstrated that the midfielder was switched on. Sherwood has that valuable capacity to support the play wherever it roams. He rarely wasted possession on Saturday, having already sized up his options, like all good players, before the ball arrived. Bearing in mind that the sometimes irksome tendencies of Leeds' Lee Bowyer in midfield carried potential for fireworks, Sherwood, for the most part, kept a lid on his fiery temperament.'

The other Mondays had further quotes from George. In a Shaun Custis story in *The Express*, he said, 'I never expected things to happen this quickly. No-one at Spurs would have thought we would be in this position, in the semi-final of the Worthington Cup and still in the FA Cup. Bloody hard work, that's what's done it.'

He also admitted: 'I came with preconceived ideas about some players, but having worked with them, it has changed my mind. Some have done a lot better than I thought, although I'm not going to tell you who they are. When I look at successful teams, and I mean successful over a sustained period, I look at the guy in charge, that is the answer. He injects his character and enthusiasm into the players' attitude. There are a million little things you can do, and you inject your general philosophy so that players know where they stand.'

George also talked about needing a good balance in midfield. 'Manchester United have Butt and Keane, Arsenal have Petit and Vieira. Sherwood does like to get forward but you have to have someone covering like Freund.' He also said, 'Spurs have always been known as a nicey-nicey push-and-run team that sometimes could be too much of a pushover. My objective is to change all that.'

Does this mean we can forget about style and glory? Remember our DNA, George. Still, it is encouraging to know that we will no longer be a pushover push-and-run team. But Sherwood and Freund are not as good as Keane and Butt, and certainly not in the same class as Petit and Vieira. No way, George. What was that famous shout from John McEnroe to the umpire? 'You CANNOT be serious!'

Tuesday 16 February
Wimbledon (a)
Worthington Cup, semi-final second leg

I fancy us to get a goal and just cannot see Wimbledon scoring two tonight. We have kept five clean sheets in our last eight games. And in four games against Wimbledon we've only let in one goal. If we win 1-0 we go through. Expect a close game. It will be tight, and physical, the most physical of the five games we've had with them. But George Graham has been down this road many times. He has been a winning manager in a lot of semi-finals.

Interesting stats: Wimbledon have not scored in their last four games and have only scored one in their last six games. Did Kinnear get it wrong by resting players and allowing his boys to take their foot off the pedal? The sartorial comparison between Kinnear and Graham could not have been starker. Why shop at Millet's when you can buy your clobber at Armani?

Changes I expect: Vega for Young (height), Nielsen for Sherwood (cup-tied), and perhaps Armstrong for Iversen, as this was Armstrong's old stomping ground.

Journey down to Selhurst Park in South London is a nightmare. It takes an hour to drive from Great Portland Street to Victoria, so we jump on a train. Atmosphere electric, like a home tie. Expectation enormous. This is what we have been waiting for! Seven years of frustration suddenly letting rip: we can't lose, we won't lose. There is too much at stake.

The game itself is much more blood-and-thunder than any of the other games. Iversen provides a good knockdown to Ferdinand, who makes a sharp turn and half-volley. Sullivan dives to his left for a good one-handed save.

Then we see the first bit of class in the match. Euell gets onto a Vega head-out, juggles it with his right foot and lashes it with his left, a dipper straight at Walker, who tips over. If the shot had gone a yard either side of Walker he could not have saved it. This is the real Wimbledon, the real committed Crazy Gang of old, the battlers who never allow you a second to settle on the ball. Tense and nail-biting, no real chances.

The pitch cuts up atrociously. After 20 minutes there are divots everywhere, but the atmosphere is fantastic. Blackwell clatters into Ferdinand in the centre circle, catching him in the face or neck with his knee, but he gets a lecture, not a yellow card from referee Gary Willard. Ginola has a run and shot, not his best, but it is deflected for a corner. We are playing functional football at a high tempo.

Then Anderton pumps a long ball down the middle, Ferdinand fails to control it, Cunningham comes in to challenge. Iversen takes one brilliant touch, then lobs perfectly over Sullivan! A class finish which belongs in *Serie A* on a Sunday afternoon. Great goal! One nil to the Tottenham! Spurs are on their way to Wembley!

At first glance Iversen looked offside but after much discussion at half-time it was found that Kenny Cunningham inadvertently knocked the ball into Iversen's path. He was a yard beyond the last defender, but it was not offside because the ball came to him off a Wimbledon player.

Terrific skill by Iversen, superb opportunism. Thanks, Gerry. You always said this lad was a footballer. But we were lucky. I don't think the linesman knew the ball came off Cunningham. He should have put his flag up. Then the referee would have had to decide whether it was a goal, depending on whether he saw the touch by Cunningham.

Let's face it: if Ferdinand had controlled the ball properly, we would not have scored that goal. And Ferdinand, right through the game, was a disgrace. On tonight's form it is hard to believe he ever played for England. Did he really cost £6 million?

Still, we are enjoying it. Everyone is singing *Are You Watching, Arsenal?* Wimbledon tried to push forward in the second half for the equaliser and they left space at the back which we should have exploited. But the quality of our counter-attacks is sadly lacking.

Nothing goes for Wimbledon. We have all the luck on the night. When Ginola cuts across Andy Roberts his heel catches Roberts, Ginola goes over and Roberts is booked, unluckily. Freund gets in a good block on a Michael Hughes shot. Then Sol gestures madly to the bench for a sub. Sinton comes on for Edinburgh, who is obviously injured.

Ian Walker does not have many saves to make. But Wimbledon keep up the pressure right to the death. Walker fields a tame header from Earle, then Earle sidefoots over the bar after a low cross from Thatcher. The only real scares come in the last couple of minutes. Gayle has a good volley just over and then, in injury time, Sinton makes a poor clearance, straight to Earle, who hits a superb shot which clips the top of the bar.

After four minutes of injury time Willard blows the final whistle and visions of the Twin Towers come flooding back. The pitch invasion is completely different to those which had taken place at the Lane against Sheffield Wednesday, Middlesbrough and Leeds. How ironic that it was Cunningham and not Ginola who would ultimately get the assist that takes us to Wembley.

This is what it is all about, Mr Sugar! The passion, the excitement, the desire – not balance sheets. Success on the pitch will lead to success off the pitch. The season has turned upside down. It's been a rollercoaster. Perhaps I should wait at the car park again, as I did after the first game of the season, just to see Sugar's reaction. He may have even anticipated me being there.

But we have a train to catch. The station is packed full of chanting Spurs fans. We cannot get on the first train back to Victoria, so we go back to East Croydon to catch a train.

The journey brings back memories of the Wolves semi-final at Hillsborough 1981. The banter, the songs, the jokes, the atmosphere, even though we were robbed during that '81 match. We are not going to let this moment pass. The songs just keep on coming. We sing *Spurs Are On Their Way To Wembley.* Brilliant, this is what it's all about. And we sing, *Que Sera Sera.* We sing *It's A Grand Old Team* and *Giorgio Armani's Blue and White Army.*

George Graham has got us to Wembley, but we still can't chant his name. The *Giorgio Armani's Blue and White Army* chorus lasts for all of two verses. Then someone pipes up, 'Hey, we can't sing that, there's too much George in that!' So we sing:

Man in a Crombie's blue and white army
Man in a raincoat's blue and white army
Man with a bald patch's blue and white army

Only when the double and the European Champions Cup sits proudly at the Lane, and Mr Graham exceeds his achievements at Arsenal, will we really accept this mercenary Gooner. And, just as a finale, we sing, *We've got our Tottenham back*. A tremendous night. Roll on Wembley! Roll on 21 March!

Wednesday 17 February

Matt Dickinson started his report in *The Times* by describing last night's pitch invasion:

'Four months ago they wanted to tear their team to shreds, yet it was in celebration last night that supporters of Tottenham Hotspur ripped the shirts from the players' backs. A place in the Worthington Cup final secured, they wanted any souvenir they could lay their hands on. Even George Graham's expensive overcoat seemed in danger at one point as thousands of supporters skipped across Selhurst Park, but the Scotsman proved a remarkably quick mover, just as he has in reconstructing Spurs from the mess he found them in.'

The six Wimbledon-Tottenham games have been an exhausting and often boring series of matches. Six games between August and February! But we won the one that mattered most last night, and we are back at Wembley for the first time in eight years. In football, eight years is a very long time. For me, those eight years have been mostly miserable, unhappy, angry years, lit up by moments of pure ecstasy like Jürgen's goal at Anfield in 1995 and our victory against Man Utd on New Year's Day 1996. Well, that's enough excitement for a decade.

Does last night make up for being thumped 4-1 by Everton at Elland Road? Not really. But you cannot live in the past. You must enjoy the present and plan for the future.

Thursday 18 February

Steve Stammers reports that the club wants to thrash out new deals with Anderton and Campbell. Anderton has one more year left after this season and Campbell has two. Pleat is quoted: 'Darren has fought hard to get over the public misconception that he had a continual injury problem. He has had a run of games and done very well. It is the kind of run of which previous managers never had the benefit. We value him as much as any other player at the club.

'He has proved he can take the toughness of the current regime and everyone at Tottenham hopes he will extend his career at White Hart Lane. As for Sol, he knows the offer of a new contract is there any time he wants to discuss it. Darren and Sol have been part of the recent past and present – we hope they will be part of the future.'

We will play Leicester at Wembley. They drew 1-1 with Sunderland after beating them 2-0 at the Stadium of Light. Tony Cottee scored their equaliser last night after scoring both goals in Sunderland. The papers emphasise that Cottee has never won anything in 16 years as a professional. This will be his last chance.

Friday 19 February

We still have not won away under George and Middlesbrough are going through a sticky patch. We have the Leeds replay coming up on Wednesday, and the players will not want to put themselves about. Middlesbrough has a lot of potential to be 0-0.

Saturday 20 February
Middlesbrough (a)

I listen to this game on the radio and, sure enough, it turns out to be a non-event. I see the TV highlights later on. We missed the first chance when Taricco, running onto a backheel from Iversen, got in and placed a powder-puff shot past Schwarzer, kicked off the line by Vickers. Carr made a sloppy return pass to Anderton which Gascoigne intercepted, and when Carr recovered to get in front of Gascoigne, our former hero scythed him down. Gazza's 11th yellow card of the season.

Ginola put in a left-wing cross which Anderton, in the centre-forward position, headed on. Ferdinand chested it down and poked the ball home but was clearly offside. Then Anderton took a free-kick which Vega headed against the base of the post with Schwarzer well beaten.

We kept Gazza quiet except when, late on, he picked up the ball on the halfway line, beat Sherwood, held off Freund, evaded Sherwood again and hit a left-foot shot which Vega deflected for a corner. There is, occasionally, a spark of life in the old Geordie.

Another Ginola cross reached the far post, but was too close to the post. Armstrong ran in with Dean Gordon and headed wide. It was, in the final analysis, a hospital cross. A fully-committed header would have been suicidal: Armstrong would have collided with the post and put himself in the nearest infirmary with a broken collarbone or a fractured skull.

We had Vega, Carr and Armstrong booked. This 0-0 draw stretches our unbeaten run to 13 games. Middlesbrough, on present form, are the worst team in the Premiership and have just lost 5-0 to Everton. A game we should have won.

But, hey, we got to Wembley this week. And our opponents Leicester were stuffed 5-0 at Arsenal today. Leicester, like Middlesbrough, are beginning to have relegation worries.

We probably had more of the game, and more chances, but maybe that's to be expected. Football is changing in that teams are playing better away from home where there is less pressure, and where they can create more openings with counter-attacks. Most teams have forgotten how to play at home. The only teams that can play well at home, and do it for 90 minutes, are Arsenal, Chelsea and United, who have won trophies and know they are good enough to win more trophies. So if a goal doesn't come in the first 20 minutes, they won't panic. They just keep playing to their system, and expect to score later.

Sunday 21 February

We play a local Jewish Cup game against a team in the division above us. Brady Maccabi are our big rivals. The match, in the Cyril Anekstein Cup, is in Greenford, a large complex with a lot of pitches, in terrible conditions: sleet, snow, wind, rain. It is 0-0 after 90 minutes and it is still 0-0 after extra-time. So it goes to penalties.

The captain Barnett Horowitz says, 'Mark, do you fancy one?' I say, 'Yeah, OK.' So he says, 'Alright, you're No 5.' Which I had taken before, a few years ago, in another pressure situation. And was successful.

They miss the first penalty, we score. Then all the remaining penalties are scored until we have to take the fifth penalty to put us through. But while the penalties are being taken someone else chirps up and says he'll take the fifth. So the captain asks me and we agree that if he wants it that desperately, we'll let him have it. So he steps up to take the fifth penalty – and the keeper saves it !

So it's 4-4 after five penalties each. Sudden death. Brady then score. So who has to take our 6th penalty to keep us in the cup? Yours truly. Their goalkeeper Joel Nathan sits two rows behind me at Tottenham. So there is a bit of banter going off with the 'keeper. He hands me the ball and tells me that if I score he's gonna gob on me for the rest of the season. I calmly place the ball, take a few steps back and sidefoot it past him. We are level. They then miss, we score. So we go through to the last eight.

Monday 22 February

The Leeds replay could be a grudge match, with Leeds chairman Peter Ridsdale sitting across from George in the directors' box, especially after the 3-3 game in September where some of our fans attacked the Leeds coach in the High Road after the game. The match will be live on Sky, and has not sold out in advance. It is the second cup-tie not covered by our season tickets, the first being the Wimbledon replay. My ticket costs £34.

The current League table shows that our Wembley opponents have a very similar record in the Premiership after the first 25 games. We have scored slightly more goals, and conceded slightly fewer.

FA Carling Premiership

		P	W	D	L	F	A	P
1	Man Utd	27	15	9	3	61	28	54
2	Chelsea	26	13	11	2	39	21	50
3	Arsenal	26	13	10	3	34	12	49
4	Aston Villa	26	12	8	6	37	27	44
5	Leeds	26	11	9	6	39	25	42
6	Liverpool	26	11	6	9	49	32	39
7	Derby	26	9	10	7	25	24	37
8	West Ham	26	10	7	9	29	38	37
9	Wimbledon	25	9	9	7	29	35	36
10	Newcastle	26	9	7	10	34	35	34
11	Middlesbrough	26	7	12	7	33	36	33
12	Sheff Wed	25	9	5	11	31	24	32
13	**Tottenham**	**25**	**7**	**11**	**7**	**29**	**31**	**32**
14	**Leicester**	**25**	**7**	**9**	**9**	**25**	**34**	**30**
15	Everton	26	6	9	11	19	28	27
16	Charlton	26	6	8	12	31	37	26
17	Blackburn	26	6	8	12	27	36	26
18	Coventry	26	6	6	14	24	37	24
19	Southampton	25	6	5	14	25	48	23
20	Nottm Forest	26	3	7	16	22	54	16

Both clubs have only won seven of their 25 games. I would love to think we could score three or four goals against Leicester, but even the class Premiership sides don't do that. Commonsense, and the stats, suggest a close final. We only beat Wimbledon by a single goal, and Wimbledon's record suggests they are on a similar level to Leicester and ourselves.

Chapter Seven

LEEDS REPLAY

Tomorrow's game will be tougher than the first game at Elland Road because Leeds are better as a counter-attacking side. Kewell and Hasselbaink have pace and exuberance. But the build-up to the game is pretty low-key, almost surreal, considering it is an FA Cup fifth round replay. Maybe both teams have their eye on the semi-final, rather than the next round, since both assume that they can knock out Barnsley. There is an underlying, unspoken feeling of: whoever wins this replay is automatically through to the last four.

Arsenal went through tonight, beating Sheffield United 2-1. It was the repeat of the match that never was when Kanu and Overmars created the 'ungentlemanly' goal, not returning the ball after Parlour's throw-in. Arsenal offered to replay it after the first game finished 2-1.

Wednesday 24 February
Leeds (h)
FA Cup, fifth round replay

I went to the game with Ian, one of my cousins, a Leeds supporter who got a ticket for the Leeds end. Arriving for the 7.45 kick-off, the game did not really feel like a big event as it should have done. It's live on Sky, so thousands of regulars have decided not to come. We have Derby on Saturday and Southampton on Tuesday as well. That is a lot of money to find. And Leeds did not sell the whole of their allocation.

This is probably the last cup-tie of the season at White Hart Lane, but there are many empty seats. It feels as if we are playing for the right to play Barnsley away in the quarter-final – that's all. The first leg against Wimbledon was very low-key because it was only half a match. The away game, which took us to Wembley, was the one which had the atmosphere. White Hart Lane did not see the decisive moments that took us to Wembley.

Even so, it's the FA Cup, where there is always a slight feeling of uncertainty. I don't feel as confident as I did against Wimbledon. This game will be more difficult. Leeds have had a blip recently, lost a couple of games, but then went to Villa and won 2-1, so they've picked up. It is an opportunity for the Leeds players and fans to show George he was wrong. That he should have stuck with what he had, rather than walk out halfway through his contract. But had George taken them as far as he could? Without the resources, without serious extra expenditure, could he have taken those players any further?

I found it amazing that David O'Leary played the Dutch youngster, Willem Korsten, on the left wing. Korsten, on loan from Vitesse Arnhem, has only been in England for a couple of months. That didn't make any sense to me at all. Why did he not play Kewell on the left and striker Alan Smith up front? I thought that was a big, big mistake. We are a tall team with strong, experienced defenders. Smith is young and small, but he's fast and very aggressive. Surprisingly, O'Leary played Radebe at centre half. In the first game he played Radebe on the right, marking Ginola, and Woodgate and Weatherall in the middle.

The match has a predictable pattern, following the first game, where the away side took the initiative for the first

20 minutes. Leeds have some half-chances during that period. We clear one off the line and Walker makes a good save with his leg. The longer the half goes on the more I am hoping for the half-time whistle, so that Graham can get in the dressing room and say: look, this is going wrong, that's going wrong.

Ginola drifts around too much and is losing the ball to players like Bowyer, Hopkin and Haaland in positions which could have killed us. There are occasions when Leeds break with three or four men and we are caught out. But they lack that killer ball, that touch of class up front. Overall, Leeds are playing more football than us. They have more ideas, more angles, better movement, brighter passing patterns. But we are more penetrating. Anderton provides a chance with a cross to the near post which Iversen heads over. An Anderton free-kick is glanced narrowly wide by Sol. Good cup action so far.

Then there is a horrific clash of heads when Carr pumps the ball up towards Iversen. Ferdinand jumps first and collides with Weatherall. A complete accident but both are laid out for four minutes. Ferdinand goes off on a stretcher, Weatherall walks off looking groggy, comes back, and is then replaced by Gunnar Halle, with Woodgate moving from right back to centre half.

A clean game so far, but Radebe picks up a yellow card for clattering into the back of Iversen's ankle after the ball has gone. Leeds get a corner, play it short, Hopkin gets to the bye-line, crosses low, Haaland gets a touch at the near post and Walker makes a pointblank save with his leg.

Then we have a chance. Anderton's corner is cleared, Freund heads the ball neatly forward, Iversen smacks a left-foot shot which is going inside the near post. But Martyn parries well. An excellent shot which lifts the crowd. At last! The tide has started to turn in the game.

We finally have something to sing about: *Come on you Spurs, come on you Spurs!*

From then until half-time the game is pretty uneventful. Neither side has any proper chances. The way we are playing is similar to the way we played under Gross and Francis, the long-ball game. You cannot play constructive football with our strikers because they cannot hold the ball up. So we play it forward to our speed-merchants, who are very hit-or-miss. You make the other team turn, you put the ball into channels and dangerous areas, and play for set-pieces. Free-kicks, corners and long throws in the last third, and we send up the big boys to head it in or win a knock-down. Nielsen, if he's playing, takes a long throw, or Edinburgh takes one, Vega goes to the near post to try to flick it on, and the strikers come in at the back post for the second ball. It's so predictable.

By contrast some of the Leeds free-kicks are innovative, but too complicated. You practice them using traffic cones. But when playing against another team instead of traffic cones it does not work. One free-kick is definitely too clever because it does not result in a shot. For George, I think, simplicity is better because he has Anderton, a very accurate dead-ball kicker. When Anderton and Ginola went over to take a short corner, the crowd start hailing and bowing, but what was the end result? When you have players like Vega, Campbell and Ferdinand, three very powerful players in the air, you've got to use them. And when you have two players who can deliver the ball right on the money, why waste it?

Graham comes down to the bench just before half-time, which is very rare. He seems to be yelling at Ginola to stay wide, rather than wander. But it doesn't do much good. Ginola pops up on the right and produces a decent cross which Armstrong heads over the bar from 12 yards.

Second half, George is on the bench as usual. When Anderton takes a short throw on the right to Ginola, he sets off on a run infield. He rides a tackle by Kewell, accelerates across the field between Hopkin and Haaland, and past Halle. I'm thinking: he's going parallel to the penalty area at full pelt! What can he do while he's running away from the goal? Can he stop and curl in a shot with his right foot?

But somehow, from just inside the penalty area, Ginola fires an incredible left-foot shot across the 'keeper. From where I am sitting it looks as if it is just drifting away, but it hits the inside of the post.

George Graham jumps off the bench and claps his hands. He's celebrating! He thinks it's a goal. But play continues as the ball rebounds right across the goal and bounces along the bye-line to Ginola again; frustrated, he smacks the ball blindly, low across the penalty area, but it's cleared. Then we get his antics, his theatrics. His body language says: why me? Is the whole world against me?

We then get a dubious free-kick. Armstrong chests the ball to Ginola, who pushes the ball past Halle, walks into him and falls over. Ginola knocks the free-kick across the field to Anderton, who is unmarked. The inexperienced Korsten has given him 12 yards of space. Anderton nudges the ball forward and slams a 30-yard shot which goes like an Exocet and flies in off the far post. What a shot! Unstoppable! Martyn had no chance. As soon as it left Anderton's boot you knew it was a goal. It is his third goal of the season, but his first in open play for two years.

We feel good now, obviously. We're 1-0 up, and it's not a Worthington Cup scenario where if they score an away goal they go through. Leeds now need two goals to win the game and I cannot see Leeds scoring two goals. One, maybe, to take it into extra-time.

The atmosphere picks up. It is *You're Not Singing Anymore* and *Que Sera, Sera*. But still no *Georgie Graham's Blue and White Army.*

Ginola starts a dribble in the inside-left position, steps inside Halle and hits another thunderous left-foot shot. It is a screamer which beats Martyn but smacks the near post, high up by the angle, and rebounds. It's not Ginola's night.

But wait! Walker kicks long down the right, Iversen pinches the ball from Radebe on the touchline, reaching round him to poke it forward, Sherwood crosses, Woodgate makes a feeble clearance, and as the ball drops centrally outside the penalty area, Ginola runs in and smashes a right-foot volley which bounces and flies into the corner.

Another spectacular goal! It is 2-0!

The ball sat up on a plate for Ginola. The defending was poor, edge of the box, 20 yards out, wallop! Thank you very much! Third time lucky. This time he didn't have to beat anybody. He just had to hit it first time and keep it down.

Leeds come back with a neat move. Hopkin pushes the ball forward, Hasselbaink touches to Kewell, who turns well and hits a ferocious half-volley but Walker makes a terrific reflex save with his left hand, a world-class save. So we are still two goals up. We may need a few more saves like that to get us to Wembley on 22 May. O'Leary brings on Alan Smith for Korsten, and Kewell soon puts Hasselbaink in on the left. He hits a good shot which Walker tips over. George brings Young on for Vega to counter Smith's pace.

Radebe stretches us with a good diagonal pass, Kewell touches to Hasselbaink whose excellent shot hits the foot of the post and rebounds off the back of the sprawling

Walker, hits Freund on the leg and is cleared by Vega, but only to Haaland. We can't get the ball away, but, thankfully, Hopkin shoots over the bar.

There are 77 minutes on the clock and we are defending now. It's a siege. But all the Leeds attacks are being funnelled down the centre. Both teams are packed round our box as they try desperately to get a goal back, with only Ginola left upfield in the centre circle with Radebe and Halle covering him. We have enough bodies in the middle to deal with the onslaught. There is no space, nobody is able to turn. When Smith has a shot, Sol blocks it.

Sinton comes on to replace Ginola, who goes off to a standing ovation. Ginola has had a superb second half. He has been the inspiration, the match-winner. His powerhouse dribble and shot against the post lifted the whole event. He is probably the only player in the Premiership who could have picked up the ball on the right, taken the North Circular route round the penalty area, and still had the strength to hit such a fantastic left-foot shot.

Right at the end, Harte takes a long throw to the near post. Walker comes out a long way and doesn't make it. A Leeds head wins the flick-on but we have three players on the line, and Edinburgh boots the ball upfield. A year ago we would not have had three players on the line, and Leeds would have scored. Game over, 2-0, roll on Barnsley.

No doubt pleasantries were exchanged between Sugar and Ridsdale, especially since Sugar was conspicuously absent for the 3-3 draw at the end of September when he was pinching the other chairman's manager. Still, Ridsdale has his £3 million compensation and is no doubt delighted to be ten points and eight places above Tottenham in the league.

I reckon Ginola and Anderton realised the Leeds midfield were all similar players. The Leeds midfielders all wanted to play in the centre, and each of them neglected their duties to mark the wide man. The whole point of keeping Anderton and Ginola wide was to spread Hopkin, Haaland and Bowyer, who are all central midfield players.

It was only after the game that I found out that Martyn had tipped the Ginola shot onto the post, a phenomenal save to stop an astonishing shot. For a player to make that run, pivot, and hit the ball with the accuracy and power that Ginola did, was truly amazing. That incredible moment of brilliance, which looked like being the goal of the season, was in fact the save of the season by Nigel Martyn. The shot had been hit so hard that nobody realised the 'keeper managed to get a touch to it.

The defenders Ginola went past were all positioned in front of the penalty area, not wide. The way to beat Leeds is on the flanks. They have no width in midfield and no width at the back. Their philosophy is to channel everything through the middle. George knew Leeds would attack like that because they haven't got any wingers, so he had his full backs tucked in. He knew nothing would come outside the full backs. The goal that Leeds scored in the first game did not come with Ian Harte going to the bye-line and crossing. It happened when Harte came inside and shot with his other foot. Harte is a very good player.

As for the injury, we heard that Ferdinand was taken to hospital in an ambulance at half-time. It always seems to happen to Ferdinand. Our strikers all seem to lack anticipation. All of them seem to be reacting a second or two after the event, always stretching, not quite getting there. It is no coincidence that all three of them have had substantial periods of time out with injuries. Iversen looked so cumbersome tonight, as though everything was an effort. He couldn't get his leg out unless the ball came straight to him.

I like Armstrong because he's a trier, a worker who puts in more effort than the other two. His tracking back was superb in the second half when he was doing some of Ginola's running. He was cutting angled balls out, and putting people under pressure. He has pace and the bottle to get in where it hurts and score goals. But, bottom line, I don't think he is skilful enough.

Once again, teams find it hard to score against us, although they don't necessarily find it that hard to defend against us. We started our Worthington Cup campaign, before George arrived, with two 3-2 wins over Brentford, but our three most recent cup scores are 0-0, 1-0 and 2-0. Those scorelines say a lot about the new Tottenham Hotspur.

Thursday 25 February

George must have been infuriated by Ginola's performance in the first half last night. He shouted down to Chris Hughton from the directors' box. He came down to the bench after 40 minutes. That is almost unique for George. He doesn't do that. He must have been really upset to do that. He must have had a go at Ginola at half-time. He must have said, 'I pay you to do a job, don't go off on frolics on your own. Don't do that till we're 5-0 up!'

Ginola is a maverick. A magnificent, maddening maverick. It is incredibly ironic that it was Gerry Francis, a slave to the 4-4-2 system, who actually signed him. Not because he felt Ginola could do a job, but as a sop to the fans. You want a star? You want flair? Here is a six-foot two-inch French god who can dribble and dribble and dribble – and shoot over the bar. It was an appeasement exercise for the fans. Give them an eye-catching winger who can turn it on once in a while, and maybe buy time to lick the rest of the team into shape. I don't believe for one minute that Gerry Francis ever thought David Ginola was a great footballer.

This 2-0 victory over Leeds sums up what George has achieved at Tottenham. He has moulded the players he inherited into a system, a shape, a pattern. He has instilled discipline in them, individually and collectively. And, clearly, the improved performances just emphasise the mismanagment and complacency of the last three years. It shows what a low ebb we had reached when the same players are able to produce performances of grit and determination.

Even so, there are still times when Ramon Vega gets the ball and I'm scared. And when a cross comes in, and Walker goes for it, my heart is in my mouth. Right at the death Walker came for a long throw, got nowhere near the ball, and was stranded. So players are still prone to make mistakes, although these are gradually being eliminated.

The goals that have been scored against us recently have been very good goals. We have only let in three goals in eleven games since 9 January. A terrific overhead kick by Robbie Earle, Matt Jansen's wonder-goal at Blackburn, and the Ian Harte equaliser from the edge of the box at Elland Road. There's not a lot you can do against strikes as good as those.

We've got our four defenders playing as a unit, and our two central midfielders playing as screens in front, and that enables Anderton and Ginola to create in the attacking third. We rely on them, and on set-pieces. We are not playing possession football, it's more power football and strategic football: the further away the ball is from our goal the better. Possession football can be high-risk, whereas power football, if it's well-rehearsed, is low-risk.

I've seen nothing at the back to suggest that Sol Campbell has become a better passer or a better reader of the game. The fact that George has brought Luke Young in is perhaps a recognition that Campbell isn't such a good distributor of the ball, and that Vega isn't. Vega is big, strong and can win balls in the air, but he lacks pace. Campbell has pace and strength but lacks passing ability like Rio Ferdinand.

Steve Carr has come on in leaps and bounds. You could always see it in him, but he just needed the right guidance. Carr has perhaps missed two years of his career because Francis and Gross retarded his development. If Carr had been playing under George or Wenger or Ferguson for the last two years he would be a Republic of Ireland regular by now. Because Gary Kelly has been injured for so long.

Last season, and the season before, fans were saying: look, you've got to get rid of the manager, he's not doing the job! The players aren't playing for the manager. So where does the buck stop? People were calling Capital Gold, calling Five Live, saying: the manager's gotta go! Nothing was done. Fans do not realise that Capital Radio pay big money for access to Tottenham.

Now, all of a sudden, George Graham is successful with the same players, so it makes Francis and Gross look bad. And it makes those supporters who wanted them out look correct in their assessment. Why were we not listened to then? Instead of being slagged off by Jonathan Pearce and Tony Gale. We were we told: give him a chance, give him time. Sorry, they *were* given time. It was clearly not working, the chemistry was not there.

Now I'm not 100% sure that the chemistry between George Graham and Tottenham Hotspur is there, but because we had sunk to such depths you could have put in Saddam Hussein and he would have done a job. Instilled certain disciplines. And, let's face it, guidance comes from the boardroom. And it is no secret that in the boardroom you have conflicts, and a director of football who has been a failed manager again and again over the last ten years.

What is David Pleat's role? What does he do? He wants the glamour but doesn't want his head in the noose. In Pleat's programme notes he says: Spurs are doing this, Spurs are doing that. He should be saying 'we' are doing this and that. It's as though he is one step removed. Is Pleat's principal role at the club to be a peacemaker between the chairman and the manager?

Pleat is another mouth to feed. Sugar talks about cutting wage bills and cutting costs but maybe we should look at the off-field personnel. And now we are taking on Stewart Houston, another first-team coach. Will we have to pay compensation to Ipswich? And what happens to Chris Hughton? Does he get sacked? If he goes, he's gotta be paid off as well.

Sugar could have appointed George Graham much sooner, after his one-year ban from the game. Two years later, having sunk to the relegation zone, Sugar did what was previously unthinkable.

In only five months George has made us rock solid and hard to beat. We knocked Wimbledon out of two cups because we kept after them with a consistent formation and a consistent team selection. We had, at last, a real, organised, hungry team, playing to the best of their ability and giving 100%.

Compare that to 1987 when Pleat was the manager. In the run-up to the FA Cup Final against Coventry, we had a few injuries, and players were rested. So when we went out at Wembley we had our first eleven on the pitch in name, but not in body. And that was the difference. The longer the game went on against Coventry, the more out of it we looked.

In the last month we have kept the same players performing consistently, and full credit to George for that. He hasn't done what Joe Kinnear did, resting players or dropping them because they might get booked and be suspended.

Recently, knocks and strains are becoming few and far between. Where in the past players have been missing with niggly injuries, groin strains and hamstrings, they now know they will be on the M25 at 5 o'clock in the afternoon after their third treatment session of the day. All of a sudden players see the Twin Towers in front of them. And this may be the last chance for some of them to play at Wembley in a domestic cup competition.

Leicester will have to be careful about this in their run-up to Wembley. They have a threadbare squad, as we've seen when Heskey and Cottee were out recently. Martin O'Neill will have to be very careful because he knows that George Graham will always play his strongest eleven. If Ferdinand is out, Armstrong will come in. If Freund or Sherwood is out, Nielsen will come in. If Ginola is injured, Sinton will play instead. But Tottenham players are not going to be rested for the sake of being rested.

When teams play Tottenham the best time to score against us is early in the game. Once we've had the first 45 minutes, and George has sussed the other team out, there's only gonna be one winner. Teams are gonna find it difficult against us in the second half of games, especially in cup competitions because the thought of extra- time, the thought of penalties, weighs heavily on their minds. George's teams at Arsenal and Leeds won a lot of games in the last ten minutes.

The next few weeks will be interesting. When teams see the way we play, will they realise there is a massive gaping hole around our left-back position? At the start of the season, when Ginola didn't track back, the central midfield player, who could even have been Anderton in those days, was having to tuck in on the left and cover the full back. And that created space in the middle.

Now we have Sherwood and Freund, who should be able to cover those gaps. Freund is an anchorman, not a midfield general. More of a midfield sergeant, somebody who keeps possession with simple ten-yard passes. His workmanlike play balances the more risky, creative flourishes of Anderton and Ginola. Not a character you can love, though. When someone's physical with Freund he starts moaning, but when he flattens somebody he yells at them to stop faking injury and get up. That is a fairly unusual trait in a British player, but not, alas, in a foreigner.

He is a poor man's Popescu. He won't give the ball away, he'll be there or thereabouts, and he tackles more than Popescu. But he doesn't have the same vision or range of passing as Popescu.

Sherwood won the championship at Blackburn and captained the team. But how many captains did that team have? They had Colin Hendry to captain the defence, Alan Shearer to captain the attack, and Sherwood to toss the coin.

The papers have a couple of Alan Sugar stories today. Nigel Dempster's column in the *Daily Mail* informed us that Sugar has decided to sell his ocean-going yacht and buy a private jet. Sugar flew to Palma, Majorca on Monday where the 165-foot yacht is having an £800,000 refit. He told Dempster the yacht, *Louisianna*, is on sale for £11 million. It has a cinema, nightclub and helicopter landing pad. It also has some history, having hosted the historic signing of Jürgen Klinsmann in Monte Carlo harbour in 1994. Sugar said he is negotiating to buy a 200-footer, but he doesn't want to end up with two yachts. Heaven forbid! The jet will cost a mere £5 million.

Tonight's *Standard* informed us that Alan Sugar is putting his personal profits back into the club. The story, by David Bond, said that Sugar has already pledged £20 million to Graham for new players. He said that Spurs revealed improved figures to the City today. Turnover was up by 20% in the six months ending 31 January. Turnover went from £18.6 million to £23.6 million in the same period last year. This was mainly due to completion of the North Stand which raised capacity from 27,000 to 36,000. Profits before tax jumped to £4.1 million. A year ago Sugar received more than £150,000 as a dividend on his 41% majority shareholding, and he is now due about £400,000 which he is re-investing in the club. The club admitted that merchandising turnover fell by £300,000 against last year. Wages shot up by 28% to £8.5 million, and Sugar has said the squad will be cut from 44 players to 35.

Friday 26 February

It is reported that Graham wants Robbie Keane of Wolves! Now you're talking, George! Robbie Keane, the 19-year-old Irish international, is possibly the most exciting young striker in Britain. He's a fast, skilful, brave, confident goalscorer, a clever dribbler, a natural footballer whose talent sticks out a mile. He is far better than Ferdinand or Armstrong and he's probably better than Iversen, even though he has never played in the Premiership.

Keane is certainly wasting his time at Wolves, but there is a queue of Premiership clubs who want him. Where are we in that queue? It's not so much a case of whether Tottenham can afford Robbie Keane. It's really a matter of: does Keane want to play for George Graham? Will he ask his pal Niall Quinn if this is the right move? Quinn played for George at Arsenal and might say: 'Don't bother, mate, you'll be chasing 70-yard punts and crashing into defenders twice your size!'

An Ian Walker quote shows that our goalkeeper is ready to own up. He said, 'What I have learned above all else under the gaffer is to work at my game. For too long I relied on my natural talent, but I knew I would have to change when the manager came in. We all knew about his reputation.'

Saturday 27 February
Derby County (h)

We stop for a pint at The Antwerp Arms, a pub near the ground. A mild afternoon with fans drinking outside, sitting on a wall. We talk to a couple of guys. One is fifty-something, the other a thirty-something whose son, a teenager, joins us a few minutes later. The lad says that in some pubs there are sporadic outbreaks of *Georgie Graham's Blue and White Army*. But they won't sing it in the ground? 'Not yet,' he says.

A pretty tepid game against Derby. It looks to me as if Wanchope wants away. He is not putting himself about. A very sterile affair in which Jim Smith has Stefan Eranio marking Ginola, which I find incredible. Eranio has to go off injured after half an hour. We huff and puff, with Derby having one or two better chances than us in the first half.

Within a minute of the second half starting we are a goal down through sloppy defending. Campbell is beaten in the air by Wanchope, who knocks the ball down, and Burton nips round the back of Vega to toe it past Walker.

The crowd try to lift the players and encourage them. But it is a very lethargic performance. Then Dominguez comes on for Armstrong and gives us a bit of inspiration. Within three minutes he cuts in from the right and plays a beautiful early pass through for Sherwood, who slots it past the 'keeper for 1-1. We then have a lot of pressure and Hoult makes a couple of excellent saves. If you are playing at home to Derby, and you don't take your chances, you don't deserve to win.

But the game had an overall feeling of After The Lord Mayor's Show, following on from Leeds and Wimbledon. The League games have been treated as less important, as games we don't have to win. Despite what people say to the contrary, it is clear that players are concerned about keeping themselves injury-free for Wembley.

And that is understandable. Whereas teams like Manchester United, competing on three fronts, have to give 100% or close to it in every game because every game is a Cup Final for them, we can only lift ourselves for the odd game in three or four, and maintain a reasonably consistent level in the other games.

So Tottenham are still a cup team, even with an Arsenal manager who was good at grinding out League points. Where we once raised our game, and turned on a bit of flair, now we play a mechanical style and just raise the tempo and the commitment to win our cup-ties. So our cup-ties are not glamour games, not spectacular, but games where we grind out a result. Especially now that there is only one replay rather than two replays or three. The replay now goes to extra-time, then penalties.

Sunday 28 February

I had a good look at yesterday's match programme. The cover is a picture of Ginola with both fists clenched, celebrating his goal against Leeds, with the Hewlett Packard logo jumping off his shirt front. Pages 2 and 3 list the board of the directors and summarise the last couple of games and welcome today's opponents. A few pictures and index.

Page 4 advertises 1,000 Sol Campbell Limited Edition fine art prints at only £20, each one signed by Sol himself with a certificate of authenticity. Page 5 is George Graham's programme notes, where he says that now he has got the basics right he wants to see a bit more self-expression in the attacking third. Pages 6 and 7 are devoted to a profile of Steffen Freund by programme editor John Fennelly.

Page 8 is the David Pleat page, then an advert page for Hewlett Packard, ad for the Football Trust on page 10, news snippets on page 11, a full-page ad for the Tottenham Hotspur Visa Card, fans letters on page 13. A typical fan letter includes a drawing of Chirpy, the club mascot: 'Could you please show my picture in the programme? Chirpy is the best mascot in the Premiership and he is always friendly to me.' Harrison Field (aged 9), Dagenham, Essex.

A full-page ad for Yorkie bars. Page 15 is an Update on trainee Glenn Poole and a small feature on referee Jeff Winter, a full-page ad for Carling, a Derby & Spurs quiz on page 17, a Junior Spurs page featurring the McDonald's logo, a full-page ad for Spurs Insurance, a page of logos for the North Stand boxholders. Analysis on reserve defender Lee Kersey, who is Luke Young's best mate, a little career factfile on Chris Hughton, whose Top

Spurs are Glenn Hoddle and Ossie Ardiles. Then an ad for the Carling Premiership and their official partners *Daily Telegraph*, Yorkie, PlayStation, McDonald's, Visa, Wilkinson Sword, Visa, Swatch, Sky Sports, Mitre, Lucozade Sports drinks and England 2006.

'Casting Shadows', a look back at past matches against Derby County. Then a four-page centre-page spread on Derby, and a breakdown of how they have scored their goals and conceded their goals, and who has yellow and red cards. A fold-out on a Spurs player with a breakdown on his entire career, This week it is Colin Calderwood: 'Manager George Graham is a great believer in strength in depth and that makes Scottish international defender Colin Calderwood a highly important member of the squad.'

If we look to see how often CC has played for GG it is eight games. He has been on the bench, but not since January. And George has never brought Calderwood on as a sub. Page 30 is Carling fans update where they talk about the Carling Opta statistics and the Carling Challenge which is the matches between the six London clubs, where we have three points from three draws thus far. A reminder that we can't even beat West Ham, Charlton and Wimbledon in the League, let alone Arsenal and Chelsea!

'Eurofile' by Keir Radnedge, on page 31, is quite educational. Though I did not realise that Nigeria and Argentina were in Europe. A Pony sponsor's page, a Centenary Club Member's logo page, an Executive Box Holders page. Then a page of Premiership stats on how clubs have scored their goals this season, from inside the penalty area or outside, from corners and so on. Red and yellow cards, a table of attendance figures (We had an average of 33,798 which is below Chelsea, Leeds, Middlesbrough and even Everton). Incredibly, another page telling us who the East Stand box-holders are, and also the Legends Executive Club companies. A nostalgia page by deaf supporter Brian Judson, who has watched 41 seasons.

Pages 38-39 feature five photos from the 0-0 draw at Middlesbrough last Saturday. Followed by a two-page ad for Vauxhall vans. A page for the Crossbar Club and the Hotspur Suite. A code of conduct page with evacuation procedures, followed by a page with three small ads for Nissan, Rainham Steel and Bee Line Transport & Distribution.

Then a Reserve and FA Premier Academy League fixture list with results so far. Then on pages 46-47 the two key pages of any programme: the 1998/99 first team match record listing all the players and subs in each game chronologically. Then two pages of box-office information about forthcoming games home and away. Page 50 is a preview of Tuesday night's game against Southampton, and page 51 is three more pictures from the glorious Leeds fifth round replay. The back page lists the Tottenham and Derby squads with the squad number of each player.

So our 52-page Official Programme, costing £2, contains 11 pages of ads and five pages of logos. We used to have the top programme in the League, with better analysis, good interviews and news about the reserves, which is always information you can't get anywhere else.

But I would only give this five out of 10. You could halve the size and not lose anything. It has stopped being a little magazine and become a merchandising tool, and a plug for the companies who buy the various corporate hospitality packages.

The football editorial has gone down and the commercial information has gone up. And it is self-perpetuating. If you give people information, and seem to care about sharing your team and your players with the fans, they might want more information. They might ask questions. But if you tell them nothing they will soon stop asking questions.

_____

Monday 1 March

George Burley has appointed John Gorman, Hoddle's No 2, at Ipswich, clearing the way for Stewart Houston's release to join us. Chris Hughton will stay on. Graham says, 'Chris will also still be here next season, but Stewart is coming in as my assistant and I'm happy with the back-room team I've now assembled.'

Les Ferdinand will not be available tomorrow. He had a brain scan last week after being carried off with head injuries in his last two games against Middlesbrough and Leeds. Les said, 'Medically, I'm not quite fit to play yet, although I feel fine. I was concussed in the Leeds cup replay, and if I were a rugby player I would have to be out for a minimum of 21 days.'

_____

Tuesday 2 March
Southampton (h)

We are unbeaten in our last 15 games but have only three Premiership victories since George arrived in October. Southampton tonight should be his fourth league win. Saints are struggling, but I saw highlights of them playing Manchester United on the box, and they looked a little unlucky in that game to come away with a 2-1 defeat.

I was surprised to arrive and find that Ostenstad, Le Tissier and Kachoul were all on the bench rather than playing. The game is played in heavy rain. We get a goal from a quickly taken free-kick by Ginola which Armstrong slots in. Southampton then try to claw their way back to into the game but I cannot really see them scoring. We then get a second goal, Iversen heading in from Ginola's cross. Dominguez comes on as a late sub and makes it 3-0 in injury time.

Wednesday 3 March

David Beckham was different class when Manchester United beat Inter Milan 2-0 in their quarter-final first leg. His crossing was brilliant. He laid on two near-post headers for Dwight Yorke. Inter's defending was poor, especially on the flanks, which had been pointed out by all and sundry before the game. United needed a 2-0 win and got it when Mr Krug disallowed a header by Simeone for shoving by Bergomi, as Baggio's corner came over. Whether United need more than a 2-0 win remains to be seen. Most people think they will get to the semi-final now. But it's not over.

Beckham, a Leytonstone lad, should be playing for us. But he was a United fan as a kid. We need more success so we will have more fans. And some of those fans will be good young footballers who want to play for Tottenham. Success is cumulative, just as failure is cumulative. Failure puts a club into a downward spiral which is very hard to arrest. Look at Manchester City. Relegated with Alan Ball in 1996, they are now in the Nationwide Second Division.

Thursday 4 March

Writing this diary has made me feel detached from the season. It's become a dissertation, a project. Inevitably, it has affected the way I think about each week and each game. Maybe when the season is over I will get back to being a fan, enjoying the ups and downs. My shouts are now less frequent and I don't get as intense as I have been.

My detachment pre-dated the start of the season, and was brought about by Alan Sugar's administration of the club. It was taken a stage further by starting this diary. Then, with the appointment of George Graham, my detachment became almost complete. It wasn't my club any more. When I speak to people and make comments they say: 'Yeah, but do you really support the club?' I do, but I take a more objective view.

I suppose I've become hypercritical, wanting more, demanding more. If we win the Worthington Cup, fine. But we will be one game away from a bigger final, the FA Cup Final. And one Worthington Cup is a meagre return from the last eight years of Alan Sugar's stewardship of Tottenham. A lot of people feel it is not their club any more. They go out of loyalty and out of habit. Because that is what they do on a Saturday, and that's what they will continue to do. They will still moan and groan, but they won't do anything about it.

What's the alternative? Well, there isn't an alternative to a football club. You just don't stop going to Tottenham one weekend and go to Arsenal the following weekend. Kids used to do that when the terraces were cheap. You went to both clubs and made your choice while you were growing up. But kids can't afford to go to a match every week now, and parents probably can't afford to send their kids to both Tottenham and Arsenal, even if they could get tickets.

Football has lost its hold on the working class, and that will continue. And the grassroots will eventually be cut off from the superstars. But as long as the media hype continues, promoting the rich clubs and the famous players, football will be the biggest sport. As long as it is on the back and front pages every day nobody will challenge the myth and the indoctrination. And the message they pump out is: watch Bergkamp and Beckham and Zola and Yorke. And, to kids, the message is: you can become a millionaire like Michael Owen.

It's all about fame and money, not about sportsmanship, camaraderie, enjoying yourself and expressing yourself. Footballers are now entertainment stars, and I think their lifespan will tend to get shorter and shorter.

Friday 5 March

Call from BBC TV South East News. They are doing a preview of tomorrow's FA Cup tie at Barnsley and want comments on how George Graham is doing, and how he has been accepted by Tottenham fans.

A crew came to my office at lunchtime.

Saturday 6 March

A catastrophic day. We were on the M1 near Northampton, going to Barnsley, when I received a call at 10.15am telling me the game was off. We were listening to Radio Five Live, expecting them to confirm this immediately because the pitch inspection was at 10am. But at 10.25 the Radio Five weatherman says he still thinks the Barnsley game will be on. We pulled off the motorway into a lay-by and waited for confirmation. At 10.30 the headline is that the game is off because of snow.

What happened at Five Live between 10am and 10.30? Knowing how many Tottenham fans would be travelling up the motorway to the game, it was an incredible own-goal by Five Live not to have a reporter there, or a local reporter phoning them to say the decision has just been made.

So I took my cousin home, dropped off my uncle, and then popped out to visit a friend in the afternoon. I was on the way to Amersham, around 1pm. It was a wet day and I was just past a junction and stationary behind two cars. The first car was turning right into a pub. I heard a screeching of brakes behind me, looked in my rearview mirror, and realised that this car was not going to stop, so I braced myself for the impact. I tried to grab the handbrake, so that I did not get pushed further forward into the other cars, but probably did not get there in time. I got smashed forward, then shunted backwards as I hit the car in front.

A four car pile-up. The car that hit me was a minicab. Two police cars and an ambulance arrive. The minicab driver had been drinking, but passed the breathalyser. He didn't even apologise! I went to Wycombe Hospital where I waited three and a half hours for a three-minute consultation. I had a sore neck, a whiplash injury. And then they said they were going to charge me for that consultation, as it was a road-traffic accident! So that really made my day. Then I came home to find that Arsenal had won their quarter-final against Derby with a last-minute goal by Kanu. Typical! Lucky, lucky Arsenal. When are we gonna get a last-minute winner?

LEEDS REPLAY

Sunday 7th March

The other two FA Cup quarter-finals? Newcastle thrash Everton 4-1. Man Utd draw 0-0 with Chelsea at Old Trafford. Then the draw is made on ITV. Once again we avoid Arsenal. We will play Newcastle, if we beat Barnsley, and Arsenal will play Man Utd or Chelsea. Newcastle is an excellent draw for us. Probably the easiest draw we could have had. George versus Ruud Gullit. Ginola and Ferdinand against their old club. Some interesting duels in prospect there. Shearer against Campbell. And the two Germans, Hamann against Freund. Gullit seems to be turning it round at Newcastle, where he probably had an even harder task than George had at Tottenham.

Previously the police said they needed two weeks' notice of a replay. Now they accommodate Chelsea v Man Utd within four days. Man Utd are in Europe, Chelsea are in Europe, and that's what counts. The European League is almost here. Pull the ladder up, we don't care who is below us. Your away games are in Amsterdam, Athens, Madrid, Milan and Kiev. If you can't afford the air fares, tough.

A graphic in *The Sunday Times* compares Beckham, Giggs and Ginola stats in the Premiership this season, courtesy of Carling Opta. A simplified version of the head-to-head table is quite illuminating:

	Beckham	Giggs	Ginola
Goals	2	3	0
Assists	13	1	8
Crosses	285	118	188
Shots on target	11	15	17
Shots off target	30	15	21
Blocked shots	13	4	13
Dribbles and runs	84	101	306

So Ginola has more dribbles and runs than Beckham and Giggs put together. But he has made a hundred fewer crosses than Beckham. Ginola has had 38 shots without scoring a goal! But no doubt he would have had more assists if he had Cole and Yorke converting his crosses.

Tuesday 9 March

We will play Newcastle at Old Trafford if we beat Barnsley. It will be a 2pm or 3pm kick-off on Sunday 11 April. That is normal for an FA Cup semi-final. But what was I saying yesterday? If Arsenal meet Chelsea it will be on a Monday night! The first FA Cup semi-final ever played on a Monday night. If Arsenal meet Manchester United it will be at Villa Park on Sunday 11 April at 12.30. But if Chelsea beat United tomorrow night's replay, they will play Arsenal at Wembley on the Monday night at Wembley.

Why? Because England play Wales in a Five Nations rugby international at Wembley on the Sunday! Monday will suit Chelsea, who will have an extra day to recover from their Cup Winners Cup tie the previous Thursday, assuming they don't lose a 3-0 lead over Valerenga of Oslo. How are fans who live outside London going to get to Wembley after work in time for kick-off? It's hard enough for an England game when the crowd is only 35,000, let alone a 75,000 sell-out as this will be.

Obviously, having the semi-finals on separate days suits armchair fans. They can enjoy one game, digest it, and tune in a day later to see who the winners will be playing. And it suits the media who can give twice as much airtime and space to each game. To hell with the loyal punters who have supported their teams from the third round onwards!

An article today says Spurs are now a good bet at 9-2 for the FA Cup. Ladbrokes rate us as a 3-1 chance. However, we are not a good bet to beat Leeds tomorrow. I think this is a match too far, and one that George won't mind losing. He would like to beat Aston Villa on Saturday, and he must beat Barnsley next Tuesday. Neither of those teams is as good as Leeds. George will expect a fiercely competitive game at Elland Road, and a hostile atmosphere. Our unbeaten Premiership record now stretches back 17 games to a 2-0 defeat by Chelsea on 19 December. But I will be amazed if we win tomorrow, which is my birthday.

Wednesday 10 March
Leeds (a)

Leeds beat us 2-0 in a game that consolidates their hold on fourth place.

Saw the goals on TV. Harry Kewell was on the right side and tried a one-two with Hasselbaink. As Hasselbaink miscontrolled the ball Kewell kept running and picked up the ball again inside the box. His shot rebounded off Walker's chest, bounced up, and Smith hooked in from eight yards. Sherwood barged Bowyer down on the edge of the box, then trampled on him just as referee Neil Barry was turning his back as he called Sherwood over to book him.

Ginola crossed from the right, Armstrong missed it, corner. Ginola crossed again to give Sherwood a header which was blocked by Martyn, who then saved Iversen's follow-up. Haaland almost scored, beating our offside trap from Hasselbaink's through-pass, but shot wide. Smith passed wide to Haaland, and when he crossed to the far post, Kewell got inside Carr and headed firmly past Walker for 2-0.

Ginola, Iversen and Anderton then departed in a triple substitution with Nielsen, Sinton and Ferdinand coming on. Nielsen will play on Saturday because Freund is suspended for the Villa game. Freund has only been here for two months and he is already suspended. Nielsen needs match practice because he will play in the Worthington Cup Final at Wembley as Sherwood is cup-tied.

So the game was predictable. Alan Smith showed why he should have started at White Hart Lane. Our 17-match unbeaten record was misleading anyway.

Manchester United outplayed Chelsea at Stamford Bridge in their FA Cup replay. They won 2-0 with Dwight Yorke scoring both goals. So the other semi-final will be Manchester United against Arsenal at Villa Park. They will play at 12.00 or 1.00 on the Sunday, and we will then play Newcastle at 3.00 at Old Trafford, if we beat Barnsley. So we have the prospect of Tottenham and Arsenal fans travelling up the M1 and the M6 at the same time. Tottenham fans will have to leave at the same time as the Arsenal fans because we have another two or three hours travelling time to get up to Manchester. It makes no sense. Another almighty cock-up by the FA. I'd like them to explain that one.

Thursday 11 March

George did not make any excuses in his after-match comments. He said, 'Leeds were better in every department. I can't think of one area where we were better. But that game has gone now. We have three very important games coming up in eight days – Aston Villa in

240

the League, Barnsley in the FA Cup and Leicester in the Worthington Cup Final and we must be ready for those.' Perhaps predictably, George said: 'It was the worst performance since I came to the club.'

Can we click back into gear against Aston Villa, beat them, and get in shape for Barnsley on Tuesday night? That might not be so easy.

Villa played Derby last night. 'Keeper Mark Bosnich came back after 24 games out with a shoulder injury, Mark Draper came back after an ankle operation, and Stan Collymore started for the first time since 2 January. On *Football Focus* last Saturday, John Gregory told Gary Lineker that Stan has stress counselling three days a week, so he doesn't normally see him until Thursday! Baiano and Burton scored, then Thompson got a goal back with a typical shot from 20 yards. Villa are a shambles at the moment with six defeats in their last seven games. They are slipping out of Champions League contention. We will never have a better chance to take three points from them.

Friday 12 March

Aston Villa signed Steve Stone from Nottingham Forest last night for £5.5 million and he will make his début against us tomorrow. Just as John Hartson played his first game for Wimbledon at White Hart Lane eight weeks ago. The last time Stone played against us was for Forest in November, when he was sent off for fouling Ginola.

Last summer John Gregory signed Thompson, the best player from a relegated team, Bolton, for £4.5 million. Now he's signed the best player from a doomed team, Nottingham Forest, who are bottom and nine points adrift of Southampton and Blackburn. I don't blame

Stone for leaving a sinking ship two weeks before the transfer deadline. Have Forest accepted relegation already? Will they spend that money on new players before the deadline?

Bosnich is also returning to the scene of a crime. He gave the Nazi salute to Klinsmann at White Hart Lane, claiming later he was impersonating Basil Fawlty. Not just an insult to our substantial Jewish following, but an insult to one of the world's great footballers, who had been clasped to the bosom of that Jewish fanbase, and been given the opportunity to resurrect his career. For Bosnich to ridicule a player, and our supporters, was disgusting. And the FA just slapped his wrist. They did the same again this season after Bosnich was in similar trouble in a match against Everton.

Will Villa play Merson just behind Joachim and Collymore? With Freund missing tomorrow, gaping holes could appear in front of our back four, where Merson likes to operate. Merson has said that unlike George, his old manager, he would never sign for Tottenham. He said, 'It's just the way you're brought up.' Merson has a chance to put one over on George.

We now have 10 league games left. How many points will we collect from those 10 remaining games? Villa at home should be three points. Leicester at home, that's six. Newcastle away, I don't fancy us, six out of nine. Arsenal at home, maybe a point, seven out of 12. Nottingham Forest away, a win, 10 out of 15. Charlton away, we will do well to get a point. So that's 11 out of 18. West Ham at home, we have to win that, 14 out of 21. Liverpool away, I don't fancy anything there because Liverpool will be pushing to get into Europe. That's 14 out of 24. Then we have Chelsea at home, and Manchester United away. Maybe one point from those two games. So I expect to get 15 out of the last 30 points available. Where will we finish if we get those 15 points? Somewhere between 8th and 13th.

Since we have not been higher than 8th all season, that would be OK.

But maybe I'm being a bit optimistic because players are taking their foot off the accelerator between cup games. If we were to reach the FA Cup Final we would be playing 14 matches in 10 weeks, a tough schedule. So perhaps George will start resting players and keeping them on the bench. That has already started to happen. The motivation for League matches is getting less, especially in away games. I think George would have preferred to play the Worthington Cup Final during our unbeaten run, rather than 11 days after losing to Leeds. We have only lost one match, but players believe results and they believe sequences.

———————————

Saturday 13 March
Aston Villa (h)

Met up with Shane Randall, editor of the fanzine *One Flew Over Seaman's Head*, in The Cockerel Bar on the High Road, just opposite the ground. The pub is packed with young blokes, some already tanked-up, singing *When The Spurs Go Marching In*, led by a young guy with glasses standing on a wooden board covering the pool table. He conducts the singing, getting them to slow the song right down, like a hymn, then speed it up into a hand-clapping, foot-stomping gallop.

There's a walled 'garden' area at the back, containing a Sixties Ford saloon car and some tables, which is quiet and sunlit. We talk about Sugar selling his yacht. A big cheery guy, a decorator, says, 'Yeah, I had to get rid of mine as well. When my council tax bill came in!' He says he's just bought Ginola shirts for his Mum, his gran and his wife, and some blue and white ribbons for his little daughter's hair. He says, 'I wish I had a pound for every time Ginola's name is mentioned in that shop. It's Ginola this, Ginola that, Ginola shirts, Ginola posters, you name it.'

Aston Villa have a good record against us in games that we need to win, Cup matches. We have a very poor record at their place. We lost 3-2 there after being 3-0 down back in November. And I can remember Dwight Yorke tormenting us both home and away in the last couple of seasons.

Villa have slipped to 5th, below Leeds, but I expect a tight game. They need a win today to keep on course for a UEFA Cup place, so it is a more crucial game for them than it is for us. Our priorities are next Tuesday and Sunday: Barnsley in the FA Cup and Leicester in the Worthington Cup Final at Wembley. So whatever George may have told his players, Aston Villa is a warm-up for the two biggest games of our season

He starts Taricco, even though he is cup-tied for the Worthington Cup Final. We dominate the first half, with Ginola putting over five good crosses, but Villa are poor. They badly miss Ehiogu, whose eye-socket was cracked by kick in the face from Shearer, and Dublin, who has a long-term groin strain.

Apart from Dublin, Gregory has bought badly. Alan Thompson? Merson? Stone? I cannot believe he's paid £5.5 million for Stone now. OK, Villa are having a very bad run. Steve Watson is injured and Gregory is desperate to stop the rot. He would not have paid £5.5 million for Stone last summer, or if they were second in the table. He has assembled a large squad of useful journeymen who are not going to challenge for the top three. Villa will just have great runs, as they did before Christmas. Like us, they lack class. Like us, they need to buy quality.

When you sell a player you have to replace him with someone who is better than the player you have offloaded. Because you can bet your bottom dollar that Manchester United, Chelsea and Arsenal will buy quality this summer. Wenger spent £4 million on Kanu recently and he has already scored two vital goals. Maybe Steve Stone will score vital goals for Villa. I doubt it. Let's wait and see.

But no wonder it is 0-0 till the 88th minute. All the strikers are incompetent. Ferdinand and Armstrong look clumsy while Collymore plays like an out-patient. Our fans are cruel, singing *You're mad and you know you are!* Merson misses the chance to put one over on George. He is anonymous, replaced by Joachim just after the hour. Then there is a feeble chorus of *Boring, boring Arsenal!* from the Villa fans. George makes a triple substitution: Iversen, Dominguez and Sinton come on for Ginola, Armstrong and Taricco.

Clearly, Iversen is an important player for us. George did not want to risk him in this game, three days before the FA Cup tie at Barnsley on Tuesday. When we need a goal he brings Iversen on in the 79th minute, and he makes a difference.

Nielsen turns away from Southgate, passes to Iversen on the edge of the box. Iversen shoots right-footed, a good low shot bouncing just in front of Bosnich, who blocks it. The ball bounces up towards Sherwood who dives forward and heads the ball against the post. The ball rebounds off Sherwood's ankles and bounces towards the goal where Alan Wright, on the line, boots it against Bosnich's leg. The ball rebounds again to Sherwood, who flicks it into the corner of the net from a yard out. What a shambolic goal! It must be our jammiest goal of the season. But it gives us three points and sends the fans home happy. And it is Sherwood's third goal in seven starts. Overall it was a typical mid-table game, even though Villa are 5th and we are 10th. We were better than them, but not much better.

Sunday 14 March

Leicester striker Tony Cottee did an interview with Joe Lovejoy in *The Sunday Times*, previewing the Worthington Cup Final. Cottee said, 'I always enjoy playing against Spurs. I scored against them on my debut for West Ham when I was 17 and I got my 100th League goal against them. Perhaps it's down to me being a West Ham boy and they're our local rivals. I think it will be an open final. I can't really see it being 1-0 because we're both attacking teams. I think there'll be a few goals in it.'

Monday 15 March

Arsenal's Petit was sent off at Everton on Saturday. It was his fourth red card of the season. The crowd put pressure on Uriah Rennie to even it up after Rennie had sent Don Hutchinson off for a mild elbow on Keown which nobody else saw. So Petit stormed off down the tunnel, allegedly saying, 'That's it! I'm finished with English football!'

That is stupid. Petit was rusty and made a couple of late tackles. He lacks sharpness after getting injured playing for France against England on 10 February.

Maybe he was hard done by. But he should stop squealing about referees driving him out of the

Premiership. This will just antagonise other refs. He might as well wear a sign that says: 'BOOK ME NOW! I'M ANOTHER DENNIS WISE!' He's put a tattoo on his forehead.

Petit should be conciliatory. He should be saying, 'I am old enough to know better. The first booking was harsh, but after that I should have stayed on my feet. I miscontrolled the ball, and over-reacted to my mistake.'

The best referees are invisible. You hardly notice them. Unfortunately, Uriah Rennie is on an ego-trip. In one of Tottenham's programmes, the one for the Manchester United game, there was a picture of Rennie in a dinner jacket, holding a microphone. Was that taken a meeting of a referees society? I don't think so. For years we have had a little blurb on the referee, saying he's got 4.2 children and a Ford Sierra. But now some refs think they are stars, like the players. Incredibly, some referees now have agents and are doing adverts in football magazines.

There is no effective check and balance on referees. In Italy they will suspend referees who are not good enough. How often has that happened here? Last season Dermott Gallagher got a one-match ban for not red carding Steve Bould. And I regard Gallagher as one of our best and most consistent referees.

Tomorrow's rearranged game at Barnsley should be a stroll. We could do with a powerful victory over the relegated team which somehow bundled us out of the FA Cup last year.

––––––––––––––––––

Tuesday 16 March
Barnsley (a)
FA Cup, sixth round

I listened to the game on Capital Gold, where Tony Gale is critical of Armstrong's technique on a couple of missed chances in the first half. Then I watched the highlights later. Taricco plays, as Edinburgh has a slight groin strain. Walker comes confidently for one cross, a very high one, and doesn't make it as Blackmore and Dyer go up. The ball goes through his hands, but, fortunately, over Dyer's head.

It seemed as if we did not have to get out of first gear because Barnsley were so bad. Ginola waltzes round the entire Barnsley defence to score the only goal. A spectacular goal, almost in the Ricky Villa class. He cuts inside, bamboozles four defenders and sidefoots past keeper Tony Bullock from ten yards. At the other end, Bruce Dyer immediately misses Barnsley's only decent chance, heading wide after a Nicky Eaden cross to the near post.

A fantastic goal by Ginola, but it is against 10 men. The referee is card-happy clown Mike Reed, who books Adie Moses for a mild obstruction on Ginola. The challenge was a free-kick, not a yellow card. Moses loses his rag, mistimes a tackle on Ferdinand and gets a second yellow a minute later.

Armstrong works a good position on the left, has time to cross, but he cannot pick out Ferdinand or Anderton, and as Anderton stretches for the ball with the left back on the bye-line, he makes contact with him. Incredibly, Reed gives Anderton a yellow. It's his 5th. He been on four for many weeks now, and to get a 5th and a one-match ban for a routine 50-50 tackle must be very annoying.

So it's another one-nil to the Tottenham. Now we know how it feels. There were, apparently, some faint chants of

Georgie Graham's Blue and White Army. Who cares? Let's enjoy the cup run while it lasts. After eight years without success you enjoy the moment. Newcastle at Old Trafford is a kinder draw than Manchester United or Arsenal, so let's make the most of it. Will it be Tottenham and Arsenal walking out together on a sunny day at Wembley? I can just see George Graham and Arsène Wenger coming out of that tunnel side by side.

Steve Carr was picked in the Republic of Ireland squad for the first time today. He gets a booking after over-running the ball, then leaving his foot in as Tinkler clears.

Ruud Gullit and Martin O'Neill watch the game. Both will have noticed that we do not have a left-footed player on the field. Both will have noted the chances Armstrong missed. They will expect Iversen to play against Leicester and Newcastle.

Wednesday 17 March

Apparently, Ginola is good value for money after the match. He plays the game after the game. Very good with the sponsors, the box-holders and their guests. His car is invariably the last to leave the indoor pitch which is reserved for staff cars on match days. He is often at White Hart Lane till 7pm. The club has gradually become the David Ginola show. The more he has moved into the spotlight, the more the others have moved into the background. Ginola now has to dribble, cross the ball, create the goals, catch the eye, and lift the crowd. Then, after the game, he does the late shift, pressing the flesh and chewing the fat with the corporate hospitality crowd. It's a one-man show for 90 minutes, followed by a one-man encore.

David Ginola: athlete, celebrity, ambassador, PR man and all-round hero. Like most superstars, he enjoys the attention, and he is running on adrenaline anyway. His wife Coroline says that, after a game, David does not unwind until 4am. He is the main man, and he enjoys being the main man. If he was to leave, where else could he be the main man? He has played for Toulon, Racing Paris, Brest and Paris St Germain, and he might fancy Marseilles for a season or two.

Thursday 18 March

Kevin Keegan picks Tim Sherwood in his first England squad for the Poland game. Everyone is surprised. There must be some history between Sherwood and Keegan. Did he score vital goals against Newcastle? Sherwood has been called up only once before. Terry Venables had him on the bench in February 1995 against Ireland in Dublin, a match which was abandoned. He was always ignored by Glenn Hoddle and once said the only way he would ever get noticed would be to go round and juggle the ball in Hoddle's back garden.

People had tipped Ray Parlour and Chris Sutton to be in the 22. Steve Guppy and Scott Sellars, two left-sided players Keegan had sold, had been watched by his scouts Arthur Cox and Derek Fazackerly. Nobody mentioned Sherwood as having a prayer. Ince is suspended, so Batty is favourite for the holding role in a 4-4-2. Since Batty and Sherwood played together for Blackburn, they could be re-united. Playing for England would give Sherwood another string to his bow, and allow him to strut around even more.

The whisper this week is that the club hopes to wear the new adidas shirts for the Chelsea game on Saturday 8

May. Contracts usually allow a new kit to be worn in the last home game. Pony aren't bothered because they are losing the contract. Pony should have said: OK, we'll walk away now if you give us £2 million. So Pony are really pinning their hopes on the FA Cup. Umbro did exactly the same in 1991, coming in at the end of the season.

Friday 19 March

A Steve Stammers story in the *Standard* is headlined 'NEW DEAL ON THE TABLE FOR GINOLA'. The story says the club look certain to offer him a new deal, beyond the two years remaining on his current contract. Talks about a new package are likely to start next week:

'Graham feels there is a lot more to come from Ginola, particularly in the goals department. "I think he could get into the penalty area more," said Graham. "I would rather that he got 15 tap-ins a year than half-a-dozen special goals. He has the strength and the presence to do that. I want him in the area when the ball is coming in from the right." '

That is common sense, and typical of George, who has always wanted end product from his wide men. He wants his wingers to produce goals and assists. When left winger Martin Hayes crossed the ball at Arsenal, George wanted David Rocastle in the box with Niall Quinn. When Rocky crossed it, he wanted Hayes in the box. George promoted Hayes from the reserves to replace Graham Rix, and Hayes scored 12 goals in open play in his first season, getting onto flick-ons and knockdowns. Rixy used to play deeper and wider, doing all his work outside the box, a bit like Ginola.

Later on, in 1990, George signed Anders Limpar when Cremonese were relegated, and Limpar blew hot and cold in a strong championship side of '90-'91. Limpar scored eight League goals in September, October and November, but then did not score again till the last day of the season, when he got a hat-trick in a 6-1 thrashing of Coventry. Wingers are often frustrating. George's quote proves that he has not changed his views about wingers. But if he wants Ginola in the box, getting on the end of crosses, he might be disappointed.

On Sunday night the players and 200 staff will have a dinner at Sopwell House, St Albans. But Campbell, Sherwood and Darren Anderton will not be there because Keegan wants his squad to report to Burnham Beeches, the England hotel, by 9.30pm.

Chapter Eight

LEICESTER AT WEMBLEY

Saturday 20th March

I cannot contemplate losing tomorrow's game against Leicester at Wembley, and I doubt if Ginola can either. He has waited a long time for a really big game. He came to England in 1995 but has never won a major trophy. Tomorrow could be a massive day for him. If we win we are in the UEFA Cup. If we lose, we are 10th in the League and in poor shape for an FA Cup semi-final against Newcastle, a team which is quicker and more creative than Leicester.

The Worthington Cup Final is set up like a normal Tottenham game, but 100 times magnified. George Graham is there to make sure the game is not lost. And David Ginola is there to win it. George organises and motivates the other ten players to make sure the game isn't lost. And Ginola scores a goal or makes a goal. Let's hope he doesn't win a penalty. If he does, we will never hear the end of it. Did he dive or was he tripped?

Darren and Sol have never won a major trophy either. Darren should not be overawed by the occasion because he has played at Wembley so many times for England. And Sol has played for England. It is familiar territory for those two. Edinburgh is the only survivor from our 1991 FA Cup team. For the others, it will be a nerve-wracking test of character. Ferdinand has played at Wembley for England, Vega and Freund have played there against England in Euro '96.

In recent weeks the strikers have been off-form and George has become reliant on Ginola. There is talk now that Footballer of the Year is between Dwight Yorke and Ginola. Leaving club loyalty to one side, I would vote for Yorke because he has played well all season, scored 20-odd goals, and has helped Man United to a Champions League semi-final against Juventus.

Having considered all angles, I cannot see us losing. It all turns on what Martin O'Neill decides to do about Ginola. Whether he stops the supply, or man-marks him. If he tries to stop the supply he will be looking to isolate Freund and Edinburgh. Leicester will have to press those two players in particular to stop them feeding Ginola. And if Ginola is starved of the ball he will wander. Perhaps O'Neill would put a marker on him. Kaamark shut down Juninho two years ago in the Littlewoods Cup Final, when Leicester beat Middlesbrough after a replay.

Will George play Ferdinand with Iversen? Or with Armstrong? He rested Iversen against Villa, we thought, so he could play him against Barnsley. But he didn't start him against Barnsley. Is that because Iversen isn't fit enough to play 90 minutes? Or because George reckoned he could beat Barnsley without Iversen, but knew Iversen would be vital against Leicester?

Ferdinand is still, it seems, his No 1 choice, and we need his aerial presence. Especially when defending set-pieces against Elliott and Walsh. Presumably Sol will mark Heskey throughout the game, but Heskey's fitness is suspect. He has a long-term back injury. Who will mark Walsh on set-pieces?

If I was Martin O'Neill I would be playing to Walsh's head. Walsh is their captain and does not mind a battle. He was the man of the match against Middlesbrough two years ago, and this final is his swansong. He joined Leicester from Wigan 13 years ago, and has scored 50 League goals in 335 games before this season, some of them as a striker. Ossie Ardiles was looking at Walsh a few years ago when he managed us. He is just the sort of defender we needed to play alongside Sol. A big strong boy, a talker, a leader. I think they've got more big strong boys than we have. Walsh, Elliott, Heskey, Frank Sinclair.

O'Neill will play Lennon and Izzet in midfield against Nielsen and Freund, and they will hustle us and play their little triangles. Whether that will be effective or not I don't know. Izzet has skill, but not pace or power. Lennon is one-paced but he is intelligent and his positional play is very good.

I doubt whether Leicester can be a potent attacking force against us. They scored two goals against us in George's first game at Filbert Street. And they were both very, very good goals. Heskey turned Vega and blasted one in, and Izzet scored with a cracking volley from the edge of the box.

Do I fancy Leicester to score against us in open play? Not really. We have our limitations, but we must be fancied to score one goal from open play. Anderton is due a decent game now. He hasn't had a good game since Leeds.

We've become a Cup side again. More of a Cup side than we ever were in our history, just peaking for the Cup games. And sometimes not even peaking. Friends who went to Barnsley said it was awful. One of the worst games of football they've ever seen.

Sadly, Ferdinand and Armstrong are just not up to it. We need two strikers, not one. There is some talk that he's looking at Alan Smith, who is out of contract at the end of the season. Obviously, George knows what wages Smith is on. But he's just a raw young kid who has arrived in a blaze of glory. We need experienced, classy strikers. I do not want to see a six-foot-seven Norwegian or Swede.

I do not expect an exciting game tomorrow. It will probably be like the Arsenal-Sheffield Wednesday finals in

1993. A lot of tension, and most of the pressure on us. We are expected to win, and Ginola and Anderton are expected to turn on a bit of style in the wide open spaces. Especially Anderton, as Wembley is a second home to him.

Leicester won this final two years ago, and have been in play-offs, so they know Wembley too. Are they the archetypal party-poopers, a side who can close a game down? Have Leicester become the Wimbledon of the '90s? Could George be out-Georged? Ground down by a relentless, stubborn, hard-tackling Leicester outfit? Martin O'Neill has already proved he is good enough to manage a bigger club. He must have been considered for the Tottenham job. He was sitting side by side with Ginola in the BBC studios in Paris during the World Cup. We should have tapped him up.

I'm getting superstitious about the L-factor. Liverpool beat us in the League Cup Final in 1982, and Luton beat Arsenal in 1988 when George was expected to retain the Littlewoods Cup, having won it the year before in his first season. Supporters get paranoid and fatalistic and look for little signs, so I wondered if Leicester would be a hat-trick of L-victories.

Sunday 21 March
Leicester
Worthington Cup Final, Wembley

Met everyone at my parents' house and drove to Wembley. It took an hour and twenty minutes. As we are driving in we see some people we know. They said, 'Have you got any spare tickets?' And we feel sorry for them because they are desperate to see the game. It was hard enough to get tickets in the early '80s, let alone the late '90s, now that the capacity has been cut. How many regular Tottenham fans could not get a ticket because there are so many people from the corporate hospitality boxes here? The fans who came by tube, and sang *We Are Tottenham, We Are Tottenham From The Lane*, are the kind of hardcore supporters who are in the Cockerel Bar on Saturdays before the game.

One of my friends, Howerd, is disabled so we are able to park right outside the Twin Towers. We get to our seats, Royal Box side, downstairs, at 2.40pm. Team selection? He will go with Vega because he knows that Heskey isn't fully fit, and he needs Vega's height because they have some big players. Dropping Armstrong to play Iversen is the right decision.

I have not been at Wembley since England v Portugal in 1996. Before that it was the 1993 semi-final against Arsenal. The chanting is *Spurs Are On Their Way To Wembley* and *Are You Watching, Arsenal?* The usual stuff with conductors in the stand getting people to sing and chant.

But they were playing loud pop music over the public address system. That showbiz hype destroys the whole atmosphere of the crowd. Thousands of blue-and-white balloons are released. Fireworks explode on either side of the tunnel as the teams walk out. Robbie Williams is screaming a rock number with the chorus *Let me entertain you!*

It is overkill, just for the TV cameras. Totally pathetic. Every year, with every big match, they find a new way of selling out the game to TV. How can the Football League, which started in 1888, ignore the traditions of the world's greatest sport? I could understand it when Coca Cola turned a football final into Disneyland. Coca Cola is an American company and I expect cheerleaders and laser beams from them. But Worthington is a British brewer which should be in touch with ordinary, red-blooded, bitter-drinking British football fans.

Why do they make it a circus? Who makes these decisions? Whose ego-trip is this? Which marketing manager took something that was not bust and decided to fix it? What planet are you on? You should resign! You are clueless! You treat us with contempt! Your technology should enhance the event, not take it over! You drown out our small voices! You dehumanise us! You charge us £40 to get in, but you spend thousands of pounds to prevent us participating in a cup final we have waited eight years for! An event that would not exist without the crowds who came through the turnstiles at all the previous Worthington Cup games. Cut the fireworks, the balloons, the hype. Don't waste that money. Give it back to us in cheaper ticket prices!

They deliberately price working-class fans out of the game, and when the stadium gets quiet they fill up the vacuum with records, DJ spiel, Jumbotron interviews and highlights. Thankfully Wembley does not have Jumbotrons.

The TV executives and marketing managers have hijacked our game. Turned us into unpaid extras in their show to exploit a captive audience for their hype, their sales pitch. They cut the capacity, crank up loud music to drown the crowd out. It's capitalism and capitalism tends to be autocratic, not democratic. It's about profit and power and bullying, not sharing and caring and a sense of community.

I am sure we will win as long as we do not concede set-pieces in dangerous positions. Corners and free-kicks, delivered by Guppy, might turn the game towards Leicester. Guppy can pinpoint the ball onto the heads of Walsh, Elliott and Heskey, and that is the only way I can see them scoring. If Heskey plays he might play with a pain-killing injection, and will not be as powerful as usual.

The first half is atrocious, as I expected. My only regret is not having a bet on it being 0-0 at half-time. When Sol misses a through ball by Savage, Vega comes in with a saving tackle on Heskey in the box. But Vega is able to reach him because Heskey is only half-fit. A fully fit Heskey would have taken one step and walloped his shot. Or he would have taken another stride, and Vega would have had to let him go or bring him down.

It is typical of us. We usually get in at half-time, George susses out the opposition, looks at their weaknesses, explains where we can tighten up, and tells the boys how to move up a gear. Then we blitz teams in the second half. But that does not happen today.

We start off badly in the second half, as if we are not at the races. Savage, with his long blond hair, is horrible. I shout, 'Why don't you go back to *Baywatch*?' The crowd round me start chants of 'Pammy! Pammy!' A reference to Pamela Anderson.

Leicester are having their best spell in the game, winning a few corners. A shot by Ullathorne which Walker fumbles, then grabs before Cottee can get to the rebound.

It is very scrappy. Sol shoves the ball across Edinburgh, who cuts into the centre circle across Savage, who bodychecks him. A tackle more appropriate to ice-hockey. He runs right into Edinburgh, knocking him over, a clear yellow-card offence. They fall, get up, have a bit of argy-bargy and verbals, Edinburgh swings an arm, a risky retaliation from a player with a notoriously short fuse.

The ref books Savage, and sends Edinburgh off. So we are now a man down with 63 minutes on the clock. But going down to ten men galvanises our players, makes everybody step up a gear. We now have less fear of losing because we have a ready-made excuse, so we stop worrying about losing and start trying to win it. After Edinburgh walked I expected George to bring Armstrong on quickly for one of the strikers. Purely to freshen it up. Because Armstrong puts himself about and does a lot of running.

Heskey goes past Sol and Vega stops him with a bad tackle. No complaints there. Vega deserves his yellow card. Ullathorne and Muzzy Izzet are excellent. Cottee is quiet, but shows that he has been a good player. The difference between Cottee's first touch and Ferdinand's first touch is chalk and cheese.

Then we get a free kick 20 yards out. I thought: Anderton must have a poke. He is closer than he was when he hit the Exocet against Leeds. I thought: this is our chance. Blast it through the wall! But he chips the ball to the back post, where Taggart heads it away. In the last few minutes there is some movement on the bench. I am surprised when Ian Marshall comes on for Heskey, but it confirms that Heskey is a long way short of fitness.

Then O'Neill takes Savage off just before the end of normal time, with tumultuous jeers and boos. I thought: this is a strange move to make just before the end of 90 minutes. It's your second substitution, so you've only got one more, and the game is going into extra-time. You don't make a substitution in the last couple of minutes of a tight game, because it might just change the balance, affect your concentration, so that someone might not pick up his man. It is a strange decision. Also, it is Savage, so there is the extra distraction of a big furore when he walks off the pitch. It is still 0-0, so the Savage-Edinburgh fracas has been the main incident.

Zagarokis comes on and everyone is resigned to extra-time. But I'm thinking: hold on! Throughout George's career there has always been a last-minute winner. A free-kick, a corner, a Mickey Thomas or an Andy Linighan. Something always happens for George Graham.

So why can't it happen for us? Why can't he bring some of that across with him to Tottenham? Because we haven't had many dramatic late goals in the past. The last time a Tottenham player scored a last-minute winner in such a crucial game was Nayim for Real Zaragoza against Arsenal in 1995. And of course he was an ex-Tottenham player by then.

So I always have the sneaking hope, as the game goes on, as the attrition had its effect, as the grind wears down Leicester's resistance, as the pressure builds up and builds up and builds up, that we could win it. The longer the game remains undecided, the more there can only be one winner: the tactician, the undisputed master of getting a result. If George Graham could play every single game just for the last five minutes, he would win the championship every year.

The fourth official holds up the little electronic board showing three minutes of stoppage time. We have to keep it going, keep the ball in their half, as far away from our goal as possible. When Ginola gets the ball near the end I think: this must be it ! He's gonna turn someone inside out, get into the penalty area and whip the ball across. Or have a dig himself and be on the front pages of the newspapers, who will make him Footballer of the Year. He hasn't done anything all day, but maybe there is still time for him to glide between Ullathorne and Lennon, sidestep Elliott and place the ball in the corner of the net. But the move comes to nothing.

Then Carr plays the ball up to Ferdinand, who knocks it wide to Iversen, who takes on Walsh about 30 yards from the penalty box. You would expect him to beat Walsh over 30 yards, and he does. He beats him for pace on the right flank. Arrowing into the penalty area, Iversen is about ten yards from the bye-line, and he scuffs his shot. It seems that Keller is waiting for a harder shot, dives too early and scoops the ball forward and up in the air. Nielsen dives forward to head in from four yards.

After that, pandemonium! Celebration city! Everyone is jumping up and down on their seats. This is the first time that we have ever won anything at the death. Probably the nearest was at Anfield when Jürgen scored.

Maybe if it had been a harder shot Keller might have done better. Or the ball would have rebounded much quicker. But he wasn't anticipating a soft shot. It was the only save Keller had to make in the game, apart from an Iversen header that was straight at him.

The goal typifies the game. After Nielsen scores we just have to play out time. It is fantastic to hear people roaring into all the old songs, *You're Not Singing Any More* and *It's a Grand Old Team To Play For* and *Glory, Glory, Tottenham Hotspur.*

Thousands of excited Lillywhites, really enjoying ourselves for a change, shaking off the despair of a decade, hardly able to believe that one priceless, priceless goal has just been scored. Every song we have ever sung comes out now, stuff like *We Only Had Ten Men* and, of course, the seven-syllable classic from down the road, *One Nil To The Tott-en-ham.*

George put Sinton on and took Ginola off to a standing ovation, even though he had a very, very quiet game. Credit to Ullathorne who had snuffed him out, aided by Savage and others.

The final whistle went and it was *Oh Teddy Teddy, Went to Man United and You Won **** All.* And, inevitably, we could not resist a chorus of *Are You Watching, Arsenal?* I do not suppose Arsène Wenger will be quaking in his boots just yet, but it feels good to win a trophy and it feels even better when it's your first trophy in eight years and we are singing, *When Sol Goes Up to Lift the Worthington Cup, We'll Be There*!

There were pockets of people trying to sing *Georgie Graham's Blue and White Army*, but the hard core still did not sing it.

Then some players throw their shirts into the crowd. A nice touch, but somewhat premature: you don't throw your shirt into the crowd before you have been up the 39 steps to collect the cup. But it was just emotional overload for the players, a release of all the pent-up feelings of the last few seasons. Joy. Relief. Past failures and injuries forgotten. Vindication. A cup waiting to be lifted, a winner's medal waiting to be collected, a door opening to Europe, a sense, maybe, of a new journey just beginning. All those things at once.

Leicester went up first to the royal box to get their medals, with the appearance of Savage triggering fierce boos, jeers and worse. Then Sol went up to lift the trophy, with Nielsen next, and Walker. And then the loud pop music started again. The DJ always wants to join in, to manipulate, to show how clever he is.

We knew the game would be rubbish, especially after George had got his retaliation in first by saying, 'Well, finals are never what they're cracked up to be.' So I was not really disappointed with the way we achieved the victory. How could I be? This is how we play. This is what we are. We are a mid-table side who play like a mid-table side, and we depend far too much on our best player. Let's face it, a winger can be closed down. A winger is often peripheral. Ginola can cross the ball, but he cannot score enough goals to influence a League season as Cantona and Zola and Bergkamp have done.

The line-ups were:
TOTTENHAM (4-4-2): Walker, Carr, Campbell, Vega, Edinburgh, Anderton, Freund, Nielsen, Ginola (Sinton 90), Ferdinand, Iversen. Subs not used: Armstrong, Dominguez, Young, Baardsen.
LEICESTER (3-5-2): Keller, Elliott, Taggart, Walsh, Ullathorne, Savage (Zagorakis 90), Lennon, Izzet, Guppy, Heskey (Marshall 75), Cottee. Subs not used: Arphexad, Campbell, Kaamark.

George Graham has given us organisation, teamwork and commitment.

But he has not raised our skill level. If anything, we played more skilful, attractive football under Gross than we do under George. Today's game showed that. We were very, very rigid. Ginola did not drift around at all. It was like the NFL, a coach's team packed with people playing to orders, playing in boxes, following a ruthlessly mapped out game plan.

Allan Nielsen, Mr Energy, the Danish dynamo who covered every blade of grass, got Man of the Match, but Robert Ullathorne deserved it. And he is out of contract at the end of the season.

Our best player was Steve Carr, who tried to bomb down the right side whenever he could, taking on two or three blue shirts, and trying to get the team going. It was a good battle between Carr and Guppy.

We were stifled by Leicester. They stopped us playing good football, and, in doing that, stopped themselves playing good football. Even so, Ginola and Anderton should have been able to pass and move, and create a few openings, but we never started to play, never created any rhythm or momentum or good moves or excitement. We missed Sherwood as the link between midfield and attack.

He does some of the link-work that Sheringham used to do. But, basically, you need strikers who can play. You cannot play good football with Les Ferdinand up front. The ball bounces off him. Please re-arrange the following words into a well-known phrase or saying: a, cement, trap, couldn't, of, bag, he.

Martin O'Neill will learn from this. The way Leicester played was nonsensical. We struggle on the left side anyway, and after Edinburgh was sent off, O'Neill should have switched to 4-4-2 and really tried to win the game in the half hour that was left. He should have moved Savage further forward to attack Campbell, who was being sucked away from Vega, which meant we were stretched at the back, with Carr and Vega covering a huge area.

We seemed to think we could beat their centre backs in the air, but that never happened. The way to do it was on the deck, but we didn't have the movement or skill to play that way. When Iversen finally put his head down and ran at them, Leicester were opened up, and we scored.

Monday 22 March

It will be bedlam if Savage appears for Leicester at White Hart Lane on 3 April. I don't think O'Neill will risk playing him, and making him the target of furious abuse. That looks like a job for Andy Impey.

I think the occasion got to Sol, who seemed very inhibited. It was one of his poorest games for a long time. Maybe he will turn in a mammoth performance when we really need it, against Newcastle. Or maybe in the FA Cup Final, if we get there, against Yorke and Cole, or against Anelka and Bergkamp.

The only thing that could help is that the FA Cup Final might not be Manchester United's last game of the season. The European Cup Final is four days later in Barcelona, so if United beat Juventus in the semi-final they will be meeting Dynamo Kiev or Bayern Munich in their biggest game since 1968.

The *Standard* says Ginola has two years left on his contract and Spurs have said he will be offered a new deal. Ginola said, 'We have the structure in place to be a great team and now it is up to the chairman to make the right choice and sometimes you have to think about getting your money out of your pocket.' He also said, 'If Tottenham give me the chance, I want to stay at this club for the rest of my career. It would be a great pleasure for me to serve them and George Graham until I finish.'

Edinburgh admitted he felt guilty about his red card. 'Come the final whistle and I was the most relieved man in the world. I don't know what I would have done if we had lost.' His three-match ban means he will miss the semi-final against Newcastle.

A Michael Hart piece in the *Standard* pointed out that George's first Championship side at Arsenal in 1989 contained seven players who had not appeared in the Littlewoods Final against Liverpool at Wembley in 1987. Graham said: 'As far as I am concerned this is the start of something, not the finish. The players have now had a taste of what it is like to win a major trophy. I hope it has made them hungry for more. I want to be successful. I want them to have big games every season, not just once in a while. I want them to be as hungry as me and I sense that they are.'

An interesting article. So will George keep four players and replace seven? And if so, which four will he keep? Will he retain Campbell, Carr, Anderton and Sherwood for his championship side of 2001?

Tuesday 23 March

A piece I had done for the Press Association is on *The Guardian* website with the headline 'GRAHAM MUST MAKE ROOM FOR SPURS CUPS':

'Tottenham fans want George Graham to go home and start clearing out his trophy cabinet of Arsenal memorabilia – to make way for some Spurs trophies instead.

'The faithful stopped short at chanting Graham's name at Wembley, but the respect is there and the days of the Spurs supporters chanting *George Graham's blue-and-white army* may not be too far away.

'A spokesman for the Tottenham Action Group said: "We are delighted that after eight years of decline, with just the odd glimmer of hope, we have finally seen a workmanlike Tottenham team pulling together and heading in the right direction.

' "We are now emerging from the shadows of our London rivals Arsenal and Chelsea and hopefully we have taken our first step back to glory.

' "It is time for George Graham to empty his trophy cupboard of all its Arsenal memorabilia and start filling it with Tottenham honours. He may even get a new patio laid with a cockerel in it and change the formation of his flowerbeds in his garden."

'The TAG believe the time will come when the fans chant Graham's name, but only when Spurs are consistently achieving at the highest level. The spokesman said: "When George was at Arsenal you could see how much he enjoyed winning things.

' "We acknowledge what he is doing but we shall not be satisfied until we are competing at the very highest level both domestically and in Europe, and this first trophy is seen as a foundation for bigger and better things."

'The TAG have also called on the Spurs board to back Graham's quest for glory by providing him with the necessary funds:

' "We cannot afford to rest on our laurels and trust that this will be the catalyst for the board of directors to give our manager every assistance to enable him to compete for the quality players our club deserves," added the spokesman.'

Some hopes! Harry Harris has a *Mirror* story headlined 'WE WON'T BREAK THE BANK TO RESTORE GLORY DAYS'. Harry reported that David Pleat last night warned supporters that Sugar would not 'pay crazy money' to bring back success.

Pleat said: 'We want progress, but we shall be selling some players and then see how much we have to spend. This club will not go into financial freefall just to return to glory, glory days that might never happen. It's got to be achieved on sound, sensible guidelines, and the club now has the football expertise to advise the chairman on how to build on the platform of winning the Worthington Cup.'

This was obviously in response to Ginola's quotes! But we were told before the season started that we had £20 million to spend. When George arrived we were told that he would have £18 million to buy players. And that was before we won the Worthington Cup and got into Europe.

Pleat continued, 'The chairman has gained experience from the first few years. Early on he had a few problems not of his making, as there was no-one on the board with a football background.Very often mediocre players were signed. Very often cover was needed for injuries and sometimes players were bought on a whim simply as cover when they weren't really up to it. Now there is confidence in the management and I'm there to provide information and keep the chairman in touch.'

Mediocre players? Name them, David! Are you talking about Johnny Metgod, the Dutchman you signed from Forest in 1987, who only started five League games? Players bought on a whim? Problems not of his making? Are these sly digs at Venables, who replaced you as manager 12 years ago? And if the board did not have enough football knowledge, whose fault was that?

Pleat said that George had made us resilient. 'The final was our third successive 1-0 win, despite a poor performance. George's man-management is first rate. He has earned the respect of the players because he is a manager who has won things in the game. If he says something the players listen because they know he can bring success. Both Gerry Francis and Christian Gross were unlucky with injuries, but George has improved things by 60 per cent.' Pleat also said that George had improved our defending from the front. 'The next thing George will be working on is creativity, and then we will be quite a formidable outfit.' Creativity? I can't wait.

Watched the video of Sunday's game. As our first League Cup Final for 17 years, and an entertainment for viewers in over 100 countries, it was very, very disappointing. Early on Savage brought down Edinburgh, who then screamed at him. So the seeds of that vendetta were sown in the sixth minute.

Our best goal attempt in the first half was after 40 minutes when Anderton's free-kick flew flat through the air and Iversen's header went straight at Keller. Terry Heilbron, a Nationwide referee, was having a decent game until Savage brought Ginola down. He gave a free-kick, not a yellow card, as many Premiership refs would have done.

It was interesting to see the Savage-Edinburgh skirmish again from another angle. Television reveals controversial incidents in forensic detail. This is what happened: Sol passed to Edinburgh, who wrong-footed Savage by coming inside. Savage could not reach the ball so he ran into Edinburgh. As they got up he shoved his shoulder into Edinburgh's chest. So Edinburgh lashed out with his hand, just catching strands of Savage's long blond hair and his neck. Savage swore at him, then turned away and leaned down, holding his face. He got a yellow card, Edinburgh got a red card.

I cannot understand why our players got so upset by a player as ordinary as Robbie Savage. Freund reacted furiously after his toe connected with Savage's knee in one 50-50 challenge. Savage over-reacted to Freund's over-reaction. Then Nielsen pushed Savage gently out of the way on the edge of the penalty area, and when Savage fell over, Nielsen nagged the ref to give him a second yellow!

Wednesday 24 March

Sherwood and Parlour were the two England players put up for interview by Keegan. Sherwood was asked: 'Are you missing captaincy since you left Blackburn?' Grinning, he said, 'I think it is a bit early for me to captain England, but maybe in the future.' A cocky character, but England need confident players. If they lose to Poland they cannot win their group. We sold Colin Calderwood to Aston Villa for £250,000. I think George had made up his mind about Calderwood months ago.

Thursday 25 March

Transfer deadline day. Suddenly, with Calderwood sold and Vega coming back from the Swiss national camp after diagnosis of a hairline fracture in his foot, we are short of centre backs. Scales has been out of action since November with a calf injury. So we sign Sheffield United defender Roger Nilsen (who?) as cover for Luke Young.

I was interviewed recently by James Kaye of the *London Jewish News*. Their story today was headlined 'BRINGING THE UK AND ISRAEL CLOSER TOGETHER'. Talked about our associate office in Tel Aviv, new projects and already needing to hire more staff. Also mentioned the Worthington Cup Final. I said, 'The atmosphere was incredible. Eight years of frustration were suddenly released when Sol lifted the trophy. George is doing the job and as long as he does well we will continue to support him. He will not necessarily be taken to heart until he surpasses what he did at a certain other north London club.'

———————————

Friday 26 March

The *Standard* says Scales is back in light training. He had a calf operation two weeks ago but is now running again. Yesterday George was desperate for a centre back who is not cup-tied. He tried to sign Richard Gough, 36, from Nottingham Forest. Gough was our captain in 1986-87, joined us from Dundee United, went to Rangers after one season, stayed nine years. Thanks for helping us out again, Mr Scholar. You signed Gough, 37 next week, on a free from San Jose Clash, he plays one game, doesn't even finish that, and you want to flog him to us for £300,000? Thanks very much! Apparently George offered £100,000. When that was turned down, he signed Roger Nilsen.

Keegan boldly announces his team the day before the Poland game.

It is: Seaman; G Neville, Keown, Campbell, Le Saux; Beckham, Sherwood, Scholes, McManaman; Shearer, Cole. An attacking team, Sherwood's début, Andy Cole's first start after four sub appearances in four years.

Another of our players has an unexpected boost to his morale. Keegan, having sent home injured strikers Chris Sutton, Michael Owen and Robbie Fowler, calls up Chris Armstrong! Chris is uncapped and has never been in the squad. How did Les Ferdinand feel when his understudy was called up by England?

Keegan paid QPR £6 million for Les in 1995. Chris had watched the whole of the Worthington Cup Final from the bench on Sunday, and been called up by England on Thursday afternoon. Like everyone else, he was gobsmacked, even though he knew he was just there to make up the numbers.

Saturday 27 March

Paul Scholes scores a hat-trick in a 3-1 win over Poland. Sherwood has a solid, responsible game but looks one-paced at times, being caught out after 53 minutes when a Pole is too quick for him. Sherwood lunges, clips him and gets a yellow card. He picks his moments to get forward. After 16 minutes Scholes nods the ball to him but he volleys over. After 90, sub Phil Neville crosses, Sherwood has time and space, a glorious chance, but heads a foot over the bar. If he had scored, Keegan would have found it hard to leave him out in Hungary next month. Sol is OK, better than he was against Leicester. Armstrong is an unused sub.

Sunday 28 March

Our next game is Leicester on Saturday, and I keep thinking about how Allan Nielsen tried to get Savage sent off. I hate to see any player holding up an imaginary card, let alone a Tottenham player. I have never seen Nielsen do that before. Is this the new, resilient Tottenham? The new siege mentality Tottenham? George changes players, changes attitudes. He is creating the paranoia, the siege mentality, that he had at Arsenal: no-one likes us, we don't care!

Monday 29 March

I hate gamesmanship. There is a difference between having highly competitive footballers who can look after themselves, and encouraging gamesmanship. Wanting to win, and being prepared to do anything to win, are two entirely different strategies. In the heat of battle, some players commit deliberate fouls. That happens at every club.

But consistent and calculated acts of gamesmanship are not acceptable at Tottenham, and never will be. To see a Spurs player holding up an imaginary yellow card, nagging a referee to send someone off, is sickening. Until now Allan Nielsen has always been a brave, energetic, honest player who tackles hard, takes a lot of knocks, and never whinges.

Really, all we can say about the Worthington Cup Final is that we won. We are now undefeated in 14 cup-ties. And we will be in the UEFA Cup next season. A team that lost 2-1 at home to Derby in the Coca Cola Cup Third Round in October '97, and lost 3-1 at Barnsley in the FA Cup in January '98, has done incredibly well to bounce back by winning the Worthington Cup in March '99. It is more than I expected.

Tuesday 30 March

Our pursuit of Frank Lampard junior, who captained the Under-21s to a 5-0 win over Poland, has upset West Ham boss Harry Redknapp. He says, 'It annoys me when I pick up the papers and read that Tottenham are going to sign Frank Lampard. Why should he go to Tottenham? We are fifth in the League. Where are they? Why shouldn't we think big? We are not second-class citizens. If we sell players like Rio Ferdinand, Frank and Joe Cole, we will never be up there with the big boys. We will just be also-rans who fluctuate between the top two divisions.'

Wednesday 31 March

Redknapp is quite right. Never betray your DNA. Keep what makes you unique. West Ham have always built their teams round home-grown talent like Moore, Hurst, Peters, Devonshire, Brooking and Cottee. Harry cannot build a team round foreigners like Di Canio and Foe. He has to build it round Frank, Rio and Joe, and keep producing loyal servants like Stevie Potts, who has played over 400 games for them.

Thursday 1 April

Duncan Ferguson is still unfit after a groin operation. He is unlikely to play against us at Old Trafford. He pulled out of a reserve comeback on Monday. This is a relief since we will face only one striker, Shearer, and Sol will not be dragged all over the field.

Friday 2 April

England coach Kevin Keegan is being candid and realistic. England's position in Group Five is precarious because Hoddle dug them into a deep hole, but Keegan is always positive. He says, 'Sweden have come out of the blocks so quickly it already looks as if the rest of us are playing for second place. It just shows that at this level you cannot afford slip-ups, because as soon as we lost to Sweden and drew at home to Bulgaria, a situation was developing which was out of our hands. Now it is completely out of our hands, but from the moment I came into the job, I knew there was a chance this could happen.'

Saturday 3 April
Leicester (h)

This was one of those angry days when we walked out through the car park, over Tottenham High Road, up Church Road, under the bridge and across the park, screaming and shouting, slandering the players.

'Ferdinand was useless! He hasn't scored since 28 December. That header he put over the bar! He scored dozens like that for QPR! He scored them every week for Newcastle! What was Fox doing out there? Why did he play Fox? Why didn't he play Dominguez? How many crosses did Ginola put over? One? Two? We missed Vega today!

Who would have thought, a year ago, that we could miss Vega so much?

Luke Young looked lightweight. He hasn't played recently. He's just come back in the side and it showed. D'you think he'll play Young on Monday night? Yes! Who else has he got? That's the double – Leicester have done the double over us this season! Were we just going through the motions? Was it just another day at the office?

We missed Sherwood! We missed Anderton as well. He's been bad in the last four games, but we missed him! Seven bookings in the game? What was Ginola booked for? Swearing at the lineswoman? Did he refuse to give her his hairdresser's phone number? We won't beat Newcastle playing like that. Newcastle are better than Leicester. They scored four today – they won 4-3 at Derby!'

And so on. That's how fans talk on a Saturday after they lose 2-0 at home to Leicester. On the way to the game we wondered whether we would parade the cup. We didn't, and that was right. But during the warm-up the big screens showed long highlights from Wembley. Why? It was such a non-event, such a boring match. We had two headers in 91 minutes – and the second header went in. Just show the goal, the cup and the celebrations!

Those Jumbotrons are a menace and a distraction and an irrelevance. Jumbotrons are the technology of instant nostalgia. Nothing is real any more unless it is on TV. Nothing is true or accepted until everybody has seen it on the screen from the same angle. We all share the same camera angle, the same edit, the same commentary, the same verdict by the pundits. We demystify football by replaying it in slow-motion and repackaging it for you in seconds, so you don't have to think or talk or argue or form your own opinions. Just let yourselves be bombarded with images and music, and we will turn you all into consumer-robots.

Leicester came out first and formed a guard of honour and applauded us onto the field. A sincere, generous gesture? Or a wind-up? Well, their applause looked half-hearted.

Martin O'Neill picked a different side. No Walsh, no Taggart, Frank Sinclair at right centre back, restored after a breach of club discipline which saw him dropped from the squad before Wembley, Ullathorne at left centre back, Impey at right wing back, Savage in central midfield, away from Edinburgh. And every touch by Savage was booed, of course.

Edinburgh is booked early on for holding Heskey, Iversen and Ferdinand miss chances, and Freund erupts into one of his theatrical tantrums, waves his arms, points, goes potty, a pathetic pantomime. He does this almost every time he gets a knock. Ginola goes over and tells Freund to shut up. Why doesn't George tell the German to adapt his game? Klinsmann stopped diving and Freund will have to stop acting.

Then, just before half-time, Leicester score in exactly the way I feared two weeks ago. Guppy takes a free-kick from the right side, left-footed into the box, and Elliott's header from 14 yards loops gently over Walker, who is off his line. Bad goalkeeping.

Heskey is far better than our strikers. He is strong, skilful and fast. He looks as if he could go through our defence on his own. Heskey makes the second goal, cutting easily inside Sol on the right wing, cruising into a shooting position, and clipping the ball across the six-yard box. Cottee makes one of his near-post runs, stabs in from four yards. Is this the first time I have seen a striker beat Sol for strength, pace and power?

Cottee had scored his first League goal against us, and his 100th, and this was his 200th. He was in tears two weeks ago, so he enjoyed this one. As a kid Cottee looked at his hero Bryan 'Pop' Robson, who had scored 200 goals, and said he thought 200 goals would be a good career. Cottee was 17 then and is 34 now. He has spent half his life scoring goals for money.

Sunday 4 April

O'Neill admitted Emile Heskey had been having treatment night and day on his back injury. He said, 'We had to give him a painkiller that would have numbed a horse at Wembley. If Heskey had been even half-fit, I would have fancied us strongly to have won the cup final.' Martin O'Neill said the guard of honour had been one of his brainwaves: 'Some of the lads didn't want to do it, but it was my idea.'

The reports on 'Derby 3 Newcastle 4' were interesting. Ruud Gullit rested Shearer and Hamann, who had minor injuries, but they are training, as is Duncan Ferguson. The reports said Rob Lee and Gary Speed were good, and the team played really creative football with Ketsbaia, Maric and Solano combining in clever moves. Derby were leading twice, but Solano volleyed in the best goal of the seven to make it 4-2. Obviously, it was wonderful entertainment. Jim Smith teams try to play good football, and they let you play. Seven goals and none of them by an Englishman: Burton 1-0; Speed 1-1; Baiano (pen) 2-1; Speed 2-2; Ketsbaia 2-3. Then half-time. Solano 2-4; Wanchope 3-4.

Newcastle played 4-4-2 with this team: Given; Hughes, Charvet, Dabizas, Griffin; Solano (Brady, 65), Lee, Speed,

Domi; Ketsbaia, Maric (Saha, 79). Gullit admitted he would be happy to play the same eleven in the semi-final. But he also said 'There is not one way I want to play, not one ideal. It depends on the opposition, on the occasion.'

Chapter Nine

NEWCASTLE AT OLD TRAFFORD

Monday 5 April
Newcastle (a)

Watch the Newcastle game on Sky. George makes six changes and Gullit makes one, bringing in unknown kid Jamie McClen for the injured Rob Lee. George drops Ginola and Ferdinand. Sinton and Armstrong come in. He also brings in Roger Nilsen for his début instead of Young, Taricco for the suspended Edinburgh, Sherwood for Nielsen and Anderton for Fox.

The composition of each team reflects the personalities of Gullit and Graham. Gullit takes more gambles on youngsters, makes more positional switches, and has more emphasis on attack and creativity, more faith in individuals doing a bit on the ball. He plays Ketsbaia with Maric, his new Croatian, who is really a midfielder, not a striker. Shearer and Hamann are obviously being saved for Sunday.

We look better with Armstrong up front against a pedestrian back four, but we miss the two best chances of the first half. Sinton crosses low from the left, Armstrong gets across Dabizas, stabs from close range, hits Given. When Carr crosses from the right, Iversen brings the ball down at the far post, hits it early and hard but straight at Given.

After 49 minutes Anderton slips Carr in down the right, Barton's right foot catches Carr's left shin inside the box, and he goes down. Ref Mike Riley gives the penalty. Anderton hits it centrally, Given dives to his right and the ball bounces over his arm and into the net.

When Carr produces another pinpoint cross Armstrong heads well, Given parries, Armstrong knocks in the rebound. But the goal is disallowed because Armstrong held down Griffin as he jumped. Solano takes a good corner, Charvet has a power header, Walker tips it over without diving. We haven't won a Premiership game away from home for six months, since we won 1-0 at Derby on 3 October. That was the first week after George arrived. But we look good for a win here.

Then Newcastle produce a good move. Domi plays a square pass inside to Ketsbaia, unmarked 30 yards out. Sol is ten yards in front of him. Ketsbaia touches the ball cleverly to tee up a half-volley, knowing that Sol cannot reach him. As Sol closes in, Ketsbaia lashes a right-foot shot from 28 yards that dips into the corner of the net off the hand of the diving Walker. A spectacular strike and a Goal of the Month candidate. But Walker could have done better. I do not think he was really concentrating.

Gary Speed crunches Iversen with a karate kick in the ribs. A wild tackle. Speed gets a yellow card and is lucky to stay on the field. Carr hits a good diagonal ball into the box for Armstrong. The ball is going away from him, but he tries to head it and gets no power. He should have brought it down and shot. The game finishes 1-1.

Newcastle's performances probably vary more than ours. They can play better than us and worse than us. Gullit's team can be very good or clueless. We tend to be more consistent.

Anderton probably deserved his man of the match award, but Freund was awful and Taricco was poor defensively, although he passes neatly. Taricco versus Solano will be an interesting duel on Sunday, and maybe a decisive one. I wonder who will mark Ginola on Sunday. I think Gullit will play Howey and Charvet at the back, not Dabizas. An FA Cup semi-final is a job for men, not boys, so Newcastle will probably line up like this, 4-4-2: Given; Barton, Howey, Charvet, Domi; Solano, Hamann, Lee, Speed; Shearer, Ketsbaia.

Old Trafford will certainly be interesting. Ketsbaia has the beating of Sol on the ground, and can score tremendous goals. Yet again, we have shown that it usually takes a special goal to score against us. The Matt Elliott goal was a bad goal in any league, but the Matt Jansen goal was spectacular, and so was the John Aloisi goal.

The Izzet goal and today's Ketsbaia rocket were also spectacular.

It is revealed that Sheffield Wednesday made a £4 million bid for Armstrong on deadline day.

Wednesday 7 April

The Champions League is now massive in terms of the amount of media coverage it commands. Tonight it is the semi-final first legs. Manchester United are outclassed by Juventus in the first half at Old Trafford and go 1-0 down to an excellent goal by right winger Conte. But they fight back well in the second half and Ryan Giggs rams in the equaliser in the 91st minute. Teddy Sheringham, coming on as a sub for the disappointing Dwight Yorke, makes a difference. Bayern Munich also battle back in Kiev, scoring two late goals to draw 3-3.

Thursday 8 April

Razor-sharp finishing by Dani against Chelsea at the Bridge. The Mallorca striker flashes onto a lovely through pass, whips round De Gooey and buries it. One of the brightest, sharpest finishes of the season. But Flo rescues Chelsea yet again and it finishes 1-1. I look forward to our exploits in Europe next season. These games are always close and tense, and usually won by one goal, or won on away goals. It's so interesting to face new opposition. Mallorca are a fine side, and we could not beat them with the team we have at the moment.

Friday 9 April

The club will launch next season's adidas kit at the West Ham game on Saturday 24 April. adidas naturally wanted David Ginola to do a photo for the publicity material. There is a rumour that he has refused. He is alleged to believe that he was badly treated by adidas last year. He apparently wanted a boot deal with them, but they said he was too old! If this was true it is hardly surprising that Ginola has not forgiven adidas for that insult.

The Department of Trade and Industry and the Monopolies and Mergers Commission have rejected BSkyB's bid for Manchester United. A great victory for passionate, articulate, well-organised supporters who believe that Manchester United is big enough to survive and prosper independently. For fans to form pressure groups like Shareholders United Against Murdoch to block a big takeover is brilliant news. BSkyB had even suggested that they would agree to be bound by strict conditions, such as opting out of negotiations on Premiership TV deals. Yeah, believe that!

Trade Secretary Stephen Byers said, 'The MMC's findings are based mainly on competition grounds where they concluded that the merger would adversely affect competition between broadcasters. But they also examined wider public interest issues concluding that the merger would damage the quality of British football. I accept these findings.' So Tony Blair's government regard the threat to broadcasting as more dangerous than the threat to football clubs.

Saturday 10 April

Watch *Match of the Day*. Ginola's winner against Barnsley is voted Goal of the Month for March, ahead of a goals by Dwight Yorke and Alan Shearer. Is this an omen for tomorrow's FA Cup semi-final? Yesterday's MMC verdict is, of course, massive news in the papers today. A leader in *The Guardian* is headlined 'Murdoch 0, Football 1'. It is a big defeat for the Dirty Digger. Tony Blair might be crossed off his Christmas card list.

Sunday 11 April
Newcastle
FA Cup semi-final, Old Trafford

A long day. I left home at 8am and drove for four hours to Manchester. We were able to park by the Munich Clocktower and walk very slowly in with Howerd, who has a walking stick. Newcastle fans have the whole of the big stand, and one corner, and we have the other three stands, so we had about 25,000 there. The atmosphere is fantastic. This is the exact opposite of 1995 at Elland Road, when we had the big stand and Everton had the rest.

Team news: we have Luke Young in defence, not Roger Nilsen, and Ferdinand with Armstrong. Where is Roger

Nilsen? He was good in the League game against Newcastle, but he is not even on the bench! He has Ledley King, on the bench . A kid who has never played for the first team and does not even have a squad number. What will happen if Sol Campbell is injured? We will be playing against Shearer and Ketsbaia with two teenage centre backs ! And what if Young is injured? The other kid will have to make his début in an FA Cup semi-final! George signed Roger Nilsen, an experienced left-footed centre back who can also play at left back. He will only be here for a few weeks on loan, and he is our cover defender. But he is not on the bench. I am mystified.

Ruud Gullit plays a back four of Griffin, Howey, Dabizas and Barton. He has Lee, Hamann, Speed and Solano in midfield, Shearer and Ketsbaia up front, and Ferguson on the bench.

Anderton hits an amazing shot in the first minute. An absolutely amazing shot. He picks up the ball and wallops it from 25 yards. It goes to the right of the 'keeper, rather than across him, as the Leeds shot did, and Shay Given makes a phenomenal save. Ginola gets in a couple of good crosses early on. When Taricco throws the ball down the line, Ferdinand wins the header, and Howey falls awkwardly, injuring his calf muscle. He soon goes off and Aron Hughes comes on. Anderton beats Ketsbaia on the right and measures his cross to the near post where Sherwood sends a looping header wide.

Shearer is having a solid, effective game. When Lee crossed he wins a knockdown against Young, but Durkin gives a foul against him. Anderton is injured after 37 minutes and goes off for treatment

Sherwood is awful, and so is Freund. Ketsbaia has a mazy run in midfield, beating three men. Incredibly, Durkin then misses a Dabizas handball when the Greek slaps a high free-kick from Sinton in the box. Durkin is five yards away, facing the defenders, but he does not see the handball. Ginola is taken off after 76 minutes, Iversen comes on, and Sinton switches to the left, so that Iversen is in the right-side position where his run won it for us at Wembley. At the same time Gullit brings Duncan Ferguson on for Solano.

In the 85th minute George jumps up and starts having a go at somebody, maybe the linesman. And that is when it happens: the fans start singing his name! All through October, November, December, January, February and March they have refused to sing his name. But now, in Manchester, on 11 April, when it is 0-0 in the FA Cup semi-final and we are desperate for a goal, they sing *Georgie Graham's Blue and White Army!*

Shearer has been using all his experience as a target man, working the flanks, mostly playing with his back to goal and holding the ball up. When a diagonal ball comes over he holds his position on the corner of the penalty area, obliging Carr to collide with him as he heads away, and Durkin gives Newcastle the free-kick. Shearer shoots over the wall but Walker saves easily.

Griffin makes a reckless lunge against Sinton's foot after the ball has gone, and gets a yellow card. Sinton, injured, goes off, Nielsen comes on. George has had to sub his sub.

Sherwood has a long diagonal free kick, Sol gets in at the far post, and heads down and wide. Carr hits a good free-kick to the far post, Armstrong wins it, knocks it down across the goal towards Nielsen, a yard out. But Given dives across and punches it away from Nielsen. Extra-time becomes a long-ball game, although Newcastle have more craft, more improvisation. Our formula football never surprises them, but we still create chances and half-chances.

The decisive moment arrives after 108 minutes. Freund fouls Hamman on the halfway line, the free-kick is headed out by Young, Sherwood doesn't really bother going for the loose ball, Speed cruises forward, gets it, and plays a one-two with Ferguson, who lifts the ball neatly up and into Speed's run into the box.

And Sol handles. Our captain handles the ball. He reaches up and touches the ball. Carr, covering danger as always, heads it away. Durkin blows his whistle. Our players do not protest the decision, and Shearer takes a good penalty, sending Walker the wrong way. So the semi-final is a bizarre tale of two handballs: one by Dabizas which is not seen by Durkin, one by Campbell which is seen, and from which Newcastle score the vital first goal.

Gullit then brings on Maric, the Croatian, who breaks down the middle and slips the ball to Griffin, who hits a strong cross-shot, but Walker makes a good save. Ferdinand wins a flick-on to Armstrong but he scuffs it to Given. Then Maric, on the left, sets up Shearer on the edge of the box. His right foot shot rises, swerves, hits the underside of the bar and goes into the net. It's 2-0 and the Toon Army goes wild. The match is over.

Five minutes from the end of extra-time my friend Howerd gets up and starts to walk out slowly. As he gets to the exit, Shearer scores the second goal and a mass exodus almost knocks him down the stairs. I run to the car and start it up, then wait for Zak, Howerd and Adam. I recognise, behind me, one of the Sugar cars, S83. Zak, Howerd and Adam get in but the cop makes us wait for half an hour. At 5.55 Alan Sugar and his entourage come out and get into an eight-seater people carrier parked right at the front of this car park. I saw Sugar but he did not see me.

I have to hand it to Ruud Gullit today. In his navy blue suit, shirt, tie and dreadlocks, he outshone Graham in the style department, and his younger team played with more spirit and ideas than we did. Everybody played a bit, everybody passed, or tried to pass, and everybody made runs to support the ball. We looked rigid and sterile.

Power football the George Graham way is the football of pressure, mistakes and rebounds. It creates a lot of half-chances, but most are missed because the guy having the shot or header is always stretching and lunging, always at the limit of his technique, so he often cannot control where the ball is going. This type of football is very hit-and-miss. It depends on the volume of pressure, the volume of chances.

Whereas passing football creates fewer openings, but better openings, as their goals showed. The move that led to the penalty was well worked. The ball from Maric to Shearer for the second was an accurate pass, which allowed him time to aim his shot properly.

Newcastle coped with the loss of Howey better than we coped with the loss of Anderton, Ketsbaia's dribbles were more threatening than Ginola's, and their substitute Maric had a far bigger impact on the game than Sinton, Iversen or Nielsen.

Gullit is a long way from putting a great team together, but he has a squad of lively players. The kid Griffin played very well. The game really changed when George took Ginola off, and Duncan Ferguson came on for them. That really wound up the Newcastle fans. It seemed as if he took Ginola off for tactical reasons, rather than because he wasn't playing well. That substitution seemed to me to be a signal that Ginola will be sold. With 15 minutes to go in a tight game, do you take off your match-winner?

As we drove home we talked about what we want to happen now. Obviously, we do not want anybody to do the

NEWCASTLE AT OLD TRAFFORD

double. So we hope Newcastle win the FA Cup, and
Manchester United win the League. I was driving a
borrowed Renault, as my own car was written off by that
mini-cab driver. There were plenty of idiots about on the
M6 and M1. It was drizzly, and I was tired, so I just took
my time, dropping off Howerd in Temple Fortune, Zak in
the West End and Adam in Stamford Hill.

Monday 12 April

We lost to Newcastle because we are not good enough.
Our strikers are not good enough. In the seven FA Cup
matches our three strikers have scored two goals. Iversen
scored two against Watford in the third round. Ginola
scored the goal against Wimbledon in the fourth round,
Sinton and Nielsen (2) scored in the replay. Sherwood
scored at Elland Road, Anderton and Ginola scored
against Leeds in the fifth round replay, and Ginola scored
against Barnsley in the sixth round.

In his whole managerial career, George has only lost a
few really big games. Luton in the Littlewoods Cup Final
at Wembley in 1988. Benfica, 3-1 in extra-time at
Highbury in the European Cup in 1991, the semi-final
against us in 1991, and this semi-final against Newcastle
at Old Trafford. So his record in big one-off games is
excellent.

In the *Standard*, a predictable headline. When are they
ever going to surprise me? The headline: 'GRAHAM: I
WANT A PREDATOR'. The Steve Stammers piece says
George will step up his search for a proven goalscorer.
George said: 'We are at present creating a lot of chances
and the statistics regarding our number of shots on target
make interesting reading. We have had a good season.

But the finishing is not up to standard and we definitely need a predator, an out-and-out goalscorer. In fact, I will be looking for lots of players.'

———————

Tuesday 13 April

The Mirror headline is 'GEORGE TO RAID HIS OLD CLUB'. Harry Harris says that George is looking at Leeds to find a goalscorer who can turn Tottenham into a major force and he might sign (*gasp!*) Alan Smith if the youngster's new contract negotiations break down at Elland Road. I think Harry knows that we will need more than Alan Smith to turn Tottenham into a major force! Harry reckons Dynamo Kiev striker Andriy Schevchenko has already signed with AC Milan for £18 million, and his partner Sergei Rebrov would cost £10 million. He also noted that Nationwide players Robbie Keane (Wolves), Lee Hughes (West Brom) and Craig Bellamy (Norwich) are also in the frame. Share price closed at 70p today.

———————

Wednesday 14 April

Maybe this summer is the time for Sugar to go. The share boom in football clubs has collapsed with the BSkyB-Man Utd deal being blocked. Sugar, in his heart of hearts, does not want to spend mega-millions on class players because the game itself, and what class players can do, does not move him enough. Irving Scholar and David Dein could feel that buzz, have a vision of a great team, a vision of excellence and excitement, but Sugar did not grow up as a football fan so he can never really feel that buzz, that thrill. He could walk away now with some dignity, saying,

'I started with a trophy in '91 and ended with a trophy in '99. I've left you with a good stadium, a strong manager and promising prospects. I've cleared the £11 million debt I inherited.'

We heard a whisper about why George substituted Ginola on Sunday. He was not playing to instructions. George told Ginola to knock the ball back instantly to Taricco, then move further forward for a pass, so he could start his dribbles 20 yards nearer the box. He did not do that. So George took him off. Ginola might argue that he missed Edinburgh, whose overlaps support him, and whose left-footed passes down the line serve him better than the right-footed passes of Tarrico.

I've decided to start a Linked With Tottenham (LWT) count, to see just how many of players we are linked with. Rebrov, Keane, Hughes and Bellamy make four.

Thursday 15 April

We are coming off a losing FA Cup semi-final, our third in a row after Arsenal at Wembley in 1993 and Everton at Elland Road in 1995. I'm glad we have an easy game on Saturday against Nottingham Forest. They are a poor side and we will not have to play especially well to beat them.

Friday 16 April

We should beat Forest in Nottingham tomorrow. They are doomed. If they lose to us they will be relegated, even if they win all their other games.

Saturday 17 April
Nottingham Forest (a)

At 2.50pm I hear the news on the radio: Ginola is on the bench at Nottingham Forest. The beginning of the end for him? George puts Ginola on the bench, but he does it in an away game, not a home game. He is not saving Ginola for a final. Is he simply punishing him for not playing to orders in the semi-final? And he is showing the other players what could happen to them?

Nielsen plays instead of Ginola, misses a penalty, gets booked and could have been sent off. George played three strikers but we only scored after Ferdinand went off at half-time and Anderton came on. That sums us up! Gough tripped Iversen in the box just before half-time and the ref pointed to the spot. But Mark Crossley saved Nielsen's feeble penalty. In the 62nd minute Iversen took the ball off their full-back Matthieu Louis-Jean on the edge area, and beat Crossley with a low shot from 15 yards. This win lifts us to 10th, so at least we are in the top half of the table. It is our first away victory in the League under George.

Sunday 18th April

Nottingham Forest now have the biggest collection of deadbeat players in their history. Yesterday was their 21st defeat of the season. Can you believe this starting line-up? Crossley, Chettle, Edwards, Gough, Harewood, Louis-Jean, Rogers, Stensaas, Woan, Bonalair, Johnson.

They sold Colin Cooper and Kevin Campbell before the season, and Steve Stone before the transfer deadline. In the meantime Kevin Campbell has come back from Turkey, signed for Everton on loan and scored four goals in their last two games! Why did they get Ron Atkinson in 13 weeks ago? In seven home games under Big Ron they have collected one point. Is that what it's about now? Big Ron cracking jokes as the ship sinks? If ever a club deserved relegation, Forest do. Nigel Wray sold his shares last week. Southampton and Charlton, who might go down with them, are better clubs with much better teams.

Monday 19 April

Today's Rumour column in *The Independent* has a handy summary of the transfer speculation in the Sunday tabloids. *The News of the World* named Chris Sutton, Ugo Ehiogu and Robbie Keane as Graham's top targets. The *Sunday People* reckoned that Alex Ferguson, who won't be allowed to spend anything like the £26 million that he spent last summer, could cash in on Solskjaer, who would cost us £10 million. And we are also watching Vincenzo Montella, the young Sampdoria striker. The *Sunday Mirror* says we are in for Willem Korsten, the Dutchman who has mysteriously refused to sign at Leeds, and Paul Ince, who could be let go for £1 million as his Liverpool contract runs out next year. So I add these six names to my Linked With Tottenham total to make 10. Maybe we should also have an Actually Made Signings (AMS) count.

Tuesday 20 April
Charlton (a)

Charlton are fighting for their lives at the bottom of the table. We had Ginola and Anderton back. The game was played in heavy rain after a delayed kick-off due to traffic jams, so I was glad I had given it a miss. Mark Kinsella scored after five minutes, a low shot into the corner after he was set up by Graham Stuart. They contained us until Iversen equalised after an hour. We then scored three in 12 minutes: Campbell dived to head in Anderton's corner for 2-1. We scored twice in the last minute. Nielsen combined with Ginola, who slipped Dominguez in and he shot neatly from a narrow angle, and then Ginola made it 4-1. A cruel scoreline. Our second away win in the Premiership under George.

Wednesday 21 April

An amazing effort by Manchester United in Turin. Inzaghi scored two early goals in the second leg of their semi-final, but United bounced back to beat Juventus 3-2 in a thriller. Roy Keane and Dwight Yorke made it 2-2 at half-time, and Andy Cole scored the winner. But Keane and Paul Scholes got yellow cards and will miss the final. Keane's card, for a slightly mistimed and harmless tackle on Zidane, was harsh. United will meet Bayern Munich in Barcelona. They have already drawn twice in group games.

Thursday 22 April

The papers reported that George has told the players not to coast through the rest of our League matches. The signs were there at the Valley, especially early on. We looked like a team that has nothing left to play for. George said, 'For the first 20 minutes Charlton started very well, and got the goal they deserved. We were a bit casual. I felt we had to play with more purpose in the second half, and we did that very well. I said a few things at half-time. The fans pay good money. At a big club like Tottenham you shouldn't be able to coast after you've won something.

'You've got to give the fans value for money and be hungry for more success and win as many games as we can. That's the way we'll approach the next season. Every game is important.' He laughed off suggestions that he will have £20 million to spend on new talent.: 'I don't know where that figure of £20 million has come from! That is not true.'

———————————

Friday 23 April

Tomorrow's game against West Ham is a nothing match, although some local pride is at stake. One of their midfielders is John Moncur, a player who didn't make it at Tottenham, and went to Swindon in 1992. They sold him to West Ham in 1994. His dad works as a scout at Spurs. Which of our strikers will be playing?

Chapter Ten

DAVID GINOLA, SUPERSTAR

Saturday 24 April
West Ham (h)

I picked up my cousin Scott from his home in Mill Hill and took him to the game. Scott is nine, a West Ham fan, and a good little footballer who is training with Watford. Our strikers are Iversen and Dominguez, who starts for the first time in 18 months. Armstrong is on the bench. So we have, really, three wingers: Ginola, Anderton and Dominguez, as we sometimes did with Francis and Gross.

West Ham are without Di Canio, but have Ian Wright up front. Steve Lomas is at right back, marking Ginola. In central midfield, Frank Lampard and Moncur.

With this formation we should be able to play more football, especially coming off a 4-1 win at Charlton, but we are rubbish. Eyal Berkovic, a playmaker we should have signed three years ago, is by far the best man on the field. Berkovic turns Freund inside out and makes the opening for their first goal after five minutes. He slips a pass through for Trevor Sinclair and Walker has to come out of his penalty area to kick the ball away. But it goes to Ian Wright, who lobs in from 30 yards, left-footed, first time. An instinctive finish from an experienced striker who scored many similar goals for Palace and Arsenal.

But it is dreadful defending by us. There is no line, no offside, a shambles. Anderton has a 30-yard Exocet just over the bar, then sends over a cross which Sherwood flicks on to Ginola, who hits a wild left-foot volley into the stand from an unpromising angle. Glory hunter! He should have knocked it back across the goal to Sherwood and Iversen. Sherwood remonstrates with Ginola. Very animated!

When Freund fouls Berkovic for the third or fourth time in the first half hour, Berkovic tells referee Uriah Rennie to book him. Rennie books Berkovic instead. Berkovic goes down in my estimation. No need for his antics. West Ham are 1-0 up and he is controlling the game. Berkovic picks out Frank Lampard's run with a wonderful lofted pass from the halfway line. Lampard tries to touch the ball past the advancing Walker from the edge of the box, but puts it wide.

Ginola's crossing is atrocious today, and Rennie books him for diving just before half-time. Once he dribbles down the left wing, ignores several chances to cross the ball, then tries to go between two defenders but dives into them for a penalty. Pathetic. Amazingly, George does not go down from the directors' box in the first half. Usually, when we lose a goal and play as badly as this, he goes down and screams and shouts and points. But he didn't go down. That proves it is a nothing match.

Second half starts, Berkovic almost makes another goal. He tees up Mark Keller, whose shot hits the far post. Dominguez is our best player. He wins the ball in midfield, touching it to Ginola, who hits a fierce shot just wide. Dominguez has a terrific shot which Shaka Hislop tips round the post.

Then Berkovic finishes us off with a slide-rule pass for Keller, who sidefoots past the advancing Walker. Good movement by Keller onto a world-class pass which allows him to run in behind Campbell. We get a free-kick from 30 yards, Anderton goes close, just past the angle.

Ginola gets a goal back after 72 minutes. A pass forward to him from Dominguez, controls it on his body, eases infield away from Lomas, smashes a right-foot shot from 25 yards, curling round Hislop's dive. One of his specials. Ginola stunk today, but he scored. And that's why George should not have taken him off at Wembley. Ginola can be useless, but still score from 25 yards.

George is on the bench for the second half, but he is not directing operations as much as usual. But, after Ginola scores, he brings on Allan Nielsen for Anderton. No surprise. Anderton has been average for weeks. The last good game he played was the Leeds replay, 12 matches ago.

When Hislop miskicks a backpass, Iversen is slow to react. He should have been anticipating the mistake. Then, after Taricco and Moncur have a 50-50, there is a huge scuffle, an explosion of argy-bargy in midfield. Rennie books Taricco and Rio Ferdinand. Then Sol has a header just wide off a free-kick. Lomas is booked for a late lunge on Ginola. Carr crosses and Iversen is injured going for a diving header. Sherwood, who has been invisible, tries an enterprising overhead kick that goes wide.

Then Moncur fouls Dominguez and another mêlée breaks out in the middle of the field. Ugly, squalid scenes. Moncur had been winding people up all day. Kicking the smallest player on the field in the 92nd minute was despicable. I was glad to see Moncur sent off.

The TV replays later showed exactly what happened. Dominguez was on the right wing. He skipped inside Keller, moved across Sinclair, and then Moncur lunged in and scythed him down as he touched the ball back to Ginola. An amateurish tackle which missed the ball by a yard. Ginola was furious when his little mate was chopped down, so he ran up pointing a finger in Moncur's face. Moncur's arm flailed out, Rennie got between them, whipping his red card out of his hip pocket and holding it up as he grabbed Moncur's shirt front. A scrum formed around them. Steve Carr steamed in, grabbed Moncur's shirt, the arm lashed out again. Other players pulled people away. Moncur walked, having spoiled a well-deserved win by his team. Referees are not all heavyweight martial arts experts like Rennie. They should not have to break up fights, stepping in between players while punches are flying.

As we walked back to the car Zak said, 'Berkovic is not Graham's type of player.' What is his type of player? Freund? Sherwood? We will certainly never win the Premiership with these two in midfield. Berkovic lives in Golders Green and would love to play for us. But he seems to be on his way to Liverpool.

Luke Young was clueless, Sol Campbell suffered because Young was so bad, Carr was way below his usual form, Taricco didn't make support runs for Ginola to take a defender away from him, as Edinburgh does. We missed Edinburgh today, again. Our midfield was abysmal. Iversen was tentative, anonymous. What chance have you got when your best player is a five-foot three-inch winger who is on the transfer list?

So West Ham, like Leicester, have completed a Premiership double over us. Harry Redknapp's Hammers showed George Graham why they are 5th and we are 10th.

Sunday 25 April

Good report by Ken Jones in *The Independent on Sunday* which starts: 'With just a few minutes left and Tottenham pressing hard for an equaliser, David Ginola provided one of those moments that polarise opinions about him. The Great Entertainer foolishly dribbled into trouble when the situation cried out for a less complicated means of putting the ball into West Ham's goalmouth.'

Jones said the supporters were less critical of Ginola than his team-mates, whose angry gestures told the story. He quoted George saying he was about to substitute the frustrating Frenchman when he scored: 'David wasn't getting anywhere. I was about to bring him off.'

Israeli manager Schlomo Sharf was there yesterday. No wonder Berkovic turned it on. Harry Redknapp said the first half was the best half Berkovic has played since he's been at West Ham. George was upset that Kevin Keegan did not consult him, as he consulted Wenger and Ferguson, before announcing his England squad. 'I can see why the top clubs in the Premier League didn't want their players picked for the Hungary game, but they shouldn't be the only clubs to be considered.' George always wants to be in control as much as possible. If other managers can veto the selection of one of their players for a friendly international, George wants that privilege as well. And who can blame him?

Some of the Sunday papers say Dwight Yorke has won tonight's PFA Player of the Year. Rob Shepherd in the *The Express on Sunday* says Yorke has won and Michael Owen is the Young Player of the Year. But later that night we hear that the winners are David Ginola and Nicolas Anelka! Aren't players always complaining that Ginola dives too much? How many defenders voted for him?

Monday 26 April

Amazing that Ginola has been voted Player of the Year by his fellow professionals last night. He pipped Dwight Yorke, who has scored 27 goals for Manchester United and Emmanuel Petit, of Arsenal, who brought his World Cup form back into the Premiership. The players also vote for Divisional Teams, and the Premiership eleven was as follows:

1	Martyn	(Leeds)
2	G Neville	(Man Utd)
3	Irwin	(Man Utd)
4	Vieira	(Arsenal)
5	Campbell	(Spurs)
6	Stam	(Man Utd)
7	Beckham	(Man Utd)
8	Yorke	(Man Utd)
9	Anelka	(Arsenal)
10	Petit	(Arsenal)
11	Ginola	(Spurs)

Remarkable, really, for a team which is 11th in the League to have two players in the PFA Premiership X1. It turns out that Sol was carrying a hamstring injury on Saturday and has dropped out of the England squad for Hungary.

This end-of-season period suits George Graham. He can put Dominguez in the shop window. And if the players don't perform in the seven games after the semi-final he can say: 'You didn't bother after Old Trafford, so I'm selling you.' And he can say to the board: 'Look, we're mid-table. We won a cup by beating Leicester, who are almost as mediocre as we are. I need big money for new players.'

George Graham and Alex Ferguson are both tough Glaswegians, but there is one big difference between them. George won't gamble on an exceptional player. He was on record as saying that Eric Cantona will let you down in big games. So he does not trust gifted players as much as Ferguson.

Ginola is clever and keeps saying he would like to finish his career at Spurs. He was on Sky News this morning. He looked like a superstar outside the Grosvenor Hotel, where the PFA dinner was held last night. In the early evening sunshine, a handsome gladiator in an immaculate dinner suit. Hyde Park in the background, cars and red London buses going down Park Lane. Autograph hunters crowding his elbows. A smart guy, he always says the right thing.

'I'm happy for Spurs, first of all,' he said. 'Because last season we struggled, to be honest. Just to have a better season was more enjoyable for us, first. And second, we won a trophy, so for the club, for the fans, I think it's something very important.' Sky News also had a soundbite from Robbie Savage, who said, 'I think the vote was after the Barnsley game, when he scored that fantastic goal.'

Ginola is a cosmopolitan star among stars. Intelligent and articulate, he knows that English football has been good for him: big money, big crowds, massive media coverage, a stimulating foreign adventure at the end of his career. The fact that Ginola often plays too selfishly has not, apparently, worried his fellow pros. But, clearly, their views are shaped by TV rather than the two games they play against Tottenham every season. The PFA members are influenced by highlights, goals, headlines and images. Ginola looks good on highlights. So does Anelka. Like Ginola, Anelka is a spectacular player. He has startling pace and scores memorable goals. Over the 90 minutes they don't look half as good.

Tuesday 27 April

Steve Stammers says we could go for Real Mallorca centreback Elena Marcelino, 27, who is rated at £5 million and wants to play in London. Marcelino looks a good player, better than Vega and much better than Young, but George Graham does not sign Latins or Slavs. He signs Swedes, Norwegians, Danes and Dutchmen. Linked With Tottenham 11 AMS 0.

Tomorrow's England match in Budapest is a unique moment in football history. Keegan has phoned up Alex Ferguson and said, 'We all know this is a joke fixture, I promise l will never play a friendly in April again. What players can you let me have?' And Fergie has given him Wes Brown, Nicky Butt and Phil Neville!

The Manchester United bench are playing for England because the first team are being saved for the Premiership title race, the FA Cup Final and the European Cup Final. Keegan has had to fill out his 22 with youngsters. Kevin Phillips of Sunderland will make his début. Republic of Ireland manager Mick McCarthy has given Steve Carr his first senior cap in the friendly against Sweden in Dublin. The Irish win 2-0. Tottenham's international players have their names etched in gilt on the board in the Oak Room, and Carr deserves to join them.

Wednesday 28 April

Luke Young made his début for England Under-21s in in Budapest. The game is almost abandoned, but starts late after a downpour. England played three centre backs and soon went 2-0 down on a pitch of puddles. But goals by Danny Mills and a penalty by Southampton's James Beattie gave us a 2-2 draw.

Can you believe this 'England' line-up? Seaman; Wes Brown, Rio Ferdinand, Keown, Phil Neville; McManaman, Batty, Sherwood, Butt; Phillips, Shearer.

The substitutes are: Jamie Redknapp, Nigel Martyn, Michael Gray, Jamie Carragher, Frank Lampard, Michael Ball, Emile Heskey and Francis Jeffers.

Shearer scores from a penalty after he is brought down in the box. McManaman, Brown and Butt don't look up to the job, and Hungary get the draw they deserve when Carragher, a sub for the injured Ferdinand, flattens one of their players 30 yards out. Defender Hrutka smacks in a Gazza-like free-kick into the top corner of Seaman's goal. Tim Sherwood played the whole 90 minutes. Well, he was on the field somewhere. The match is a waste of time. Is this a sign of things to come? When United and Arsenal will be so much bigger than England that international games are almost an irrelevance?

Thursday 29 April

Leeds left back David Robertson condemns the managerial methods of George Graham, who signed him from Rangers in 1997. Robertson has hardly played because of injuries, and sounds a bitter man.

'Leeds are doing so well under David O'Leary just now and the style of football they play is so enjoyable to watch. That wasn't the case under George Graham and even before I got injured things weren't going well for me. I'd been playing football a certain way for 12 years when George signed me and all of a sudden he wanted me to change. It was the same for a few of the other players at the club but it's impossible to change your game overnight.' Haven't we heard the same story from Tony Adams? Adams said before Christmas that he would not want to play for George again, having now played under Wenger.

Robertson also said, 'There is no doubt he did a lot for Leeds in his time at the club and he did stabilise them after a poor couple of years. But it wasn't enjoyable to play for him, and his brand of football certainly wasn't pretty to watch or play. When he was here I was really down and my desire and appetite for the game had dwindled totally.' Maybe George is really just a structural engineer who lacks the ability to design the interior and put the finishing touches to a house.

Last night Keegan announced that he was taking the England job full-time, and thus distracted the media from saying how pointless the game in Hungary was and how poorly England had played. He had initially said he would take charge for four games until early June before going back to finish the job at Fulham. He said that it was working with the England players that finally made up his mind. Keegan said, 'We've got to stop messing around. I've needed time to think about it, and weigh it up, but the more I've worked with the players, the more I've wanted to do it.'

Friday 30 April

It was announced tonight that Sir Alf Ramsey had died. He was 79. Alf was a superb right back for Tottenham in the great push-and-run team of the Fifties, and later became a thoughtful, original manager of Ipswich. He then managed England for 11 years, winning the World Cup in 1966.

Alan Mullery played for Sir Alf in the 1970 World Cup in Mexico. Mullery said, 'He was the best manager England have ever had. He was such a nice man and I don't think we will see another like him. When he said something he said it quietly but you listened. Otherwise you didn't play in the next game. Once when England were playing Brazil in the great Maracana stadium, I was meant to be marking Pele. Alf saw me looking nervous and said to me, "If you were not good enough to play against this fella you would be back home watching it on the telly." It helped me, and I went out and played one of the best games I have ever played.' Now that is class management.

———————

Saturday 1 May
Liverpool (a)

We lost 3-2 at Anfield after being 2-0 up. George rested Ginola and Sherwood, who were on the bench, and kept Dominguez in the shop window. George was not at the match, so Stewart Houston was in charge. I watched highlights on *Match of the Day*.

Liverpool used Matteo, a tall central defender, at left back, and we soon exploited that weakness. Iversen broke down the right, crossed low to Armstrong at the near post, and the ball went in off Carragher. Then Kvarme fouled Dominguez,Anderton knocked in the free-kick from the left side, and Iversen got in front of Friedel to head in from three yards. Bad goalkeeping not to claim that inswinging ball.

This Iversen looked a different player to the Iversen we saw against West Ham on a pre-international Saturday. Iversen played for Norway in midweek and scored the first goal in a 4-1 win in Georgia in a Euro 2000 qualifier. Flo got two, and Solskjaer the other. Taricco was booked for fouling Leonardsen after 37 minutes. Then, seconds before half-time, Taricco brought McManaman down near the corner flag. The cameraman was asleep, so we did not see the incident, but referee Steven Lodge sent him off. Three minutes into the second half Riedle dribbled into the box in exactly the position Taricco would have been defending. Ian Walker stupidly slid out feet first and clattered him by the side of the penalty area. Walker should not have been out there! Riedle played for it, but a clear penalty. More bad goalkeeping. Redknapp banged it in.

Even so we held out until 12 minutes from time. McManaman won a corner off Carr, took it short to Redknapp and he crossed for Ince, a glancing header which made it 2-2. Then Liverpool scored the winner a minute later when a ball was floated over the head of little Dominguez to Rigobert Song, who crossed from the bye-line. McManaman took one touch and smacked in a curling right-foot shot.

Both teams played 4-5-1:

LIVERPOOL: Friedel; Kvarme (Gerrard, 46), Carragher, Staunton, Matteo; Thompson (Bjornebye, 88), Redknapp, Leonhardsen (Song, 75), Ince, McManaman; Riedle. Substitutes not used: James, Dundee.

TOTTENHAM: Walker; Carr, Campbell, Nilsen, Taricco; Dominguez (Fox, 83), Clemence (King, 46), Iversen, Anderton, Freund (Sherwood, 66); Armstrong. Substitutes not used: Baardsen, Ginola.

If George had been there he might have been able to re-organise and get a draw with ten men. Or even a win. Where was Luke Young? Roger Nilsen can play left back! When Taricco was sent off, Young could have come on, and Nilsen switched to left back, taking a midfield player off. A boob by Stewart Houston?

Three points would have been nice because our next three opponents are better sides than Liverpool: Arsenal, Chelsea and Man Utd. I can't see us getting another point this season. We could lose the last four games and finish 14th or worse. Where was George? A spying mission? What country? What match? Which player?

Sunday 2 May

Our performances have tailed off since the Worthington Cup, as I expected. We've just conceded three goals to a Liverpool team without Fowler and Owen! Arsenal had just tonked Wimbledon 5-1 and Middlesbrough 6-1, so people were expecting goals when they played Derby at Highbury. But Arsenal only beat Derby 1-0 and seemed to be saving something for Wednesday night at White Hart Lane. Anelka scored after 14 minutes. Bergkamp was on the bench after a stomach strain. He came on for Kanu after 62 minutes but didn't do much.

I'm looking forward to Wednesday night, but also dreading it. You always feel ambivalent about playing Arsenal. I'd like to go into the game with more confidence. Will our fans sing *Georgie Graham's Blue And White Army*, just to wind-up the Arsenal supporters? If we go a goal down, the Gooners might start singing *Georgie Graham's Blue and White Army*. I can see that happening. It will just be a battle. We are looking at bookings and red cards. The most important player will be the referee. If Arsenal wind up Freund he will get booked after five minutes and then he won't be able to tackle anybody. Ginola will resume his long-standing duel with Lee Dixon, which started back in 1994 when he played for PSG in the Cup Winners' Cup.

The Sunday Times news section has a story headlined 'ARSENAL GOES TO TOP OF THE LUVVIE LEAGUE'. It is written by Arts editor Richard Brooks.

'Traditionally, it has been renowned as the most boring club in football. But Arsenal are turning the corner. The Gunners have become the passion of some of Britain's trendiest media stars. A new book will reveal how the likes of Lord (Melvyn) Bragg, Clive Anderson and society hostess Jennifer D'Abo have devoted themselves to Highbury. Laurence Marks, the television screenwriter who created *Birds of a Feather* and the *New Statesman*, was "nearly killed" when he was with Bragg during a crowd stampede at a European game in Lens as French police charged fans.

"I swore I'd never go again to a soccer game," said Marks. But he did, and now he has decided to publish his private football diary.'

The forthcoming book, *A Man for All Seasons*, describes two years at Arsenal, where celebrity supporters include Ray Davies of The Kinks, comedian Rory McGrath, Anthony Holden, biographer of the Prince of Wales, and Sir Frank Kermode, the literary critic and former Cambridge professor.

What tosh! Has decided to publish his private football diary? A professional screenwriter knocks out a Nick Hornby-type fan book? So what? Clive Anderson admits he rarely goes to Highbury. Does Jennifer D'Abo know Lee Dixon from Kerry Dixon? I doubt it. Bragg, Hornby, Davies, Holden, Kermode, McGrath? 38,000 people and only six celebrities? I'm sure Chelsea and even Tottenham have more celebs than that!

Marks gushingly describes Wenger as the 'Sigmund Freud of football managers'. He says Wenger is cheered each time he walks into the San Daniele, a restaurant near the ground. Marks also gasps, 'Coming back on the plane from Kiev he was sitting there quietly, reading Andre Malraux. Can you imagine any other manager in the world doing that?'

Brooks said that, after a match, celebrities gather at the restaurant. In fact, most music business people, and Melvyn Bragg, have lunch before the game on a Saturday. Pop lawyer Alexis Grower was joking with Bragg about *The Sunday Times* article before today's Derby game. Grower said, 'If prices go up, I'm blaming you!'

Joe Lovejoy has an interview feature with Martin Keown in the same paper. Keown said he felt unfulfilled under George Graham and would not want to play for him again. He said that Graham's strength was keeping his players aware of the importance of winning every game. He admitted that under Graham he was a spoiler who did his best to turn matches into non-events. He admitted he had a few clashes with him.

Keown said, 'There are some managers who are very close to their players and others who keep their distance. Wenger and Graham are chalk and cheese, but they are both very successful. I prefer to work in an environment which is more comfortable and relaxed, and after a couple of games under Kevin Keegan I can see him duplicating the sort of atmosphere we've got at Arsenal. Nice guys can win things; Arsène proved that last season. George works another way, and you have to say it has been successful for him, but you don't have to be at each other's throats all the time within a football club.'

Monday 3 May

We are reported to have signed Najwan Grayeb, the Israeli left back, for £1.3 million.

Reports in *The Mirror* and *Independent* spell his name wrongly, as Gharib. A phone call establishes that Grayeb is an Arab boy, 25, an exciting player, the fastest footballer in Israel. Very good coming forward, has scored three or four goals for Israel in about 14 appearances. It's good that he is quick. Playing behind Ginola, he will have a lot of ground to cover. Maybe Grayeb will be a gem, a bargain player who is as good as Hasselbaink (£2 million) or Boateng (£250,000) or Anelka (£500,000). So AMS is off the mark. Actually Made Signings: 1

George collected centre halves at Arsenal. Adams, Bould, Keown, Andy Linighan,Colin Pates, Scott Marshall. Now he has come to Tottenham he is collecting left backs. Edinburgh, Wilson, Taricco, Grayeb. Maybe he will sign a couple more in the summer. Stuart Pearce, stay by that phone!

It turns out that *The Sun* had a story on Saturday suggesting George might ditch Anderton in the summer. The whisper is that Sol and Ginola will sign new contracts soon, but Anderton has a parity clause. He's believed to be top earner on £25,000 a week, and if Sol and Ginola get pay rises to £27,000, Anderton would get the same without extending his contract.

And, allegedly, George is not too happy about that. Allegedly. We can never really know the truth about such internal matters.

Sugar must dread the Arsenal games, and his comments about Bergkamp coming back to haunt him. What a classic quote that was back in August 1995. I always re-read it when I want a laugh: 'As the season progresses and the fog, ice and cold arrive, his approach could change, especially when someone gives him a good kicking, an elbow in the ribs or a whack in the earhole. Arsenal have taken an almighty risk. There's no way Bergkamp is going to have the same impact as Klinsmann. If he thinks he's going to set the word, alight, he can forget it. Arsenal got him because they needed a bit of cosmetic marketing. It is a known fact that Bergkamp was offered to us first – so too were Gullit and Ginola.' Enough said!

Tuesday 4 May

My partner in Israel says Grayeb created a scandal last month when he did not sing the national anthem before an international.

We play Arsenal at White Hart Lane tomorrow night. It is crucial that we get at least a point and dent their title aspirations. They went top after beating Derby on Sunday. I'm approaching the game with trepidation and fear. George will pick almost the same team that started against Liverpool, with Ginola and Sherwood coming in for Dominguez and Clemence. So he will play Carr, Young for his pace, Campbell, and Taricco, though I would like to see Edinburgh at left back if he has finished his suspension, because he is used to playing derbies. Midfield will be Anderton, Sherwood, Freund, Ginola, and up front Armstrong and Iversen.

Wednesday 5 May
Arsenal (h)

We got there quite early. The atmosphere seemed muted, somewhat tense on what is a big occasion for both teams. Obviously a bigger occasion for Arsenal than for us. Our team was what I expected.

Incredibly, the minute silence for Sir Alf Ramsey was not introduced over the public address. Everyone knew why the players were standing around the centre circle

312

DAVID GINOLA, SUPERSTAR

because everybody knew Sir Alf had died last week. The papers had been full of tributes and obituaries.

The announcer should have written a script. He should have given us a brief summary of the man's career. Alf Ramsey played for our club! He played right back for Tottenham in the great push-and-run team that Arthur Rowe put together, managed Ipswich to promotion from the Third Division South and from the Second Division, and Ipswich won the championship in 1962.

What did we do? Nothing. We use our public address system and Jumbotron for hype and commercialism, but when a little gravitas is needed, a little taste, the disc jockey goes AWOL. Pathetic! No tribute, career summary, nothing to place one of England's sporting heroes in context. Younger fans do not know that Alf Ramsey played for Tottenham. And there were only two lines in the programme! A full obituary was promised in the next programme. Martin Peters, our director, played for Ramsey for seven years. Could Peters not write a tribute to England's greatest manager? Apparently not. But he did a piece for *The News of the World*.

When the game started we were playing five in midfield with Iversen on the right wing, probably to counter Overmars. But this detracted from our shape and balance. We had Anderton in central midfield, so we had three against two there, but Vieira and Petit were too good.

In the first minute Ginola took Dixon on, and it seemed as if he would show the way. But it was a false dawn. Ginola flattered to deceive throughout, picked the ball up far too deep from Taricco, who gave him virtually no overlap support. After that it was men against boys, an absolute disgrace. Which of the four players George Graham has signed would get into the Arsenal team? Who would even sit on their bench? The only Spurs player who would get into their team is Campbell.

Bergkamp made goals for Petit and Anelka, then Anderton scored with a free-kick which somehow bounced under Seaman and went into the bottom corner just before half-time. Our fans sang *Let's all do a Seaman!*

With 15 minutes to go we were 2-1 down, and George took Ginola off. In a home game, you take off your match-winner? A guy who kept two Arsenal players occupied? Ginola can always unleash a 25-yard rocket that saves the game. Not only that, Wenger had taken Parlour off and brought Vivas on to help Dixon, who had just been booked ten minutes before, also for fouling Ginola. So why did he take Ginola off? Was he watching the same game as us? He should have brought Dominguez on for Armstrong.

Two seconds into the second half. Anderton tangled with Vieira from the kick-off, Vieira fell, and with the ball yards away, Sherwood came in and stamped on Viera's thigh while he was on the ground. That kind of foul may be acceptable at Watford, Norwich and Blackburn, Sherwood's previous clubs, but it is wholly unacceptable at White Hart Lane. Tottenham players should never, never stamp on opponents who are on the ground. That is not football. The incident looked like a vendetta from the Blackburn-Arsenal game last October when Chris Sutton was sent off for a vicious tackle on Vieira.

The referee Steve Dunn was good. He gave players the benefit of the doubt for the first ten minutes. He let Winterburn get away with a bad tackle on Armstrong and he let Freund get away with one. Then, when Parlour whacked Ginola, he thought: enough's enough, I'm gonna start. So he booked Parlour. After the Sherwood-Vieira incident, when Petit decided to get involved, fighting Vieira's battles, Dunn took Petit aside and booked him.

Our defence was terrible. If George is such a great tactician, why were we ripped to shreds? He got it wrong today. And he got it wrong in the semi-final. You do not play Iversen on the wing. Especially when your striker can't control the ball. If it's gonna bounce off him you at least want another striker sniffing around him for a knockdown, not 30 yards away. It was a real Band-Aid job in midfield. He knows Freund and Sherwood aren't good enough, so he reinforces them with Anderton, and puts Iversen wide, so we have no attack!

Arsène Wenger said, 'We had a great first half today. Our passing was excellent, our runs were great, and every time we got through the first defending of Tottenham we were dangerous. So to go back in with 2-1 was very difficult. We needed to be very strong mentally. We came back to the dressing room thinking it should have been 4-0, and it is 2-1.

'Of course we expected a reaction of Tottenham in the second half. They fought very hard, and we had to be strong and well-organised in the second half and wait for our chance. Again we missed chances in the first 20 minutes, but after Kanu came on we scored the third goal. That killed it.'

Wenger was asked if there was a key to the victory.

'The key was that maybe they played very high, and we found the space behind them with Dennis dropping off, and finding Marc Overmars, Ray Parlour and Nicholas Anelka with their runs. Because they played in a very high position. So as long as we could find Dennis when we won the ball, and he could feed our strikers, we were very dangerous.'

George's comments suggested we had been competing when, in fact, we had been outclassed:

'A very good game. I thought Arsenal, in the first half, were outstanding. On the break they were real, real quality tonight, especially in the first half. We got into the game just before half-time with a good free-kick, which gave us a lift. I told the boys, second half, to be more positive. Second half, for a half an hour, 35 minutes, I thought we did well. I thought we did very well. And then they broke again with real quality players.'

George was asked who he would like to win the championship.

'To be quite honest, I'm so focused on the job here, I don't care who wins the championship. I don't know who will win it. It's not even entered my head. I'm more concerned about getting it right here, which is gonna be a long hard job, because the quality that you see from the teams at the top, they are way ahead of the rest of us. Whoever wins it, wins it. And whoever wins it deserves to win it. But the best teams, I think, are way way ahead of the rest of us. Whoever wins the championship, good luck to them.'

Will you keep Dominguez next season?

'It's an interesting question. He's played very well when I've brought him on. I thought he did well tonight in little spasms. But there's a lot of work to be done here. Next season, to get into the top six, there's gotta be a lotta changes. I anticipate a lot of changes, hopefully. And the next stage will be to get into the top six. Tonight we saw the opposition, the quality of the players, that's how far we've got to go.'

Is it just Arsenal and Man Utd?

'I would throw Chelsea in. I think Leeds have a lovely little team there. Whether they can get the squad of the other teams, I can't answer that. But they've got a good side just now, Leeds. Very good. I thought some of the defending tonight was schoolboy. I really did. I thought it was disgraceful. I thought the first goal – on the training pitch I would sort it out in no time. And the last goal, terrible defending. There were too many chances. Arsenal had lots of chances tonight. I thought the back four were not good enough. But I'd give Arsenal credit for assembling a very strong squad there. Not only talented, but physically very strong, so they can take you on, whatever way you wanna play it, they've got the answer to you.'

Meanwhile, at Anfield, Manchester United draw 2-2 after being 2-0 down. Referee David Elleray awards a controversial penalty against Blomqvist, and gives Denis Irwin a second yellow card for kicking the ball away, so Irwin will miss the FA Cup Final against Newcastle.

Thursday 6 May

George needs eight players, not four or five. He can make do with Walker, Carr and Campbell. He needs another centre half and a left back. He's probably gonna off-load Anderton. The whispers about Ginola for Fulham are getting louder and louder. Al-Fayed's probably gonna say: name your price. Because he can use him at Harrods as well. And if George was offered £4 million for Ginola he would not hesitate.

Ginola would have more time off, so he could spend more time with his family. He doesn't need the training regime under George Graham. He could play 20 minutes a match in the Nationwide, and help Fulham get into the Premiership. Be the hero. He could live in town, overlooking the Thames, and train when he wants to, and when he's not on the training pitch he'll be on the catwalk, modelling Harrods clobber.

We are light years behind Arsenal, Chelsea and United. This was our third defeat on the trot. West Ham at home,

2-1, Liverpool away, 3-2, Arsenal at home, 3-1. Spurs used to be stylish and Arsenal used to be efficient. But Arsenal have been genetically modified by Wenger. They now play with stylish efficiency.

Our next two games are Chelsea at home on Tuesday night, and Manchester United away on the last Sunday of the season. What about Anderton? Does George want to give him a new contract? If he doesn't, Anderton can sit it out next season and go on a free, like McManaman, a £10 million asset walking away for nothing. If George wants to offload him, Darren can say: 'OK, find me a club that I want to go to!'

Last night's programme contained details of an increase in ticket prices for next season. My ticket has gone up from £684 to £795. An increase of 14%. So I will be paying £111 more. Renewal forms will be sent out soon. David Pleat's column contained this last paragraph:

'The next couple of weeks are quite significant. The retained list is finalised; Chelsea are our last visitors after this evening. They are a club that has had a superb season, but it has been recently reported that they have a salary increase of around 80% from the previous season. It seems quite incredible some of the lengths to which clubs are prepared to go to achieve elusive success. We have made it clear at Tottenham that, although we will help George Graham's attempts to bring us back former glories, we will not give monies that would lead us into a suicidal financial position. We want glory, we want success like every club, but we will not be bamboozled into wild spending.'

Chelsea beat Leeds 1-0 last night to make sure of their place in the Champions League. Their 'wild spending' has resulted in them winning an FA Cup in 1997, and a Cup Winners' Cup in 1998, as well as a place alongside the big boys of Europe.

DAVID GINOLA, SUPERSTAR

Friday 7 May

Incredibly, the journalists have made David Ginola their Footballer of the Year. Ginola is the first Spurs player to pick up both prizes since Clive Allen in 1987. He said, 'The writers asked me, "What is your feeling to be alongside Stanley Matthews, Bobby Charlton, players like that?" and I am very proud. I am also very surprised because I don't play in a team like Manchester United or Arsenal or Chelsea, who are fighting for the title. It's just amazing.'

George took Ginola off in the Worthington Cup Final, took him off in the FA Cup semi-final, and took him off again last night. So he obviously does not share the hacks' high regard for Ginola. Maybe it was a sympathy vote. Maybe the reporters reckon George wants to offload him, so they wanted to make it harder for George to do that. I would have given it to Keane or Yorke. Ginola beat Dwight Yorke and David Beckham into second and third place respectively.

Paul Hayward, in *The Daily Telegraph*, managed to shed some light on an award which mystified millions of fans:

'While the Manchester United vote split no fewer than seven ways, 35 per cent of FWA members are thought to have voted for Ginola ahead of the likes of Dwight Yorke and David Beckham.

' "Art for Art's Sake" might become the FWA's new motto. It is unusual for such an unsentimental profession to reward aesthetic virtue over the more traditional combination of talent mixed with hard work.

The players and critics are as one. Ginola has been showered in starlight for doing things most mortal kickers of the sacred orb would never attempt to do: dribble past people with both feet, score spectacular goals cutting in from the wing and defy George Graham's bellowed orders to track back and tuck-in and fight to regain the ball. That amount of defiance deserves an award in itself.'

Saturday 8 May

This is the fifth year running that the Football Writers Association award has been won by a foreign player, and four of those foreigners played for London clubs. Recent winners were:

> 1994 Alan Shearer
> 1995 Eric Cantona
> 1996 Jürgen Klinsmann
> 1997 Gianfranco Zola
> 1998 Dennis Bergkamp
> 1999 David Ginola

Sunday 9 May

A good Sunday for newspaper stories. A Rob Shepherd exclusive in *The Express on Sunday* says Ginola is leaving Tottenham, and that Graham had told Sugar he needs £25 million worth of new talent. Shepherd pointed out that Ginola will never do well in big games because he will always have two men on him.

Another story is that George has said he fancies international management. He said, 'I've got a lot more enjoyable things still to do in football but becoming an international manager could probably come towards the end of your career as a club manager.' Is this a come-and-get-me quote? International manager? Where would he go? George is a Londoner who thinks Yorkshire is abroad.

So how could he manage Scotland while living in Hampstead? Or Australia? Or Norway? The mind boggles. What did Sugar say when he read that?

Rob Draper in *The Mail on Sunday* says Sol Campbell will not commit himself to a new long-term contract until 'off-the-field' issues are resolved. His current deal runs out in 2001. Draper reckons we will sign £2m-rated left winger Willem Korsten, 24, this summer from Vitesse Arnhem. Korsten had a loan spell at Leeds but failed to agree personal terms. Left winger? Isn't that where Ginola plays? We will soon have more left wingers in our squad than New Labour.

'Aston Villa thought they had clinched Grayeb until Spurs officials arrived at Heathrow to hijack the deal. Villa are currently considering whether to make an official complaint and challenge former Spurs striker Ronnie Rosenthal's role as Grayeb's unofficial agent. Leeds are also investigating the collapse of their talks with Korsten. Elland Road officials believed they had tabled the terms Korsten wanted but the player insisted he had changed his mind.'

Other papers have stories saying Leeds are furious that Korsten has been pinched by us. It looks as if we are hijacking players who are on their way to other clubs, rather than finding undiscovered gems. As far as we know, no big club wanted Jimmy Floyd Hassselbaink when he was at Boavista, or was prepared to pay him as much as Leeds were. Signing Hasselbaink, a very good but little-known Dutch goalscorer, was a coup. But maybe good strikers are in shorter supply than they were two years ago. Draper's story says Pleat has admitted that we are unlikely to spend huge sums without first off-loading high earners. And that Sol wants assurances that we are serious about closing the gap on Arsenal.

Campbell is quoted: 'I don't know if we're going to spend money. That's up to the manager and the chairman. But George Graham has the track record. He's said that he wants to sign top-quality players. He's a winner and I've got confidence in him. Next year we have to build. We have to keep the core of the side and add players to it. With Europe, there are three cups and the League to go for, so we must have a squad who can compete.'

Monday 10 May
Chelsea (h)

Reports say Nielsen and Ferdinand will have fitness tests before our last home match. We have lost the last three games, and have a bad record against Chelsea. We have never beaten them in the Premiership. They thrashed us 6-1 here last season. In fact, we have not beaten them in the League since 1990. But at least, with George in charge, fans can be sure of one thing: we will not lose 6-1 tonight.

The Mirror headline is: 'GINOLA: I'M GUNNER HELP FRENCH PALS'.

'It is the presence of fellow Frenchmen Arsène Wenger, Emmanuel Petit, Patrick Vieira and Nicolas Anelka at Highbury which has led Ginola to favour Arsenal for the title.

'He said: "I have watched Manchester United so many times this year and they're really a fantastic team. Then we played Arsenal and I can say they're very good as well, while I don't want to forget Chelsea. But because there is more of a French connection at Arsenal, I will say Arsenal – for Arsène, Manu, Patrick and Nicolas. There are no Frenchmen at all in Manchester!" '

Yet again, great diplomacy, David. Do you have a short memory or just a forgiving nature? Only two weeks ago those three French players boycotted your PFA dinner! Ginola also said, 'Playing at Old Trafford is a big challenge. It might be the game which decides the title, but when you come out on to the pitch, you always try to do well. That's the respect you have to show your job and the game.'

Meanwhile George told Steve Stammers in the *Standard* that we are five years behind Arsenal and Chelsea. He said that the big three clubs can spend the big money they will earn from 12 group games in the expanded Champions League next season, assuming Chelsea get through their qualifying round. This season Manchester United and Arsenal played six group games.

George said, 'If those three clubs spend, let's say, another £12 million each on new players for next season, then the rest of us have a long wait before we can hope to catch them up. And I'm talking at least four and possibly five years. That's the way it's going in the Premiership and there is very little the rest of the teams can do about it. Those three are just going to move further and further away. Massive funds are going to be needed – and I mean massive – to get on a par with them.'

That was our optimistic build-up to a major London derby. George got his retaliation in first, as usual, by saying we are a long way behind Chelsea, and will continue to be a long way behind.

Our new adidas shirts are big and baggy. We produce a gritty, workmanlike effort, one of our better performances. Iversen still plays on the right wing for most of the game. Hitchcock hardly has a save to make, and neither does Walker. I am very disappointed with Chelsea. Morris and Wise have good games, with Freund and Sherwood running around chasing shadows, but because they are playing so deep it does not really matter.

It is quite clear that the game means absolutely nothing to Chelsea. The match means more to us because it is our last home game. We do not dare to lose our last three home games. With our final League game coming up at Old Trafford on Sunday, it does not look as if we will finish in the top half of the table.

Flo turns Scales a couple of times. Scales does not know what day of the week it is. Anderton is covering a lot of ground but is not being especially effective. He should be crossing the ball, not Carr. Walker is at fault for the first goal, headed in by Poyet from Zola's free-kick in the fourth minute. Walker should have come out, punched the ball and Poyet as well, but he gets nowhere near it. Taricco is as bad as usual. He makes so many bad passes. He has no left foot.

Iversen makes it 1-1 after a short corner. Anderton pushes it to Ginola, who shuffles, waits for Iversen to move back, away from the goal, and picks him out at the near post, where Iversen flicks in from six yards. A tasty, well-worked goal. Ginola has two wild shots and the Chelsea supporters taunt him with a chorus of 'You'll never play for France!' Zola is disappointing and Forssell replaces him early in the second half.

Then Leboeuf drops a clanger and we go ahead. Ginola hits a pass which does not reach Anderton out wide. Leboeuf heads it to Le Saux, who plays it square inside to Morris, who plays it back to Leboeuf, who dribbles away from Anderton, who chases him. Leboeuf holds off Anderton and passes short and square to Wise, a suicidal pass which is intercepted by Ginola, who is then one on one with Desailly. Ginola swerves past Desailly, who falls over, and rams a right-foot shot into the bottom corner.

Ginola was in the D, but Hitchcock was wrong-footed and did not dive.

Desailly is angry now because Chelsea are 2-1 down, and maybe because of who has scored. As Armstrong shields the ball, keeping possession annoyingly near the corner flag, Desailly scythes away his standing leg and gets a booking.

Then Goldbaek makes it 2-2 after 73 minutes. Ginola is really, really pissed off, but Goldbaek's shot is unbelievable. It is like Anderton's Exocet against Leeds, but maybe even harder. Ginola, the nearest player to him, does not close him down. That area is our problem zone and always will be when Ginola is playing.

Still, we attack after Goldbaek's goal and try to win it. Iversen wriggles through and slides a shot wide. Ferrer, who had already been booked, brings Taricco down near the side of the penalty area, but Elleray just gives a free-kick. Poyet trips Carr and gets a yellow, Scales miscues a header over off Anderton's free-kick, Sherwood makes a run and skies his shot. Clemence comes on for Freund, who sprints off and goes into the dug-out.

Armstrong goes wide, hooks the ball over Le Saux's head, gets to the bye-line, but cuts the ball back just behind Iversen, who has to stop. His shot is blocked by Di Matteo and breaks for Anderton, who stabs inches over the far angle, a sharpish chance from eight yards which he has to hit instantly.

Then the No 14 is held up. Our star is being taken off yet again. This is the 22nd time he has been substituted this season, but the first time he has been substituted at home since winning the two awards. Ginola stands there, almost in the middle of the field, apparently thinking about whether he will come off or not, giving us time to wonder whether he will react angrily to being humiliated again.

Eventually, after an eternity of seconds, he applauds the fans, jogs over, hugs his little pal Dominguez, and goes down the tunnel. He had arrived at White Hart Lane as a passenger in Jose's little car. They are friends. Clearly, David would like to play with Jose, not be subbed by him.

So we drew 2-2 with Chelsea and all four goals were scored by foreigners. I left a minute before the end because I certainly did not want to watch a 'lap of honour'.

The match showed Ginola at his best and worst. He can dribble and shoot and cross, but he cannot mark. He can score the winner after 64 minutes, and then lose two points by failing to challenge an opponent in a dangerous position ten yards away.

Yes, Ginola made our first goal and scored our second goal. We were winning 2-1 after 73 minutes, so we either needed to score again or defend effectively for 17 minutes. But Ginola did not close down Goldbaek, so Chelsea scored. Ginola then looked mortified. He stood in the middle of the field with his hands on his hips, disgusted that his headlines had been stolen. But it was his own fault for his aristocratic attitude of: let somebody else do the donkey work. He gave Goldbaek time for three touches before he hit the ball. It was like shooting practice. Nobody reacted except Scales, and by the time he threw himself forward, turning his back, the shot was already flying into the net.

At the press conference George said we had deserved three points. 'I thought it was a good performance tonight. We deserved to win the game against a very talented Chelsea side. We gave them a goal start and I don't think you can give good teams that. It was a mistake by Ian Walker, he came for it. Then I thought we outplayed them. And I was delighted with the performance.'

Will Ginola be here next year?

'He's got another two years on his contract after the end of the season. If he leaves here it will be only for financial reasons. If he's not happy. I want to keep David Ginola here.'

If he's got so long to go on his contract, why start renegotiating now?

'Why not? I think he deserves more money.'

This comment provoked astonishment and laughter. 'I didn't say how much more,' added George. 'I think Tottenham is in the same league and has the same pay structure as Manchester United and Arsenal. And they have a wage structure, a very sensible one. And I think Tottenham are in that bracket. So they will be paid accordingly. The players here will be in similar situations as the players at Manchester United and Arsenal. So it's not as if they're not getting the same as players of equal ability. We will be offering top salaries which are in line with other big clubs.'

Hang on, George! Did you not say yesterday that our team development is five years behind Manchester United and Arsenal? Those players have won trophies and generated big money. Why should ours earn the same without achieving the same? Because 'Tottenham are in the same bracket?' Do you think paying Chris Armstrong more will make him a better player? Asked about Grayeb, the Israeli, George said, 'Negotiations are going on.'

Vialli's comments were more humble and apologetic. He said, 'I think it was quite exciting for the supporters. We didn't give our best performance. We can play much better. Maybe it was also because of Tottenham, they did reasonably well. But, again, we could have done better. At the end I think a draw is a fair result.

'But I'm not totally happy about our performance. We were too sloppy in too many situations. It's got something to do with concentration. And I accept all the responsibility for that because as a manager you've got to make sure that all your players are fully concentrated. And so when they are not, it's your fault. So maybe I should have done something different in the last few days, or today before the match. Certainly something wasn't spot-on, and it was mainly the concentration.'

Vialli was asked about the Champions League Qualifying Round and told that Arsène Wenger had said that if Arsenal were in the Qualifying Round he wouldn't know how much money he could spend on new players. Does this apply to you?

'I don't think that will make any big difference. But before we make any change we want to be 100% certain we are signing the right players. Looking at the Chelsea squad at the moment I can see only top-class players, used to English football, which is something very important. So we don't wanna make changes just for the sake of it. So let's finish the season and see if there's something available better than who we've got at the moment, which is quite difficult. And also we are trying our best to keep our best players. You mustn't forget that to keep your best players is also difficult. We've got plenty of offers for a few of our best players, and to keep them will be a success as well.'

The programme tells us that the Fans Forum, which was due on Friday, has now been postponed until early next season 'due to the unavailability of a suitable panel'. Do the club really want to listen to us? Or just go through the motions by arranging a token meeting?

———————

DAVID GINOLA, SUPERSTAR

The papers enjoy themselves with Ginola pay stories and speculation about whether he will stay or go. *The Mirror* says Ginola is on £14,000 a week and has been offered £21,000 a week to stay, but wants more. Last night*'s Standard* said he was on £16,000 a week. *The Mirror* story said Campbell, Ferdinand and Anderton earn around £21,000 a week:

'But Ginola admits that his future at White Hart Lane is in the balance because he feels he should be earning around £24,000 a week to put him in the same league as other French stars in London. And Ginola last night demanded his future gets thrashed out in the next fortnight.'

Ginola agrees that Tottenham is an ideal stage for him, and repeated that he wants to finish his career with us. He said, 'I have to stay. Where else could I go and play? Look at what's around me, they love me. I can't leave them to go somewhere else. I've had two years in London when most people were expecting me to enjoy the night life more than the football life. I've had doubts in the past but I enjoy working with George Graham. I work well with him even though we have two strong personalities.'

The *Daily Mail* headline, above a story by Ivan Speck, was 'GRAHAM'S IRON WILL HOLDING KEY TO GINOLA PAY DEMAND'.

'When the parties representing George Graham and David Ginola square up across the negotiating table, the question underpinning the clash of these mighty personalities will simply be: "Is Tottenham big enough for the two of them?" If the answer is no, it is not difficult to envisage Graham's iron will prevailing over Ginola's Gallic desire for his just reward.'

Speck said Ginola wants a three-year contract on £24,000 per week, and quoted him saying, 'I work well with George Graham. I'm quite happy working with someone who has his attitude but I have to think about my family and future. Playing for Tottenham in the next few years is most important, but I have to think of my life beyond that. I want everything sorted out before I go on holiday so my head is clear. If Tottenham don't increase my contract, I will just say there's no way for me to stay, and I'll leave. If they react like that, it's because they don't want to keep me. But I think they realise what is good for the club – and at the moment I think I am a good thing for the club.'

How many more days of this will we have? Negotiation by tabloid. It is significant that Ginola did not say, 'I am a good thing for the team.' He said, 'I am a good thing for the club.'

He realises his merchandising value. The club's sales departments are taking hundreds of orders every day for new adidas shirts which will be mailed out the day before the kit is available in the shops. No numbers or names can be printed on shirts at the moment because the player might not be here. But Ginola knows he sells far more shirts than anybody else, and that is worth big money to Tottenham.

Ferdinand and Campbell were on the C4's *Big Breakfast* two weeks ago, promoting the £43 shirts, and Sol actually said, 'They'll sell more when David wears one.'

Everybody is still writing about Ginola. Over at 'www. Football365.com', Patrick Barclay was talking about his goal against Chelsea:

'It was by no means Ginola's goal of the season. Leeds United, Barnsley and Manchester United have all been on the wrong end of better ones. So his claim to footballing genius is irresistible. Yet it is still considered something of a twin freak that both the football writers and his fellow professionals have voted Ginola their player of the year.

We know why. Both here and across the channel, his commitment to the team ethic is deemed suspect. He tends to dwell on the ball unduly. His goals, while usually spectacular, are too infrequent. All of which conspires to form the view that Tottenham's improvement has owed more to the organisation of manager George Graham than the flair of their most charismatic individual, who indeed contributed little to the Worthington Cup triumph at Wembley.'

A PA story quoted Korsten's agent Bob Maaskant saying that five clubs, including Leeds, Tottenham and Feyonoord, want to sign Korsten from Vitesse Arnhem.

Thursday 13 May

A *Standard* story by David Bond, headlined 'GINOLA SAYS "OUI" TO £23,000 A WEEK', proved that Alan Sugar knows what it takes to get the season-ticket renewal money from the fans by the end of this month:

'David Ginola today ended speculation about his future by signing a new three-year deal worth £3.6 million – a contract which will make him the highest paid player at Tottenham. But in a shock move Spurs team-mate Darren Anderton, whose current contract expires next summer, has rejected the same £23,000-a-week offer raising serious doubts about his long-term commitment to the north London club.'

Anderton appears to have been earning a third more than Ginola this season. If it's true that Anderton has a parity clause (giving him an automatic pay rise when another player is given more money than him), he should be happy with £23,000 a week.

Blackburn needed to beat Manchester United at Ewood Park tonight to escape relegation. The game finished in a 1-1 draw, so United must beat us at Old Trafford on Sunday to regain the Premiership. If we beat United, Arsenal will be champions if they beat Aston Villa at Highbury. If we draw with United, and Arsenal win, Arsenal will win it by one point. An interesting final day!

Went to a recording of *The Sports Show* at Pearson's Studios, just off Tottenham Court Road. The programme goes out tonight on ITV at 11.30pm. A friend who works at a City law firm came with me. We arrived about 8pm, they sat everyone down, and host Eamonn Holmes introduced the guests. Mike Atherton was wearing slacks while George Graham was immaculate in a navy suit and gold tie. Holmes introduced Terry Venables as the 'irrepressible cheeky chappie'. Venables was bright red, as if he had been on a sunbed, and wearing suedey shoes which looked like carpet slippers.

Holmes told us what he was going to be talking about, and asked for a copy of the *Standard*, which had the 'GINOLA SAYS "OUI" TO £23,000 A WEEK' headline, and then it just kicked off. George was given a relatively warm reception from everyone, including the Arsenal supporters who were there.

Graham was asked about Sunday's game and he said, 'We're gonna go up there and do our best. And we're gonna play Jose Dominguez in goal.' A punter asked George about money to strengthen the team. 'Will the cash be there? If it's not, will you be there?' George said, 'I hope the money will be there. I've explained to them what is needed.' Did he explain it in joined-up writing?

That word 'hope' was one I did not want to hear. If George is only saying, 'I hope the money will be there,' then my suspicions about Sugar's strategy are probably well-founded.

On the subject of our reluctant-to-sign England winger, George said, 'Darren Anderton will have to fall in line with the wage structure at the club.' I did not want to say anything, except in the third part of the programme, when George mentioned Taricco and how well he was doing. I was tempted to say, 'OK then, why have you just signed an Israeli left back?'

The best line of the night came when Holmes asked Venables, 'What are you doing these days?' That got a good laugh. Venables smiled and said, 'I do a lot of sitting.' He also said he was doing a bit of television and setting up coaching schemes abroad. Yeah, right! I can just imagine Tel setting up a coaching school in Namibia or somewhere far from the TV cameras.

George was not really convincing in what he said, partly because it was a light entertainment programme, a bit of topical fun. When talk turned to Ginola, Holmes asked, 'Do you really, really like him?''' George grinned and said, 'Love him!' When Holmes asked about international management he repeated what he said ten years ago, 'I'm too young!' George was asked again whether Spurs would be trying on Sunday and he gave predictable answers like, 'The championship is won over 38 games in the season.'

Afterwards I went upstairs to the lounge and chatted to three Tottenham supporters, testing the water very gently.

'I suppose you're delighted with George's performance here tonight?' I said. And they were.

'It's gotta be done bit by bit, in stages,' they said. 'It's gonna take time.'

'Why?' I said, 'What have we been doing for the last ten years?'

'What would you do?'

'I'd get rid of that chairman tomorrow. He should put his money where his mouth is. If he thinks Graham is the right manager he should back him.'

'We'll be happy with top six next season,' a guy said.

'Why can't we go for top one? And if we don't win the League we will finish second or third and get into the Champions League. I'd go out and sign two world-class strikers!'

'And what else?' he said.

'Then I'd sign a central midfield player who can play football. And then I'd sign a centre half and a left back.'

'So five players?'

'No, I think we should sign six world-class players and start competing.'

The poor dears were a bit gobsmacked by this. One of them actually told me he thought Steffen Freund is a good player !

Bernie Kingsley from TISA was there with his sidekick Steve Davis. The two of them went off to chat with Graham and Venables. I chatted to Holmes, a Manchester United fan, who was quite interesting.

'Everyone's talking about Tottenham not winning the game on Sunday,' I said. 'But what about the scenario where United lose and Arsenal lose. That will suit everyone, wouldn't it?'

He said, 'Well, it would certainly suit us.'

I said, 'Why don't we have two 0-0s on Sunday and then everyone will be happy, apart from Arsenal supporters. Would you be pleased with that?'

He said, 'I'd be delighted with that.'

Then we talked about my club.

'What d'you think is going down at Tottenham?' Holmes said.

'I don't think George Graham will be there in a year's time,' I said. 'He'll just get pissed off because he's not getting the finances, and he'll go.'

'Well, why don't you get rid of the chairman?' he said.

'We've tried,' I said.

I went up to Venables and said, 'I've got a bit of an apology to make. When you were at Tottenham I had a go at you.' He said, 'Oh, I don't remember any of that.' He said, 'Well, that's gone now.'

George was there listening to this. So I said, 'Welcome to Tottenham. Congratulations on last season. I hope you can take us to the next level.'

'I hope so too,' said George. 'Thanks a lot.'

I shook his hand.

'Let's hope that the chairman gets his chequebook out,' I said.

'I hope so too,' said George.

Friday 14 May

Found myself thinking about last night's programme. It was like a coffee morning. Atherton was dressed casually, and George and Tel were just going through the motions, with no intention of telling us anything new. Wallpaper TV, totally unmemorable. It just scratched the surface. Just a regurgitation of what's been said in the tabloids and on TV. If you tell people something often enough they will eventually believe it.

The Sports Show is not sport or current affairs. It is light entertainment, a hybrid which helps to dumb down people's ability to think. It is another nail being driven into the coffin of reality. Instead of broadening the debate these programmes narrow the debate. Most TV debates about football are shallow and topical and flippant, so Venables and Graham are ideal guests. If Terry Venables says something it must be gospel, so the real issues are never addressed.

Eamonn Holmes can hold himself well in front of the camera. He says the right thing, smiles at the right time and is relatively photogenic, but I don't think he is really the right kind of front man for the programme. It would be far better if it was hosted by genuine supporters, who were involved and had an alternative view. Because all you get is bog-standard lines.

When George Graham was a successful manager at Arsenal he always refused to appear on *The Footballer's Football Show* and talk shows like last night. He wanted to play the games and win the games, not talk about it. Such programmes took George away from what he was good at, so he conserved his energy, kept his own counsel, and left the topical waffle to others. That increased the impact of anything he did say as Arsenal manager. He made sure he was never over-exposed.

Venables, more of a delegator, never focused his whole attention on his team in the same single-minded way. He loves being on TV and loves being paid big money for five minutes of chat on Champions League nights. Terry and George were a slightly odd couple, a double act whose rapport seems to have faded. Maybe it will be rekindled if the two old actors some day do a theatre tour reminiscing about the good old days. A hour of humorous anecdotes and one-liners we have heard 50 times before.

Chapter Eleven

OH, TEDDY, TEDDY!

Saturday 15 May

The spotlight is on George tomorrow, so he will have to field his strongest team. Except, of course, Dominguez in goal! Can we find gloves small enough to fit him? What do I expect tomorrow afternoon? Waves of United attacks, backs to the wall defending by Sol and the boys, and a defeat.

I just cannot understand Spurs fans who say they want us to win at United. How can Richard Littlejohn even contemplate a scenario where Arsenal win the championship again? I could not bear another season of *We Are The Champions* in a certain neighbourhood of North London. When are we going to hear that song over the PA system at White Hart Lane?

Nielsen has put in a transfer request, according to *The Mirror*. He had a bust-up with Graham and has been banned from training with the first team. Nielsen has had a back injury for three weeks and was not allowed to train with his team-mates on Thursday. He is very keen to regain full match fitness in time for Denmark's Euro 2000 qualifiers with Wales and Belarus in June.

He said: 'It's a purely personal thing that made me hand in my written transfer request. Something personal has happened between George Graham and myself but I don't want to be the one to tell people about it. If George Graham chooses to tell his side of the case then I will do it because I've got witnesses on everything that happened between us. I still have a contract for three years with

Tottenham and I was sure my football future was with the club.'

———————————

Sunday 16 May
Manchester United (a)

Our final game of the season is a championship decider – for Manchester United. I watch it on Sky. The big team news is that Jaap Stam is out with an achilles injury, and Les Ferdinand will start. So their most powerful defender will be missing against our most powerful striker. No Armstrong, who is not even on the bench.

Obviously, I do not want Arsenal to win the Championship, even if it means Teddy Sheringham winning a Championship medal with United. Wearing our old Pony kit, we start quite brightly and positively. Then Ian Walker kicks a clearance against Dwight Yorke, who is closing him down. The ball rebounds towards the goal, but Walker gets away with the mistake. Then Ginola is pushed in the back by Gary Neville as he dribbles towards our goal near the halfway line. Ginola appears to pull a muscle. He goes off after four minutes and Dominguez comes on three minutes later. Strange that Ginola, who has been kicked black and blue all season, but has still been fit enough to start 43 games, should be injured by a push in the back.

Then an amazing thing happens after 24 minutes. We score against the run of play! Walker hoists the ball down the middle, Iversen outjumps David May and heads on to Ferdinand, who powers past Ronny Johnsen on the left side of the penalty area and flicks the bouncing ball up and across Schmeichel into the far corner. Schmeichel stumbles back into the net. A good stretch by Ferdinand

and a well-controlled flick with the outside of his right foot. An excellent goal but he does not celebrate! It is as if he is thinking: what have I done? Will they lynch me in Enfield? Will I ever dare to show my face in Hertfordshire again?

Or maybe Ferdinand was in shock, since this is his first goal in 19 appearances. Maybe he knew it might be his last for Tottenham.

Walker makes a double save from Scholes, Beckham heads a sitter over the bar, and Keane dispossesses Sherwood by tanking right through him and charging on into the penalty area. His low cross is hit by Yorke but Carr blocks. United play with spirit and tempo, and only Campbell can really live with them. Sol is always good in an all-action game like this where defensive heroics are needed. When Sheringham fouls Campbell, Sol just gets up and walks away, while Teddy is booked. What a temperament! And how Ferguson would love him at Old Trafford.

When a team attacks with such momentum they often get away with a foul or two, and this is what happens. Scholes clearly clatters Sherwood, the ball breaks for Giggs, who gives to it Scholes, who feeds Beckham, who is unmarked. Edinburgh is ten yards away and Beckham has time to place his angled shot just inside the far post for 1-1. The half-time score at Highbury is Arsenal 0 Aston Villa 0, so the Gooners are not winning either.

Our midfield is totally over-run. Freund scuttles around, never getting near the ball. Alex Ferguson brings on Andy Cole for Sheringham at half-time, and within three minutes Cole scores when Scales plays him onside. Cole takes two touches and hooks the ball over Walker to make it 2-1.

Interesting that Cole was sold by Graham to Bristol City for £500,000 in 1992 when he was a youngster and fourth in line behind Ian Wright, Alan Smith and Kevin Campbell. George said, 'Andy has come a long way since he was with me at Arsenal. He was only a baby when I had him. I didn't think he would reach the standard he has, or I wouldn't have sold him. But it was a great sale at the time.'

United are champions, Arsenal are second a point behind. Chelsea are third, Leeds are fourth and West Ham fifth.

FA Carling Premiership Final Table

			HOME				AWAY						
	P	W	D	L	F	A	W	D	L	F	A	Pts	GD
1 Manchester United	38	14	4	1	45	18	8	9	2	35	19	79	43
2 Arsenal	38	14	5	0	34	5	8	7	4	25	12	78	42
3 Chelsea	38	12	6	1	29	13	8	9	2	28	17	75	27
4 Leeds United	38	12	5	2	32	9	6	8	5	30	25	67	28
5 West Ham United	38	11	3	5	32	26	5	6	8	14	27	57	-7
6 Aston Villa	38	10	3	6	33	28	5	7	7	18	18	55	5
7 Liverpool	38	10	5	4	44	24	5	4	10	24	25	54	19
8 Derby County	38	8	7	4	22	19	5	6	8	18	26	52	-5
9 Middlesbrough	38	7	9	3	25	18	5	6	8	23	36	51	-6
10 Leicester City	38	7	6	6	25	25	5	7	7	15	21	49	-6
11 Tottenham	**38**	**7**	**7**	**5**	**28**	**26**	**4**	**7**	**8**	**19**	**24**	**47**	**-3**
12 Sheffield Wednesday	38	7	5	7	20	15	6	2	11	21	27	46	-1
13 Newcastle United	38	7	6	6	26	25	4	7	8	22	29	46	- 6
14 Everton	38	6	8	5	22	12	5	2	12	20	35	43	-5
15 Coventry City	38	8	6	5	26	21	3	3	13	13	30	42	-12
16 Wimbledon	38	7	7	5	22	21	3	5	11	18	42	42	-23
17 Southampton	38	9	4	6	29	26	2	4	13	8	38	41	-27
18 Charlton Athletic	38	4	7	8	20	20	4	5	10	21	36	36	-15
19 Blackburn Rovers	38	6	5	8	21	24	1	9	9	17	28	35	-14
20 Nottingham Forest	38	3	7	9	18	31	4	2	13	17	38	30	-34

We were 11th when George Graham took over in October, and we have finished the season in 11th place. We will never know where we might have finished if Christian Gross had stayed. At least we were safe from relegation long before the final weekend. The last five games have told their own story: we only took one point out of 15 from those five games against West Ham, Liverpool, Arsenal, Chelsea and Manchester United. Only one point from a 2-2 draw against Chelsea. And who have we beaten in the league? Everton twice, Nottingham Forest twice, Southampton, Liverpool, Blackburn, Charlton, Derby, Newcastle and Aston Villa. Four of those victories came against teams who were relegated. So we finished 11 points off relegation and 20 off automatic qualification for Europe.

Monday 17 May

We buy Willem Korsten from Vitesse Arnhem for £1.5 million. He has signed a four-year contract. A PA Sport story describes his three-month loan spell at Leeds, and negotiations there.

'When talks began, however, Leeds chairman Peter Ridsdale described Korsten's original salary demands as "preposterous", which ultimately changed following negotiations. After a period of reflection Ridsdale then agreed to the new terms only to be told Korsten no longer found them acceptable because the club "had not given in to his demands" at the first meeting.

'Speaking to PA Sport from his home in Holland, Korsten said: "It was hugely disappointing I didn't join Leeds, I felt they were the perfect club for me because they were doing very well. To play in a team that's doing so well is a great deal easier than with a team that is struggling, and I don't think I did too badly. I was very excited that they wanted to sign me, but it wasn't meant to be." '

So we have signed a 24-year-old squad player. Korsten is not a full international. He is unproven left winger who has achieved almost nothing. We should be improving our team, George, not our squad. Korsten is just an understudy to keep Ginola on his toes.

———————

Tuesday 18 May

An *Independent* story by Nicholas Spencer quotes Korsten's agent, Bob Maaskant, saying, 'It was an easy choice once I told him of Tottenham's interest. Having played at White Hart Lane, he was very impressed by what he saw.' The *Daily Mail* reports that Korsten will challenge David Ginola, the double player of the year, for his place in the team. Korsten said, 'At Leeds I was competing with Kewell, so I am up for competition. It doesn't matter to me. I can also play behind the strikers, or even up front.' Bob Maaskant and George obviously get on well. They have known each other for some time because Maaskant is also Hasselbaink's agent.

———————

Wednesday 19 May

Watched the Lazio-Real Mallorca Cup Winners' Cup Final on the box. Not impressed by Eriksson's team selection. He had both his wingers on the bench, Lombardo and Conceicao. Amazed that he played Mancini in midfield. I would have taken Mancini off after five minutes and put De La Pena on. He is a quality player who would have helped Almeyda hold the midfield together. We should go for De La Pena, whose style is halfway between Ardiles and Gascoigne. But George has never signed Latin players.

Mallorca were as good as Lazio, but bottled it. They did not realise Lazio were there for the taking. Vieri scored with a header off a 40-yard ball down the middle with Argentine keeper Roa in no man's land. Dani equalised after ten minutes. Centreback Nesta was superb, but Salas and Nedved were abysmal. Eriksson was about to take Nedved off and bring on Lombardo when Nedved scored the winner with a volley off a loose ball at the edge of the box. He still took him off.

Thursday 20 May

The Mirror says we will offer Armstrong in part-exchange for Sutton, who is rated at £12m by Blackburn. Aston Villa also want Sutton, and may offer Riccardo Scimeca as part of the deal. Chelsea's main target is said to be Marco Delvecchio of Roma, but they are also said to be interested in Sutton. I don't want Sutton. He is a target man and if we get him we will play too much long ball. He's 26 and should be in his prime, but where was he when Blackburn were fighting relegation? He was injured. He has a relegation clause in his contract. I hope we do not give players relegation clauses. If we go down, you can leave? What a disincentive! Ridiculous. That is player power gone mad, the tail wagging the dog.

The *Daily Mail* has a worrying story by John Richardson and Graham Hunter:

'Tottenham manager George Graham has moved in for Liverpool's deeply unsettled Norway midfielder Oyvind Leonhardsen. Sources close to Leonhardsen confirmed last night that Graham is willing to pay £2 million for a player who has been so miserable at Anfield that he felt forced to advertise his services on the Internet.

343

Leonhardsen could play on the right flank of Graham's midfield – the position filled by England international Darren Anderton – and they will also need cover if they accept Allan Nielsen's transfer request.'

Liverpool to sell Leonhardsen to us? Is this their revenge for selling them Neil Ruddock and Paul Stewart? Leonardsen has been a flop at Liverpool. How many players have left Wimbledon and been successful? Only two: Nigel Winterburn and Dennis Wise.

Friday 21 May

It is incredible to look back at some of the things the club has said in the last year. At the start of the season, on 20 August 1998, David Pleat said, 'For Spurs now it is either the best from around the world or the most promising young British players.' Does Pleat think we have forgotten what he promised nine months ago? Does he expect to be taken seriously? Is Freund one of the best from around the world? Is Sherwood one of the most promising young British players? Did Pleat not tell us on 25 September that we would buy three class players for £6 million each? A year ago, in the summer of 1998, fundamental mistakes were made by Alan Sugar. He should have paid off Christian Gross and said, 'Thanks for keeping us up.' Then he should have hired a proven manager and invested in some class players.

Saturday 22 May

Teddy Sheringham was man of the match in the FA Cup final. Alex Ferguson started with Cole and Solskjaer, but

OH, TEDDY, TEDDY!

Teddy came on as sub soon after Roy Keane was injured by Gary Speed in the fourth minute.

Ruud Gullit surprisingly selected local kid Steve Harper, who was Newcastle's fifth choice keeper until recently. He should have picked Shay Given, since Harper had only played ten games. Given has played in many big games, like Eire v Belgium in Brussels. It was Given's wonder save from Anderton in the first minute of the semi-final that kept them in it. If Anderton had scored we might have been at Wembley today.

Newcastle had a go for the first ten minutes in each half, then bottled it. Gullit admits Charvet is not a centre half, and Charvet proved it in front of a global audience of billions. He had not played for six weeks and was asleep when the first goal was scored after eleven minutes. A precise through ball from Scholes, an ambling run from Sheringham, no challenge, a simple shot through Harper's legs, 1-0. Newcastle dithered, had no shape, no defence. It was no contest, a non-event, an embarrassment.

Teddy laid on the second goal for Scholes, a shot from the edge of the box after 52 minutes, and later hit the bar with a chip-shot. His England buddy Alan Shearer trundled around like a weary old soldier. There were no crosses for him. Newcastle never worked the ball out wide, never supported their wide players, never got crosses in, never demonstrated any shape, good habits or confidence. They have some decent players, but no team, not even a glimpse of a team.

As it turned out the match was not really an FA Cup final, just a victory parade for the Premiership champions. The Red Devils did a lap of honour after playing an exhibition match. Their third Double in six years, but the Double is devalued now. It was hard for Tottenham and Arsenal to win their Doubles in 1961 and 1971.

The most memorable FA Cup finals are the upsets. When Sunderland beat the mighty Leeds in 1973 the whole country was shocked. Ipswich beat Arsenal in 1978 with a goal by Roger Osborne, a player who was never heard of again. Millions of football fans knew that Spurs had never lost an FA Cup final, but then, in 1987, we lost 3-2 to Coventry in extra time. A year later Wimbledon surprised the all-conquering Liverpool when Lawrie Sanchez scored the only goal of the game.

Nowadays the underdogs do not seem to have a chance. Feeble performances by losing teams are common. Liverpool turned up in white suits in 1996, got changed but did not play. Newcastle flopped dismally in the last two finals.

So Teddy went to Manchester and won the Double and could even win the Treble. I do not want Sol Campbell to do the same.

Sunday 23 May

The club has sent me the brochure containing Season Ticket Information 1999-2000 and renewal forms. The cover is a colour photo of the Worthington Cup being held proudly aloft by Sol Campbell and a grinning blond man. Allan Nielsen. The Wembley hero who has now had a row with George Graham and put in a transfer request. Should I renew my season ticket? Despite our Cup runs, Tottenham seems a very dull club these days. There are only three personalities, Sugar, Graham and Ginola, and they seem held together only by commercial and contractual necessity.

OH, TEDDY, TEDDY!

Monday 24 May

Saw Ginola on the TV news in a dinner suit at the Cannes Film festival. He was better-looking than the movie stars. Some fans are surprised Ginola is still with us. Many Arsenal fans expected George to do what he did with their favourite, Charlie Nicholas: sell him as soon as possible. Once Charlie Nicholas was sold, nobody else in that Arsenal side had any charisma. The only star at Highbury was George Graham and he kept it that way for eight years. He never signed a big star who might fall out with him, put in a transfer request, move to another club, play brilliantly and prove him wrong.

I look back over the season. A football season means a lot of different things to different people. But some things are shared by everyone. Fans always share the memories of great goals, important victories and bitter defeats.

I remember thinking we could get a last-minute winner before Allan Nielsen dived forward to head that ball past Kasey Keller at Wembley. I remember the *Evening Standard* newsstand poster 'SUGAR SHOCK FOR SPURS', when we thought he was going to sell the club on 25 August. I remember Ferdinand's reaction when he scored against United at Old Trafford. I remember Gross standing by the emergency exit at Selhurst Park. I remember Darren Anderton's cannonball against Leeds and Ginola's crossfield dribble when he hit the post.

I remember having a car crash in Amersham when I should have been in Barnsley. I remember Sugar telling me to 'Fuck off!' I remember Sugar at the AGM saying, 'Does Mark Jacob speak for anybody here?' I remember coming down the motorway from Manchester after the semi-final thinking Ginola would be sold. And I remember *The Sports Show* and George shaking my hand and saying, 'I hope so too.'

Chapter Twelve

CHEAP 'N' CHIGWELL

Tuesday 25 May

Have studied the brochure. Our leader's letter to the faithful says that Premiership wages have gone up 40% in 1997-98, and that Tottenham's total revenue from ticket sales does not come near the cost of the players' wages, so prices are going up by 12% across the board. Our season books will include tickets for our first four cup games, which will include UEFA Cup games.

Without making any promises I can inform you that George Graham has been allocated an amount of money to acquire players to further strengthen the squad. Hopefully, there will be significant movements in and out of the Club during the close season.

Our season ticket list was at a record high for the Club this season and will no doubt increase further next. So please remember that in order to guarantee your renewal we must receive your application by 28th May 1999.

Next season is our centenary at White Hart Lane; I hope you take this opportunity to celebrate it with us.

Yours faithfully,
Alan Sugar
Chairman

So Sugar has made no promises and he can only hope there will be significant movements. It's all hope, hope, hope. Football lives on hope and anticipation, but we finished 11th in the table. We need more than hope. We need bold, imaginative action by the chairman and the manager.

Wednesday 26 May

Tonight's European Cup Final pits Bayern Munich coach Ottmar Hitzfeld against Manchester United's Alex Ferguson. Both clubs were runners-up in their respective leagues last season, but they call it the Champions League. Hitzfeld, the man who recommended Gross to Sugar, won the trophy two years ago with Borussia Dortmund. They beat United in the semi-final and then beat Juventus 3-1 in Munich.

Ferguson picks the wrong team in the Nou Camp. He has the best pair of wingers in Europe, but he plays them both out of position. In the absence of the suspended Keane and Scholes, he plays Giggs on the right and Blomqvist on the left, with Beckham and Butt in the middle. After five minutes Basler puts Bayern ahead with a free-kick round the wall when Schmeichel is expecting it to go over the wall. United stutter, and the Germans sit back, launching a few counter-attacks which also stutter because Effenberg has nobody to play with until Scholl comes on. Ferguson admits the error of his team selection, takes Blomqvist off and puts Sheringham on the left side after 67 minutes.

All the action is in the last ten minutes. Scholl hits the post, Matthaus goes off, Solskjaer comes on, Jancker hits the bar with an overhead kick, Basler goes off, and the trophy is brought down to pitch side with Bayern's ribbons on it. Then, in injury time, a corner by Beckham, goalkeeper Schmeichel comes up for it, the ball is half-cleared to Giggs, who half-hits a bouncing shot from the edge of the box, Sheringham swivels and knocks it in. Then another corner on the left, Beckham hits an inswinger which Sheringham flicks on, Solskjaer sticks out his foot and the ball flies into the roof of the net.

Amazing drama! United have won a historic treble with two goals in the last 109 seconds. What a week for Teddy Sheringham! Oh, Teddy, Teddy, went to Man Utd and you won it all. You were sold to Man Utd for £3.5 million by a club who paid £4.2 million for Ruel Fox and £6 million for Les Ferdinand.

Thursday 27 May

We need six new players. Who will they be? Will they be the quality players our club deserves or functional B-internationals who won't cost Sugar too much money ? Will they be as talented as Ossie Ardiles and Steve Archibald and Chris Waddle and Paul Gascoigne and Gary Lineker and Jürgen Klinsmann?

David Ginola is our star player, but you cannot build a team round a 32-year-old winger. Ginola can only win so many matches for us. He had to stay at Tottenham and we had to keep him. It now seems to me that Alan Sugar, George Graham and David Ginola are bound together in an uneasy alliance, needing each other but wishing they did not need each other. When Ginola left Newcastle, Spurs was his best option. When Graham left Leeds, Spurs was his best option. For Sugar, last September, Graham was his best option. Ginola needed a stage, Graham needed a London job, and Sugar needed to stay in the Premiership. Have you heard the one about the Scotsman, the Englishman and the Frenchman? They formed a *ménage à trois* to prop up a fading football club in North London.

Clearly, the work ethic instilled by George Graham means we will avoid defeat in many games we cannot win. But, ultimately, we will be found out, so a quantum leap has to be made. And that costs big money.

That is where the crunch will come. When George says: I've modified my principles, I understand that football has moved on, I now need to start spending big money. Sugar and Graham will continue in their alliance of convenience for a while, but how much further can that take us? Will the fans be satisfied with a Leeds scenario, top six and a UEFA Cup run? Graham claims that the Leeds board didn't back him financially. The day he says that at Tottenham will be the day that their amnesty ends and open conflict begins. You can only buy so many Freunds and Sherwoods and Tariccos. After that you have to start buying a Klinsmann or a Bergkamp or a Zola or a Batistuta. You can't go on buying Chris Armstrongs. If he buys British it has to be one of the up-and-coming kids, like Robbie Keane. Next season we want to see good football again. We will not put up with boring, mechanical football and 1-0 victories.

Is the chairman willing to spend the money to bridge the gap, so that Tottenham can compete with Manchester United, Arsenal and Chelsea? We ground out wins over Brentford, Northampton, Liverpool, Manchester United and Wimbledon to get to Wembley where we won with a late goal. Next season we want more than that.

At the moment we are one injury-time goal better than Leicester City. That is all.

———————————

351

Friday 28th May

Sent off my season-ticket renewal form yesterday. I will now sit back and wait for some world-class players to arrive, and contemplate an exciting new season kicking off in two months' time.

See you in the Stade de France for the European Champions League Final ...

2001: A Spurs Odyssey.